Implementing Business and Human Rights Norms in Africa

This book examines the contemporary and contentious question of the critical connections between business and human rights, and the implementation of socially responsible norms in developing countries, with particular reference to Kenya, Nigeria, and South Africa. Business enterprises and transnational corporate actors operate in a complex global environment, especially when operating in high risks sectors such as oil and gas, mining, construction, banking, and health care amongst others. Understanding human rights responsibilities, impacts, and socially responsible behaviour for companies is therefore an essential component of corporate risk management in our current world. The release of the United Nations Guiding Principles on Business and Human Rights, an instrument consisting of 31 principles on this issue, has further underscored the emergence of a rapidly developing set of international law norms on human rights responsibilities of businesses and transnational corporations. It has also shaped the discourse on corporate accountability for human rights. In addition to minimizing litigation, financial and reputational risks, understanding and demonstrating corporate respect for human rights is vital to building a culture of trust and integrity amongst local communities, investors, and shareholders. While Africa has been at the receiving end of deleterious activities of corporate actors, it has failed to address corporate impunity and human rights violations by non-state actors. Questions abound revolving around the underpinnings of a corporate responsibility to respect human rights, that is, how non-western and particularly African conceptions of respect may help develop a beyond do no net harm approach to respect; policy discourses on human rights due diligence, human rights impact assessment; mandating corporate respect for human rights in both domestic and international law.

This book examines, clarifies, and unpacks the guiding principles of a rights-based approach to development and social inclusion. It offers an excellent exposition of regulatory capacity, institutional efficacy, and democratic legitimacy of governance institutions that shape development including a comprehensive analysis of how states are shaping business and human rights discourses locally to develop a critical understanding of identified issues by exploring the latest theories through comparative lenses.

Oyeniyi Abe is Lecturer in Law at Huddersfield Business School, University of Huddersfield, United Kingdom. His areas of expertise are business, trade and human rights in Africa, extractive resource governance, investment law and sustainable development. He is also a Research Associate at the Centre for Comparative Law in Africa, University of Cape Town, South Africa.

Routledge Research in Corporate Law

Available titles in this series include

Employee Rights in Corporate Insolvency
A UK and US Perspective
Hamiisi Junior Nsubuga

Shareholder Protection Reconsidered
Derivative Action in the UK, Germany and Greece
Georgios Zouridakis

Corporate Takeover, Management Discipline and the Law
Francis Okanigbuan Jnr

Shareholder Activism and the Law
The Future of US Corporate Governance
Ekrem Solak

The Law and Governance of Decentralised Business Models
Between Hierarchies and Markets
Edited by Roger M Barker and Iris H-Y Chiu

The Enlightened Shareholder Value and Corporate Social Responsibility
A theoretical and qualitative analysis
Taskin Iqbal

Adjudicating Global Business in and with India
International Commercial and Investment Disputes Settlement
Leïla Choukroune and Rahul Donde

Implementing Business and Human Rights Norms in Africa: Law and Policy Interventions
Oyeniyi Abe

For more information about this series, please visit: www.routledge.com

Implementing Business and Human Rights Norms in Africa

Law and Policy Interventions

Oyeniyi Abe

Routledge
Taylor & Francis Group
LONDON AND NEW YORK

First published 2022
by Routledge
4 Park Square, Milton Park, Abingdon, Oxon OX14 4RN

and by Routledge
605 Third Avenue, New York, NY 10158

Routledge is an imprint of the Taylor & Francis Group, an informa business

British Library Cataloguing-in-Publication Data
A catalogue record for this book is available from the British Library

Library of Congress Cataloging-in-Publication Data
A catalog record for this book has been requested

ISBN: 978-0-367-71101-6 (hbk)
ISBN: 978-1-032-26830-9 (pbk)
ISBN: 978-1-003-29012-4 (ebk)

DOI: 10.4324/9781003290124

Typeset in Times New Roman
by Apex CoVantage, LLC

To: ***Oluwadamilola, Oluwademilade, and Ruth***

Contents

Preface xii
Acknowledgements xvi
List of abbreviations xvii

Introduction 1

PART I
Introductory context and principles 3

1 Introduction 5

1.1 Background 5
1.2 Business and human rights in Africa: legal context, challenges, and overview 6
1.3 Nature, aim, and scope of the book 10
1.4 Justification for the book 12
1.5 Structure of the book 14
1.6 Conclusion 15

2 Nature and scope of business and human rights challenges in Africa 20

2.1 Introduction 20
2.2 A third world approach to business and human rights in Africa 20
2.3 Country case studies 22
2.3.1 Niger-Delta: the Ogoni experience 22
2.3.2 The Marikana incident (South Africa) 23
2.3.3 Lake Turkana Wind Power Project (Kenya) 24
2.4 The role of the African Union 26
2.5 Africa's trade regime and human rights implications 27
2.6 Conclusion 29

3 Corporate governance paradigms and regulatory framework 35

3.1 Introduction 35
3.2 Theoretical basis for implementing business and human rights principles 35
3.3 Competing theories of corporate governance 37
3.3.1 Social change as a system of corporate transformation 38
A. Business respect for human rights 38
3.3.2 Shareholder value principle 39
3.3.3 Stakeholder theory 42
3.4 Stakeholder value approach 44
3.5 The board structure of a firm: correlative rights and duties between corporations and local communities 45
3.5.1 Social license validates the responsibility and power of firms 46
3.5.2 Transparency and accountability are sine-qua-non for obtaining social licence to operate 46
3.5.3 Cost-benefit analysis and environmental impact assessments prevent unmitigated violation of human rights 47
3.5.4 Firms as moral agents owe society social service responsibility 47
3.6 Sustainable approach to business and human rights principles 47
3.6.1 Incentivizing socially responsible projects 48
3.7 Conclusion 49

PART II
Human rights-based approach to business and human rights in Africa 55

4 Corporate duty to respect human rights 57

4.1 Introduction 57
4.2 Corporate Human Rights Due Diligence (HRDD) 57
4.3 Corporate Human Rights Impact Assessment (HRIA) 60
4.4 Conclusion 61

5 Integrating a rights-based approach to developmental projects 64

5.1 Introduction 64
5.2 A human rights-based approach to developmental governance 64

5.3 What is a human rights-based approach to developmental governance? 66
5.4 Adaptation of HRBA to development projects 67
5.4.1 Participation 68
A. The nature of participation 70
B. Scope of participation 70
C. How is participation occurring? 72
5.4.2 Accountability and transparency 77
5.4.3 Access to information 82
5.4.4 Non-discrimination and fairness 83
5.5 Conclusion 84

6 Access to effective judicial and non-judicial remedies 90

6.1 Introduction 90
6.2 Legitimacy and the question of access 90
6.3 Effective judicial and non-judicial mechanism 91
6.4 Elements of access to remedies 94
6.4.1 Effective administration of justice 94
6.4.2 Creating a standard legal framework for corporate liability 95
6.4.3 Access to appropriate forums 96
6.5 Conclusion 101

PART III
Implementing the protect, respect, remedy framework in Africa's energy and extractive sectors 105

7 Policy and legal framework in Nigeria 107

7.1 Introduction 107
7.2 Constitution (1999) 107
7.3 The Petroleum Industry Act (2021) 110
7.3.1 Regulatory and institutional reforms 111
7.3.2 Establishment of a host community development trust 111
7.3.3 Environment management plan 112
7.3.4 Gas flaring 112
7.3.5 Access to information 113
7.3.6 Transparency and accountability 115
7.3.7 Abandonment, decommissioning, and disposal 115
7.4 Transitional provisions 116
7.4.1 Petroleum Act (1969) 116

A. The Environmental Guidelines and Standards for the Petroleum Industry in Nigeria (EGASPIN) 118
7.4.2 Oil Pipelines Act (1956) 118
7.5 Environmental Impact Assessment Act (1992) 120
7.6 The Land Use Act (1978) 123
7.7 Companies and Allied Matters Act (CAMA) 2020 124
7.7.1 Human Rights Due Diligence (HRDD) 126
7.8 The National Oil Spill Detection and Response Agency (NOSDRA) 127
7.9 Niger-Delta Development Commission (NDDC) 128
7.10 National Environmental Standards and Regulations Enforcement Agency (Establishment) Act 2007 (NESREA Act) 128
7.11 Nigerian National Human Rights Commission Act (1995) 129
7.12 Corporate criminal jurisdiction 129
7.13 Conclusion 130

8 Policy and legal framework in South Africa 138

8.1 Introduction 138
8.2 Constitution of the Republic of South Africa (1996) 138
8.3 Companies Act (2008) 140
8.4 Mineral and Petroleum Resources Development Act 28 of 2002 (amended in 2008) (MPRDA) 141
8.4.1 Social and labour plan 142
8.4.2 Closure and abandonment 143
8.4.3 Mineral rights ownership 143
8.5 The National Environmental Management Act 107 of 1998 (NEMA) 144
8.6 Environmental impact assessment 145
8.7 South African Human Rights Commission (SAHRC) 145
8.8 Conclusion 147

9 Policy and legal framework in Kenya 151

9.1 Introduction 151
9.2 Constitution of Kenya (2010) 151
9.3 Companies Act (2015) 152
9.4 The Petroleum Act (2019) 153
9.5 Mining Act (2016) 153
9.5.1 Environmental rehabilitation and restoration plan 154
9.6 Business and human rights challenges in Kenya 154

9.7 National Action Plan (NAP) on business and human rights 156
9.8 Conclusion 157

10 The future of business and human rights in Africa 162

10.1 Introduction 162
10.2 Global adaptation of business and human rights principles 163
10.3 The future of business and human rights 163
10.3.1 Global Memorandum of Understanding (GMOUs) 164
10.3.2 Business and Human Rights Unit (BHRU) 165
10.4 Challenges to implementation of business and human rights principles 166
10.4.1 Gender disparities 166
10.4.2 Developing national action plans 167
10.4.3 Political will 168
10.4.4 Environmental democratisation 168
10.5 Conclusion 169

Index 172

Preface

The business and human rights agenda is constantly reshaped by global events. This book comes at a time of urgent international security and health emergencies as well as critical structural challenges. The COVID-19 pandemic, climate change, global economic slowdown, and domestic political tensions, particularly in Africa brings to fore the inability of states to protect and respect human rights. Societal expectations of companies are changing, so also is the power and role of corporations in society constantly escalating. Safeguarding corporate respect for human rights is fundamental to dependable business practice and understanding the obligations and responsibilities of businesses in this context is one of the most significant challenges for state leaders in developing countries. The Guiding Principles on Business and Human Rights were devised specifically to tackle global governance gaps brought by unchecked activities and impact of corporations and lack of political leaders to protect human rights.

The book clarifies and unpacks the respective duties and responsibilities of state and businesses to prevent, mitigate, and remedy adverse human rights impact of corporate activities. It addressed challenges of implementing business and human rights in developing countries, with particular reference to Africa and how states can increase their obligations under various international human rights instruments. The common challenges in key sectors such as energy, extractive, and finance are identified, and solutions are provided. The book is a reviewed version of the author's doctoral thesis and a reflection of the author's academic and practical experience in the business and human rights field. The book will create a platform for stakeholders, especially academics, corporate lawyers, and non-lawyers in business, economic and financial spheres, as well as government and policy leaders, community leaders, experts, researchers, and academics, to discuss, debate, and clarify how to support businesses in this emerging area. The book is divided into three sections and ten chapters.

Section 1 provides the introductory context, and it contains three chapters. Chapter 1 discusses the background, nature, scope, and content of business and human rights agenda in Africa, and how the various challenges in diverse sectors have been impacted by corporate practice. The chapter sets the tone for the discussion in subsequent chapters of the book. The chapter provides an overview of the body of legislation, regulatory framework, guiding principles, institutional arrangements, and industry guidelines that govern developmental projects such as oil, gas, and solid minerals in Africa. In arguing for the justification of the book, the chapter argues that while many countries have developed standards of operation for MNCs – including the Guiding Principles, existing research has not considered the feasibility and viability of countries agreeing to give constitutional recognition to such strong rights-based principles.

Chapter 2 examines business and human rights challenges from an African perspective. It provides an overview of classical cases of business and human rights violations in Africa, highlighting their importance and the necessity for a heightened scrutiny and punitive measures for irresponsible corporate practices in Africa. The chapter further unpacks Africa's approach to the business and human rights discourse. There is the tendency to believe that African states have outsourced the control and responsibility over multinational companies to home states. From a third world approach to international law perspective, this chapter considers the challenges of regulating MNCs in Africa noting the exclusionary, discriminatory, and inequitable characteristics of current global order that is stacked against Africa. The chapter also reframes the business and human rights discourse from an African legal and political landscape. It highlights that the entrenched state interests have prevented the realization of positive outcomes in the development of Africa's resources. Chapter 2 also examines the role of the African Union in developing an African Union Policy Framework on Business and Human Rights, and the importance of integrating business and human rights into trade agreements such as the African Continental Free Trade Area Agreement (AfCFTA).

In Chapter 3, the book provides a systematic examination of the applicable theories and regimes underpinning corporate social responsibility (CSR) in Africa. In doing so, it deals with several complicated matters relating to the competing theories of CSR. First, it contextualizes the discourse by ascertaining the parallels between BHRs and CSR. It then reviews the diverse theories that have been put forward to clarify whether BHRs challenges are within the purview of corporate entities, especially with regards to the shareholder-centric approach of companies.

Section 2 examines the human rights based approach to business and human rights in Africa. Chapter 4 discusses the fundamental key elements of corporate duty to respect human rights: corporate human rights due diligence, and corporate human rights impact assessment. Heightening readers' understanding of the sources and scope of business and human rights norms, this chapter clarifies how businesses can efficiently detect, mitigate, and avert legal and business risks when investing in weak zones, particularly African countries.

Chapter 5 considers the innovative legal methodologies and mechanisms needed to achieve a sustainable and rights-based approach to development projects. This chapter discusses the drivers for corporate accountability and how human rights-based approaches can be integrated to business and human rights standards and principles. Key elements of a rights-based approach extensively discussed include participation, accountability and transparency, access to information, non-discrimination, and fairness. The methodical and fundamental injustice host communities in Africa are subjected to has made any subsequent distribution of income from development projects contentious. The stymied growth in weakly governed countries arises from the lack of an ideological roadmap to develop critical industries in Africa.

Chapter 6 examines the judicial and non-judicial process of obtaining remedy. It highlights states and corporate responsibility to guarantee effective remedial mechanisms for victims of corporate induced human rights violations. The importance of non-judicial grievance mechanisms to remedy corporate-related human rights violations is the hallmark of the business and human rights debate. While highlighting the central features of access to remedies, the chapter constructs a standard legal framework for corporate liability in Africa.

Section 3 discusses the implementation of business and human rights standards in Africa using three geographically located countries as case studies. Chapter 7 highlights the legal framework in Nigeria's energy and extractive sector. It focuses on the regime created in the country to enable sustainable development of its critical extractive sector. A key feature of the legal regime in Nigeria is the recently enacted Petroleum Industry Act which guarantees host community development fund and sustainable development of the oil and gas sector. While these frameworks are innovative, the challenge appears to be inadequate protection of human rights which creates challenges to the implementation of business and human rights principles.

The focus of Chapter 8 is South Africa. South Africa is critical to the business and human rights discourse for a number of reasons. First, it has a robust legal regime through which business and human rights can be met. Second, the judicial branch has, over the years, progressively realized human rights and given justice for victims of human rights violations. Third, South Africa operates a hybrid legal system. Its legal system is an admixture of civil law, common law, and African customary law. Although, the legal procedure for enacting laws follows the English common law system. Fourth, South Africa was one of the countries that called for the process of producing a busines and human rights treaty. This chapter examines the adequacy of domestic laws, practices that can be replicated in other emerging economies, especially with regards to mining projects that impacts the local communities.

The ninth chapter examines business and human rights in Kenya. Kenya is the first African country to adopt a National Action Plan on Business and Human Rights. Its mineral deposits make it an attractive destination country for foreign direct investment. However, human rights concerns associated with resource exploitation have been widespread. On the one hand, the history of the social and ecological structures currently contributes to a thriving environment for the exploitation of natural resources and the chance for economic development, while, on the other, human rights abuse has led to the impoverishment and marginalization of rural communities, and systemic gender discrimination. This chapter examines the legal and institutional framework regulating business and human rights regime in Kenya's energy and extractive sector and considers whether Kenya's legal framework has a strong normative foundation establishing both vertical and horizontal human rights obligations, and a clear legal mechanism for redress in the event of violation of those rights.

The tenth chapter is the conclusion and discusses the future of business and human rights in Africa. It considers that a rights-based approach to development projects provides a just and ethical path towards developing social expectations that corporations ought to make a proactive contribution to solving grave communal problems associated with their activities. For emerging economies, human rights perspective to legal framework is fundamental, otherwise, business enterprises risk exacerbating harm in host communities. In this chapter, an attempt is made to contrast the earlier works on business and human rights which have focussed on the weaknesses inherent in normative instruments, with the current approach which adapts a rights-based approach to development projects. This could help emerging economies, such as Africa achieve holistic sustainable development of its resources, where the rights of the local community are guaranteed, and fundamental human rights protection is integrated into extant laws.

Acknowledgements

An academic writing of this nature requires significant preparation and development. I am thankful to the several helping hands that have helped achieved the completion of this book. My thanks and appreciation to God for being my fortress and pillar throughout the writing and completion of this work. My personal experience from this research exposed me to the realization that the completion of this research was not my sole accomplishment. God granted me good health, for which I am eternally grateful.

My debt of appreciation to the community of business and human rights scholars. Endless thanks to Professor Ada Ordor of the Centre for Comparative Law in Africa, University of Cape Town, South Africa, for her research guidance during my doctoral studies and an excellent academic mentor. I am equally indebted to Professors James Gathii and Spencer Weber Waller, who agreed to serve as my Fulbright supervisors and mentors while at Loyola University, Chicago School of Law. Many ideas in this book were conceived while at Loyola. They made my Fulbright stay highly rewarding and engaging, and offered invaluable advice, support, and encouragement. Many thanks to Julienne E. Grant, the Reference Librarian at the Loyola University Law Library whose kind assistance facilitated my research in Chicago.

I found immense support while preparing this book from the resources at the University of Huddersfield, United Kingdom. I am particularly grateful to Professor Kasim Sheikh, Head of the Law School, for his guidance and support.

To my parents who have always been a source of inspiration, I say a big thank you for your prayers, love, and support. I am grateful to my siblings, for their encouragement and prayerful support.

Finally, thanks are due to my family who supported me as I completed this project and kept reminding me that life consists much more than the world of business and human rights. Many thanks to Oluwadamilola, Oluwademilade, and Osalele for their love, support, and inspiration.

Abbreviations

AfCFTA	African Continental Free Trade Area Agreement
ATS	Alien Tort Statute
AU	African Union
BBBEE	Broad-Based Black Economic Empowerment.
BHR	Business and Human Rights
BIT	Bilateral Investment Treaty
CAMA	Companies and Allied Matters Act
CEMIRIDE	Centre for Minority Rights Development
CESR	Center for Economic and Social Rights
CSR	Corporate Social Responsibility
DIHR	Danish Institute for Human Rights
EAP	Environmental Assessment Practitioner.
ECOWAS	Economic Community of West African States
EIA	Environmental Impact Assessment.
EMP	Environmental Management Plan
ESIA	Environmental and Social Impact Assessment
EU	European Union
FDI	Foreign Direct Investment (FDI)
FPIC	Free, Prior and Informed Consent
GATT	General Agreement on Tariffs and Trade
GMOU	Global Memorandum of Understanding.
GPs	Guiding Principles
HRBA	Human Rights Based Approach
HRC	Human Rights Council
HRDD	Human Rights Due Diligence
HRIA	Human Rights Impact Assessment
ILO	International Labour Organisation
LTWP	Lake Turkana Wind Power Project
LUA	Land Use Act
MOSOP	Movement for the Survival of the Ogoni People
MPRDA	Mineral and Petroleum Resources Development Act
MRGI	Minority Rights Group International
NAPs	National Action Plan

NDDC	Niger-Delta Development Commission
NESREA	National Environmental Standards and Regulations Enforcement Agency
NGOs	Non-Governmental Organisations
NHRI	National Human Rights Institution.
NNPC	Nigerian National Petroleum Corporation
OGPP	Kwale Oil-Gas Processing Plant
RECs	Regional Economic Communities.
SAHRC	South African Human Rights Commission
SDGs	Sustainable Development Goals
SERAC	Social and Economic Rights Action Committee
SLO	Social License to Operate
SLP	Social and Labour Plan
SPDC	Shell Petroleum Development Corporation
SRSG	Special Representative on Business and Human Rights
SVP	Shareholder Value Principle
UN	United Nations
UNGPs	United Nations Guiding Principles
WTO	World Trade Organization

Introduction

Globalization has unified the world by creating a new scope for sharing commonalities. Within this space, business enterprises and transnational corporate actors operate in a complex global environment, especially in high-risk sectors such as mining, oil and gas, telecommunications, construction, banking, and health care amongst others. Understanding human rights responsibilities, impacts, and socially responsible behavior for companies is therefore an essential component of corporate risk management in our current world. The release of the United Nations Guiding Principles on Business and Human Rights by the United Nations, Human Rights Council in 2011, an instrument consisting of 31 principles on this issue, has further underscored the emergence of a rapidly developing set of international law norms on human rights responsibilities of businesses and multinational corporations. In addition to minimizing litigation, financial and reputational risks, understanding and demonstrating corporate respect for human rights is vital to building a culture of trust and integrity amongst local communities, investors, and shareholders. Furthermore, the challenges and opportunities for leveraging resources for sustainable development are as critical as ever. The most pressing problems in the fields of governance and development are evident in the manner in which development scholars and practitioners grapple with the ways in which power, interests, incentives, and characteristics of political systems shape how various human rights impact business activities, the impacts of governance interventions, and the ultimate outcomes of both.

With these questions and contexts in mind, this book examines, clarifies, and unpacks the nature, scope and practical implications of emerging business and human rights norms in international law. It investigates the prospects and potentials of implementing business and human rights norms, in trade, investment, extractive, energy, and diverse sectorial projects in developing countries, with particular perspectives from Kenya, Nigeria, and South Africa. Using the elements of the rights-based approach, this book evaluates what international human rights standards currently regulate corporate conduct as opposed to the conduct of states and individuals, and to clarify the corresponding roles of states and businesses in safeguarding these rights. Business and human rights norms present a valuable roadmap for strengthening institutions to ensure that business activities in various sectors are not devoid of pertinent human rights considerations.

DOI: 10.4324/9781003290124-1

Part I

Introductory context and principles

1 Introduction

1.1 Background

This book examines the potential and challenges associated with adopting business and human rights principles as a legal and institutional framework for addressing human rights questions in development projects in Africa, using Nigeria, South Africa, and Kenya as key focal countries. The book provides an overview of the body of legislation, regulatory framework, guiding principles, institutional arrangements, and industry guidelines that govern developmental projects such as oil, gas, and solid minerals in Africa.

On 16 June 2011, the United Nations Human Rights Council, unanimously endorsed the United Nations Guiding Principles on Business and Human Rights (UNGPs).[1] The UNGPs rest on three pillars: the State duty to protect against human rights violations; the corporate responsibility to respect human rights in their operations; and greater access by victims to effective remedy, both judicial and non-judicial, for human rights violations. The UNGPs thus becomes instructive as a rights-based approach to safeguarding governance challenges in Africa. The book adopts the UNGPs as a Human Rights Based Approach (HRBA) in providing a multijurisdictional and general assessment of the legal and institutional framework designed to manage developmental projects across the focal countries. It further discusses the importance of integrating human rights protection into extant relevant laws and considers how human rights protection can be effectively implanted into domestic laws, regulations, and corporate practices. In so doing, it examines the practicality of implementing business and human rights principles through adaptation of legal and practical structures. Anchored on the HRBA, the book investigates how key developments and strategies have adopted and integrated human rights norms into corporate practice.[2] The objective is to ensure that the implementation of business and human rights (BHRs) principles will ensure positive extractive resource governance, while at the same time guaranteeing that state and corporate actors are held liable for breaching their human rights obligations. The effect will be to create a synergy between key stakeholders in the extractive resource industry: state, corporations, and local communities.

The book offers a fundamental paradigm change in approach to existing literature that has precluded African scholarship.[3] It focusses on efforts to expand the regulatory capacity, institutional efficacy, and democratic legitimacy of

DOI: 10.4324/9781003290124-3

governance institutions that shape development. While existing literature have grappled with the ways in which power, interests, and characteristics of political systems shape how development projects are developed, the impacts of governance interventions, and the ultimate outcomes of both, the goal of this book is to develop a critical understanding of BHR principles and the challenges of economic transformation through social change.

Section 1.2 of this chapter provides the background to the issues identified. It highlights the vital challenges that necessitates vigorous legal solutions in Africa's developmental paradigms, most especially legal challenges relating to business, human rights, and the extractive industry. While the developed nations have done well, developing nations – mainly Sub-Saharan African countries – are still struggling to find a way of securing the desired dividends of developmental projects.[4] Ranging from civil wars arising in diamond conflicts to environmental degradation to mineral exploitation, the stories are of woe, conflict, and further impoverishment for the indigenes of resource rich communities.[5] Harnessing the benefits of resource extraction has become so problematic, that the challenges far outweigh the desired results. Not only has this led to the impoverishment of African citizens, but it has exacerbated wars and ethnic conflicts. The activities of multinational companies (MNCs) are rarely felt in a positive way;[6] the state cares little about improving lives in local communities.[7] These teething problems, which are unique to developing countries,[8] foreground the need for a more comprehensive understanding of shared communal responsibility within a local context. With this approach, companies, local communities, and the state will have a common and shared responsibility to co-exist with one another.[9]

This chapter begins with a contextual analysis of the earliest attempts to regulate corporate activities in key sectors of the economy, and how those attempts have failed. It further examines the importance of the proactive implementation of business and human rights principles in the economies of focal economies. Thereafter, it reveals how these challenges can create a "smart mix" approach:[10] where soft-law instruments will, over time, metamorphose into legally binding instruments – thereby creating cross-cutting synergies between business, human rights, and policy measures.

1.2 Business and human rights in Africa: legal context, challenges, and overview

The energy, extractives, financial, and telecommunications industries have mostly been the strength of African economies.[11] For a number of African countries, oil and gas has constituted part of their gross domestic product (GDP). For instance, oil has been Nigeria's main revenue earning sector. Yet, Nigerians continue to suffer untold hardships arising from activities involving corporate related human rights violations. The 2011 United Nations Environment Programme (UNEP) Report,[12] revealed that the activities of Shell and other oil companies have systematically contaminated the vast majority of Ogoniland. These have serious consequences for human life and well-being. The extent of environmental degradation as evidenced in the Report can be summarized as follows: large-scale evidence of contamination of land and underground water courses, high levels of harmful substances and pollutants, such as benzene, found in community drinking water, residues of harmful substances still found on sites claimed to have been cleaned by the oil companies, failure of the oil companies to operate according to Nigerian standards or any recognized global standard.[13] No doubt, oil exploration in Ogoniland has resulted in severe environmental degradation, oil pollution and grave injustices to the people of Ogoniland.[14] The Report further states that it will require $1 billion for the first five years and between 25 to 30 years to complete any environmental restoration in Ogoniland, once ongoing pollution is stopped.[15] The various human rights violations evident in this Report shows a long overdue restoration of host communities to Nigeria's extractive projects.[16]

Resource governance has been a challenging task in Africa. Flagrant pollution of the air and environment has continued without abatement. Multinational organisations (MNCs) are more concerned with the benefits derived from exploration rather than the impact of their activities on the immediate environment. The idea of wealth maximization at the detriment of sustainable development seems to be the companies' guiding principles. African societies are increasingly concerned that the rise of MNCs in wealth and influence has not seen a commensurate rise in addressing human rights concerns, poverty, unequal treatment of workers, environmental damage, and pollution.[17] This book, therefore, considers the corporate irresponsibility that has pervaded Africa's developmental landscape and human rights concerns associated with corporate practice.

Observing human rights principles in business continues to be one of the greatest challenges facing the current generation. Over the years, concern over human rights violations by businesses has increased exponentially. Indeed, "human rights are not so much an inheritance to preserve as an intervention to make".[18] Yet, the concept of human rights is both simple and powerful. The simplicity and power of human rights lies in the idea that every person is endowed with inherent dignity, and has equal and inalienable rights.[19] Traditionally, human rights were conceived and "designed as a set of rules" and practices to defend citizens from the excessive powers of the state. As a result, states are obliged to ensure that their citizens live a life of dignity. Several human rights instruments have been enacted since 1948 to protect the inviolability of human lives.[20] These mechanisms, collectively referred to as the International Bill of Rights, did not however specifically provide for corporate-related human rights abuses. The idea that "business enterprises must have human rights responsibilities backed by legal requirements in their spheres of operation, is relatively new and is still not universally accepted."[21] Much has been said about states adopting policy measures aimed at responsible natural resource extraction, but the tendency has been to describe the problem rather than profer solutions.[22]

There have been various attempts since the 1960s to regulate the activities of corporate actors and their impact on human rights. The United Nations (UN), through several treaties and conventions, has continued to urge MNCs to observe minimum, basic, human rights protection in their activities. The disparities in the response to these instruments is evident in the attitude of the MNCs which adhere to the basic protection of human rights in developed countries – but which turn a blind eye to such protection in developing countries. The countries of the Global North have shaped corporate behavior through legal and institutional frameworks. Their legal systems enhance corporate responsibility by mandating parallel checks on authorities and offering a medium for vertical claims by citizens. In the African continent, perceptions on the discourses surrounding business and human rights have been lacking, despite the adverse impact of non-state actors and human rights violations on the continent. African states need to reinforce and strengthen their courts (including prosecutors and police); oversight institutions (ombudsmen, anti-corruption agencies, and human rights commissions). Not only should these institutions be more accessible to the people, but they must also be effective in handling complaints and grievance mechanisms. While the Global North appears to have strengthened their oversight over corporate entities, Africa, where the effect of corporate activities is felt is still lacking behind. While the Guiding Principles are a normative construct, African institutions must begin to create innovative pathways to framing claims, employ necessary rhetorics, to hold non-state actors accountable under international law.[23] Perhaps, the lack of a binding business and human rights treaty, and moral frameworks to guide the behaviour of MNCs, has emerged as one of the global socio-economic problems of developing countries in the 21st century.[24] It is thus essential to examine how existing human rights frameworks can be integrated into national and international efforts to reduce irresponsible resource governance and other corporate catastrophes caused by human activity.

In a slightly symmetrical development, the UN sought to regulate corporate actors. In 1974, the UN established a Centre for Transnational Corporations, to "draft a Multinational Code of Conduct for Transnational Corporations."[25] Part A of the Draft Code was concluded in 1983, while Part B was finalised in 1990. The Code placed a tremendous obligation on MNCs to "not only respect the laws of the host states, but also to desist from any form of political or economic interference in the domestic policies" of such states.[26] Few years later, the Organization for Economic Cooperation and Development (OECD), suggested some rules for corporate actors.[27] The OECD guidelines epitomized a comprehensive effort at regulating MNCs during that period. The Guidelines instruct corporations to respect human rights in any country in which they might operate. However, the Guidelines were "intended to be non-binding."[28] Furthermore, the MNCs were involved in the sustained growth of the economies of the developed states within the OECD.[29]

Numerous other initiatives have called for more openness in extractive resource management. The Kimberley Process Certification Scheme was one of the first initiatives to track the illicit sale of diamonds (referred to as "blood diamonds" which are exploited by MNCs, with the proceeds funding rebel governments and their allies against legitimate governments), from being imported from states involved in conflicts or ethnic wars. State parties would have to "certify that any diamonds to be exported are conflict-free – before they can enter the international market."[30] The Extractive Industries Transparency Initiative (EITI) is a multi-stakeholder approach which promotes openness, transparency, and accountability in the management of natural resources in the decision-making process.[31] A significant objective of this initiative is that member states "agree to disclose information on tax payments, licences and contracts."[32] Nigeria is a signatory to the initiative, having voluntarily signed up to the global initiative. To show its commitment, Nigeria passed the EITI Act, 2007,[33] to enforce implementation of the initiative in the country. It became the first country in the world to support this voluntary implementation with legislation.[34] Nigeria has shown meaningful progress in implementing the aims of the initiative. However, South Africa is not a signatory to the initiative. It is important to stress that the purpose of the initiative is to reconcile the information given by the company with that obtained from the government. As will be argued in later chapters, this is a clear indication that soft-law instruments could be used as a yardstick for controlling MNCs, in order to ensure extractive resource governance.[35]

In 2003, the UN adopted the "Draft Norms on the Responsibilities of Transnational Corporations and Other Business Enterprises with Regard to Human Rights."[36] This instrument was approved on 13 August 2003 by the United Nations Sub-Commission on the Promotion and Protection of Human Rights.[37] However, as inventive as these treaties and instruments may be, their realization at national and international levels has been met with challenges. Fears around these domestic applications have propelled the debate on an approach that integrates human rights protection with extractive resource governance, and corporate practice and conduct.[38]

In July 2005, then UN Secretary General Kofi Annan appointed Professor John G. Ruggie as his Special Representative on Business and Human Rights (SRSG).[39] Initially, Ruggie's duty was to "identify and clarify standards of corporate responsibility and accountability regarding human rights, elaborate on states' roles in regulating and adjudicating corporate activities, clarify concepts such as "complicity" and sphere of influence, develop methodologies for human rights impact assessments and consider state and corporate best practices."[40] The SRSG, after widespread consultations, eventually produced the UN Guiding Principles (GPs) on Business and Human Rights.[41] The GPs provide an allocation of tasks between the states (as duty bearers of protecting and realizing human rights established in international treaties) and companies, who are duty-bound to respect the rights and apply due diligence in their activities – especially when they are operating in weak zones.[42] This resolution doubtless marks a turning point in terms of creating an inclusive standard for MNCs liability for business-induced human rights violations.[43] The GPs re-emphasized the significance of states' existing obligations in protecting human rights, the need for businesses to comply with domestic laws and rules, and providing adequate remedies to victims of human rights violations.[44] Applying these Principles to the various sectors of economic development in Africa, the GPs seek to enhance corporate practices in order to achieve concrete results for victims of human rights violations – as well as communities that are host to development projects and which are recipients of a corporate-induced environmental disaster.[45]

The initiatives discussed in this section illustrate the efforts aimed at ensuring that businesses positively impact on human rights in their areas of operation. The effectiveness of these initiatives lies in the responsiveness of corporate actors relative to understanding the precariousness and unpredictability of their activities which impact tremendously on human rights in weak zones. Indeed, this latest attempt is not a "silver bullet" panacea for the business and human rights dilemma.[46] Instead, and depending on the side of the aisle, it gives stakeholders an opportunity to demand their rights and insist that corporate responsibility involves respecting human rights. Furthermore, evidence has shown that Africa suffers from huge infrastructural decline and lax enforcement of laws and policies.[47]

Undeniably, the business and human rights principles have suffered from a fair amount of criticism.[48] While these criticisms may be plausible in that the GPs give companies wide discretion to cherry-pick human rights provisions of their choice and at their own pace, they do not weaken the potentials of the GPs in any way. The GPs are currently in their eleventh year. The fact that they have outlived earlier initiatives suggests potential for mitigating and reducing adverse human rights violations in the energy and extractive industry – particularly in Africa. Certainly, the GPs do not provide a "silver bullet" resolution to the corporate abuse of human rights. However, they have again triggered a discussion on the dangers of the intractable clarification of corporate responsibility and on the need for developing a framework that would mainstream human rights protection into corporate practice and culture. This book builds on this foundation and takes the debate on integrating human rights further by conducting a socio-legal approach to the implementation of business and human rights in Africa's resource economy.

1.3 Nature, aim, and scope of the book

Harnessing the dividends of various resources in Africa has not only remained challenging – but has also led to civil wars, ethnic conflicts, and rent seeking. Resource governance in Sub-Saharan Africa has created many human rights challenges, including land displacement by citizens to make room for extractive projects. This is particularly important when local communities have spiritual and traditional attachments to their land. Other issues include locating projects in local communities that lack infrastructural amenities, and which are poor and vulnerable, lack of local community consultation and participation in the decision-making process, lack of transparency and accountability, and having little or no access to judicial remedies for victims of human rights violations. Related to these challenges is the debate over who owns the natural resources, and, therefore, in whose interest the extraction should accrue to. Most constitutional and domestic regimes have been able to craft legislation in a way that gives absolute right over natural resources to the state; however, the state is expected to utilise those resources for the benefit of the people. The various challenges related to extractive resources do not seem to have adequate solutions. Using an admixture of various rights-based approaches to resource governance, as well as multijurisdictional perspectives and assessment of crosscutting themes, laws, institutions that practically applies the GPs, have not been considered extensively in the literature.

The question then arises: what legal, policy, and institutional frameworks at the domestic level would facilitate the integration of business and human rights principles into resource projects approval and implementation? What are the practical challenges and prospects of adopting a rights-based approach to resource governance? What is the legal justification and value of incorporating the rights-based approach into corporate governance models? Engaging with these questions will determine how developing countries can craft policies and programmes that will not only incentivize corporate responsibility but facilitate the social license to operate (SLO). The capacity of local communities to structure their environment in their own way, to be represented in governance, and to be able to voice their concerns about development projects is absent from the debates on the implementation of business and human rights principles.

The presumption is that MNCs typically prefer to violate human rights than to remedy or mitigate adverse human rights violations – even where the need to respect human rights is glaringly obvious. Various corporate disasters: Bhopal (1984 – India), Shell (1997 – Nigeria), Marikana (2012 – South Africa), and Rana Plaza (2013 – Bangladesh), have shown that companies will continue to double down on their dislike for compliance with human rights. Corporate entities do not have effective complaints processes for grievances related to their activities.[49] Victims of human rights violations on the other hand find it difficult to hold MNCs accountable – either in the domestic courts due to court delays, judicial corruption, and ineptitude, prohibitive costs, and weak enforcement of laws, or at international level, due to the principle of *forum non-convenience*.[50] Global and national efforts are needed to limit the misuse of natural resources in developing countries – which is often excessive.

Furthermore, MNCs hardly ever admit any wrongdoing when victims demand compensation but are quick to claim sabotage and local community violence.[51] While some pay fines as compensation, they do not accept that human rights violations were caused by their activities. For instance, Shell (Nigeria) has and continues to pay huge sums of money in out-of-court settlements, and yet it still engages in massively corrupt practices and extreme violations of human rights.[52] Nevertheless, where innovative approaches are taken, fair, timely, and transparent remedies can be found in domestic courts through torts claims such as negligence.[53]

MNCs understand they must comply with host state laws. However, these companies have established over time that complying with legal norms may not guarantee their prosperity – especially in developing countries like Nigeria and Kenya with weak enforcement capabilities. Some companies with reports of human rights compliance cannot produce any evidence to support their claim.[54] Home and host-state regulations have not checked on the excesses of these MNCs. The inability of the international community to craft regulations that would guide corporate practices and mitigate adverse human rights violations, could have serious implications for the effective implementation of business and human rights principles. Weak economies lower human rights standards so that MNCs find it attractive to function in the states concerned.[55] Short-term gains in these countries are, however, illusory – and they weaken longer-term recovery.[56] The protracted and unrestrained governance gaps encourage MNCs to operate without sanctions or caution.

Current research suggests that resource wealth can go together with unstable development, macroeconomic instability,[57] "high unemployment, poverty and inequality."[58] Developed countries have however shown the commitment and capacity to enforce their laws, so mandating their companies to be involved in responsible behaviours wherever they operate. Given its centrality to African economies, there is a growing demand for research into resource governance and its leverage for sustainable development. The rallying point is administering resource governance in a way that positively contributes to the SDGs.[59]

The inherent problems are massive displacement without adequate consultation or compensation when making way for development projects, lack of participation, and inadequate or non-existent access to judicial remedies for victims of human rights violations. These instances are a stark reminder that corporate disasters represent state failure to address corporate impunity and failure to assume "duty" in respect of respect human rights under national and international laws. While it is envisaged that integrating human rights protection into domestic laws and policies would be the panacea to these intractable challenges, a rights-based approach to resource governance would be a holistic framework that would safeguard future generations from corporate-related human rights abuses and climate disaster.

MNCs are not subject to any single global regulator, and thus the difficulties in integrating human rights standards into the operations of development enterprises constitutes a growing concern for victims of corporate-related abuses, national bodies, and the international community. Not only do victims of human rights abuses face the daily challenges of living, they also are denied access to justice through the courts. States, on the other hand, lack the political will to enforce laws due to Foreign Direct Investment (FDI) from development projects. The task, therefore, is to ascertain what international human rights standards currently regulate corporate conduct as opposed to the conduct of states and individuals, and to clarify the corresponding roles of states and businesses in safeguarding these rights. The lack of a legal and institutional framework to integrate human rights protections has prevented communities which host extractive projects from realizing their human rights.

This research considers the impact of extractive companies on their host communities and how this has affected the ability of such communities to develop in an environmentally sustainable way. Drawing significant lessons from South Africa – due to its proactive legislation imposing human rights compliance on companies – this book examines the potential of implementing the GPs in Nigeria's extractive resource industry.

1.4 Justification for the book

Many countries have developed standards of operation for MNCs – including the GPs.[60] While these have shown tremendous promise, adequate steps need to be taken to ensure that these recommendations are effective in practice. For example, the UN Commission on Transnational Corporations failed after almost 20 years of regulating MNCs activities. Existing research has not considered the feasibility and viability of countries agreeing to give constitutional recognition to such strong rights-based principles. This book attempts to fill this gap.

While home state regulations have been instructive in controlling MNCs, host states have not yet understood the urgency of developing new rules or adapting emerging rules to the local context. This book therefore examines emerging debates on the alternative approaches for ensuring the integration of human rights norms into business conduct and corporate culture.[61] Thus the question is how best to incorporate and implement the GPs. This is particularly important when it is considered that the GPs are voluntary. The main task is identifying the means through which states can address human rights concerns in development projects through laws, policies, regulations, and judicial pronouncements. In implementing the GPs, companies need to be proactive and more involved in the protection and realization of human rights. The obligation to achieve this depends on the moral imperatives of companies in terms of being involved in human rights respect. Hence, can there be incentives for companies to address these human rights concerns? This book investigates the relationship between corporate accountability and human rights.

The linkages between human rights and business are here to stay. States and corporate actors both share control and authority. A system must be put in place to address the linkages between human rights and trade, investment, and socio-economic development. For example, the Nigerian legal regime does not admit of corporate human rights obligations or refer to international human rights treaties on human rights. However, it is the norm that if a state starts to enforce a strict set of regulations, MNCs can simply relocate and reincorporate somewhere else. There is therefore a need to balance the interests of states and MNCs. However, there have been no studies on the usefulness of these business and human rights principles in resource governance development in Africa. Hence this book.

As noted earlier, most of the existing legal scholarship have focused on specific and sectorial issues in the Global North and have not provided a multijurisdictional assessment in Africa. This analytical divergence has not allowed for complete and multisector evaluations on key regional, national, and local actors and bodies who are actively engaged in promoting a human rights-based approach to resource governance in Africa. Given the corresponding and divergent legal, institutional, and human rights challenges facing the resource industry in the continent, a complete and logical investigation of governance and institutional settings, including prospects for multisector alliances is warranted. This book fills the gap. It offers a thorough and book length clarification of the legal regimes and institutional paradigms in select African resource industry from a holistic standpoint that has not been offered in existing literature.

The book offers a useful and analytical discourse on the implementation of business and human rights principles in select African countries. To achieve this, the book adopts a lesson learned and continental approach which does not necessarily focus on one country. The book unpacks the nature, scope, drivers, contours, and gaps with respect to business and human rights norms in Africa. The lessons learned approach operates at the highly analytical and conceptual level, while using examples from Kenya, Nigeria, and South Africa, each country representing sub-Saharan African regions to strengthen the analysis made.

It is undoubtedly acknowledged that the substantive chapters cannot unpack and explore every applicable legislation and instruments in all African countries. The essential unifying principle and objective of this book therefore is to enhance an understanding of the guiding principles of laws, and institutions that govern Africa's developmental trajectory; investigate detailed sustainability issues such as human rights-based approach; offer realistic perspectives on how corporations can recognize, alleviate, and avoid human rights risks in development projects across Africa.

1.5 Structure of the book

This book is organized into three parts to reflect a transition from conceptual and theoretical issues to practical and substantive issues. Part I consists of three chapters. Chapter 1 is the introductory chapter which highlights the background to the study, nature, aim, and scope of the book, and justification for the research. Chapter 2 examines nature and scope of business and human rights challenges in Africa. It discusses three case studies, each from Kenya, Nigeria, and South Africa, highlighting the imperative of adopting human rights standards in corporate practices in Africa. It discusses these challenges through a third world approach to business and human rights in Africa. The chapter concludes with an exposition on African Union's approach to contextualize business and human rights in the continent. Chapter 3 reviews corporate governance paradigms and regulatory framework. It discussed the theoretical framework for implementing business and human rights in Africa, identifying applicable and relevant competing theories and sustainable approach to implementing business respect for human rights. It argues for a local community stakeholder connection with MNCs as the only basis for granting social license to operate – thereby ensuring that the aims and objectives of the UNGPs are attained. While companies continue to be involved in CSR initiatives, states are to give them direction and to incentivize any beneficial programmes for communities. Business and human rights build on this and offers a closer nexus between various stakeholders in managing the relationship between companies and their host communities. The chapter further critically examines the effectiveness of incentives for compliance with human rights norms, and also the adequacy of penalties for promoting deterrence.

Part II consists of three chapters, and it examines the human rights-based approach to business and human rights in Africa. Chapter 4 examines the corporate duty to respect human rights. It extensively discusses the imperatives of adopting corporate human rights due diligence and human rights impact assessment in business practice and management. Chapter 5 further discusses the elements of a human rights-based approach. Extending the discussions from Chapter 4, Chapter 5 discusses emerging approaches to integrating human rights into state laws, policies, rules, and regulations. The chapter considers the idea of mainstreaming human rights norms under international law – through the application of the core provision of a Human Rights-Based Approach (HRBA). It also discusses how they can be implanted into local legislation – thereby driving corporate conduct in terms of respecting human rights. One of the challenges facing the global corporate community is securing a mandatory legal regime as it concerns human rights fulfilment. This chapter examines the strategies adopted by the HRBA and how they can be utilized in understanding and implementing the UNGPs. The strategies have also sharpened the quest for an international legal order for human rights in business. Chapter 6 considers access to effective remedies for victims of corporate induced human rights violations. It highlights the systemic shortcomings in existing efforts at addressing access to remedies within the business and human rights debate. It further analysed range of mechanisms guaranteed by effective remedial mechanisms – from state-based judicial and non-judicial mechanisms to non-state-based remediation and operational level grievance mechanisms involving businesses, and other stakeholders.

Part III discusses the implementation of the Protect, Respect, and Remedy Framework, with particular focus on Africa's energy and extractive industries. It considers the development of, or reform of legal and institutional framework that will guide the implementation of business and human rights in the identified focal countries. Chapter 7 considers the policy and legal framework in Nigeria's extractive sector and how these frameworks can be adapted to the realities of business and human rights challenges. Chapter 8 focuses on the legal and policy regime in South Africa, and how the regime is shaping implementation of business and human rights norms. Chapter 9 discusses Kenya's approach to business and human rights. It examines its policy and legal framework as well as efforts to develop a National Action Plan on Business and Human Rights. Chapter 10 concludes the book. It provides a roadmap for developing a National Action Plan for African states and adopts a lesson learned approach from global best practices in realizing busines and human rights norms. The chapter also highlights the future of business and human rights in Africa, opportunities for further engagement and offers some key practical recommendations.

1.6 Conclusion

There are rich prospects for cross fertilization and interchange of best practices between the key actors, organizations, investors, and stakeholders operating in Africa's development sector. For example, in Nigeria, Kenya, and South Africa that have robust regulation on resource governance, key lessons on how governance and supervisory measures may be enriched in resource development to avoid the recurrent consequences in resource sector management will be pivotal. Furthermore, the focus on a human rights-based approach is predicated on the fact that human rights tests have proceeded beyond setting standards and implementation. They now focus more on the social inclusion of key stakeholders. A systemic, multi sector and robust examination of human rights standards and norms into the design, approval, and implementation of extractive projects will safeguard a coordinated, transformed, well informed, and effective lessons from extant governance arrangements. The next chapter discusses the nature, aim, and scope of business and human rights in Africa through a third world approach to mainstreaming corporate human rights standards and norms.

Notes

1 Human Rights Council, "Guiding Principles on Business and Human Rights: Implementing the United Nations "Protect, Respect and Remedy' Framework" Report of the Special Representative of the Secretary-General on the Issue of Human Rights and Transnational Corporations and Other Business Enterprises, UN Doc. A/HRC/17/31 (21 March 2011) [UNGPs].
2 See: "The Human Rights Based Approach to Development Cooperation: Towards a Common Understanding among UN Agencies" <https://unsdg.un.org/resources/human-rights-based-approach-development-cooperation-towards-common-understanding-among-un> accessed 15 October 2020.
3 Considering its importance to the African economy, this book focuses on certain businesses such as extractives and energy industries.
4 Claudia Pérez, & Oscar Claveria, "Natural Resources and Human Development: Evidence from Mineral-Dependent African Countries Using Exploratory Graphical Analysis" (2020) 65 *Resources Policy* 1; Yannis Arvanitis, & Maxime Weigert, "Turning Resource Curse into Development Dividends in Guinea-Bissau" (2017) *Resources Policy* 226.
5 In the year 2000, the United Nations condemned illicit trade in diamonds that had helped fuel conflicts in war-torn Sierra Leone. The UN called on the business community in diamond trade, to establish a legal regime for demarcating diamonds from legitimate sources. See the following UN Documents: SC Res 1173, UN SCOR, 53rd sess, 3891st mtg, UN Doc S/RES/1173 (12 June 1998); SC Res 1295, UN SCOR, 55th sess, 4129th mtg, UN Doc S/RES/1295 (18 April 2000) ['The Situation in Angola']; SC Res 1306, UN SCOR, 55th sess, 4168th mtg, UN Doc S/RES/1306 (5 July 2000) ['The Situation in Sierra Leone']; SC Res 1343, UN SCOR, 56th sess, 4287th mtg, UN Doc S/RES/1343 (7 March 2001) ['The Situation in Liberia'].
6 In the context of this work, multinational corporations (MNCs) shall be used interchangeably with transnational corporations (TNCs). An MNCs is an organisation, which owns or controls production of goods or services in one or more countries – other than the home country. See further "Multinational Corporations" <http://www2.econ.iastate.edu/classes/econ355/choi/mul.htm> accessed 29 June 2021.
7 Amy Copley, "Figure of the Week: Extractive Resource Governance in Africa" *Brookings* (6 July 2017) <www.brookings.edu/blog/africa-in-focus/2017/07/06/figure-of-the-week-extractive-resource-governance-in-africa/> accessed 9 May 2020; see further Stewart Patrick, *Fragile States, Global Threats, and International Security* (2011).
8 Ibid.
9 Salar Ghahramani, "Sovereigns, Socially Responsible Investing, and the Enforcement of International Law through Portfolio Investment and Shareholder Activism: The Three Models" (2014) *U of Penn J Int'l L* 1073 [Social activism, along with socially responsible investing (SRI), has a long history among individuals and private institutional investors].
10 In the context of business and human rights, "smart mix approach" are approaches that utilize a combination of voluntary and regulatory measures in addressing human rights concerns in business activities. See further Daniel Kinderman, "Time for a Reality Check: Is Business Willing to Support a Smart Mix of Complementary Regulation in

Private Governance?" (2016) *Policy and Society* 29–42; Jolyon Ford, & Justine Nolan, "Regulating Transparency on Human Rights and Modern Slavery in Corporate Supply Chains: The Discrepancy between Human Rights Due Diligence and the Social Audit" (2020) 26(1) *Australian Journal of Human Rights* 28.

11 D. Olawuyi, *Extractives Industry Law in Africa* (2018) 5.

12 UNEP, "Environmental Assessment of Ogoniland" (2011) <https://postconflict.unep.ch/publications/OEA/UNEP_OEA.pdf> accessed 9 May 2021.

13 Ibid.

14 Ibid.

15 Ibid. at pages 15, 211.

16 See further, Mercy Makpor, & Regina Leite, "The Nigerian Oil Industry: Assessing Community Development and Sustainability" (2017) *International Journal of Business and Management* 66. [noting the positive impact when development takes place in host communities and sustainability is attained]; Kola Odeku, "Effective Implementation of Environmental Management Plan for Sustainable Mining" (2017) *Environmental Economics* 26–35. [arguing for environmental protection in the process of mining operations and highlighting the importance of sustainable mining in order to ensure that mining is conducted sensibly and responsibly].

17 N. Sinkovics, & J. Archie-acheampong, "The Social Value Creation of MNEs: A Literature Review across Multiple Academic Fields" (2020) 16(1) *Critical Perspectives on International Business* 8.

18 Samuel Moyn, *The Last Utopia: Human Rights in History* (2010) 9.

19 Preamble to the Stockholm Declaration on the Human Environment (1972).

20 The International Bill of Right refers to the Universal Declaration of Human Rights (UDHR), 1948; International Covenant on Civil and Political Rights (ICCPR) 1966; International Covenant on Economic, Social and Cultural Rights (ICESCR) 1966. See also O. Abe, "The Feasibility of Implementing the United Nations Guiding Principles on Business and Human Rights in the Extractive Industry in Nigeria" (2016) *Journal of Sustainable Development Law and Policy* 138.

21 Abe, above (n 20) 138. See further John G. Ruggie, *Just Business: Multinational Corporations and Human Rights* (2013).

22 Some of the problems related to human rights violations in the context of resource extraction include land grabs, access to information, water and air pollution, displacement of citizens from their ancestral lands, and lack of participation by locals in development initiatives.

23 Stuart Kirsch, *Mining Capitalism: The Relationship between Corporations and Their Critics* (2014).

24 N. Bernaz, "Conceptualizing Corporate Accountability in International Law: Models for a Business and Human Rights Treaty" (2021) 22 *Human Rights Review* 45; J. Kolieb, "Advancing the Business and Human Rights Treaty Project through International Criminal Law: Assessing the Options for Legally-Binding Corporate Human Rights Obligations" (2018) 50 *Georgia Journal of International Law* 789.

25 See: UN Code of Conduct on Transnational Corporations, 23 I.L.M. 626 (1984).

26 Steven Ratner, "Corporations and Human Rights: A Theory of Legal Responsibility" (2001) 111 *Yale Law Journal* 467 at 519.

27 OECD, "OECD Guidelines for Multinational Enterprises" (2011) <www.oecd.org/daf/inv/mne/48004323.pdf> accessed 16 October 2020. The Guidelines were updated in 2011 for the fifth time since they were first adopted in 1976.

28 See Larry C. Backer, "Transnational Corporations" Outward Expression of Inward Self-Constitution: The Enforcement of Human Rights by Apple, Inc." (2013) 20 *Indiana J of Global Legal Std* 827. [Arguing that the system of managing corporate behaviour outside imperatives of local laws creates three governance systems arising from multi-faceted arrangement between states, international organizations, and global actors].

29 See Gunther Teubner, "Self-Constitutionalizing TNCs? On the Linkage of 'Private' and 'Public' Corporate Codes of Conduct" (2011) 18 *Indiana J Global Legal Std* 635.

[noting that the codes are constitutional instincts which impacts TNC drastically. Their metamorphosis into binding constitutional standards is beyond state instrumentality but inner workings within private organizations]; see also George K. Foster, “Investors, States, and Stakeholders: Power Asymmetries in International Investment and the Stabilizing Potential of Investment Treaties” (2013) 17 *Lewis & Clark L Rev* 361. [arguing that investors owe self-imposed obligations toward local stakeholders such as OECD].

30 General Assembly Resolution 55/56, A/ RES/55/56 (29 January 2001); See “Kimberly Process Core Document” <www.kimberleyprocess.com/en/kpcs-core-document> accessed 13 October 2020; See also Holly Cullen, “The Irresistible Rise of Human Rights Due Diligence: Conflict Minerals and Beyond” (2015) 48 *George Washington Int'l Law Review* 743 [noting that activities of NGOs exposed the relationship between sales from diamonds to finance armed rebel groups].

31 See “What We Do” <https://eiti.org/About> accessed 15 October 2020.

32 See “How We Work” <https://eiti.org/about/how-we-work> accessed 15 October 2020.

33 See “NEITI: Nigeria” <https://eiti.org/nigeria> accessed 15 October 2020. [Nigeria domesticated its version of this initiative and made it imperative on agencies in the extractive industry to ensure reporting, disclosure, and transparency in all revenues from the extractive industry].

34 Ibid.

35 Other initiatives include Publish What You Pay (PWYP) coalition launched as a bid to avoid the resource curse pandemic. It does this through three pillars: publish why you pay and how you extract, publish what you pay, and publish what you earn and how you spend. Nigeria, South Africa, and Kenya have representations in the organization. See further “Who We Are” <www.publishwhatyoupay.org/about/> accessed 15 October 2020. The Open Government Partnership (OGP) is a multilateral partnership, which aims to “secure concrete commitments from governments to promote transparency, empower citizens, fight corruption, and harness new technologies to strengthen governance”. Nigeria is currently implementing 16 commitments from their 2019–2022 action plan. Kenya and South Africa have delivered their 2020–2022 action plan. See “About Open Government Partnership” <www.opengovpartnership.org/about/> accessed 26 April 2021. See further the UN Global Compact, <www.unglobalcompact.org/what-is-gc/mission/principles>; Voluntary Principles for Security and Human Rights (2000); Code of Conduct for Private Security Service Providers (2010), the OECD Due Diligence Guidelines for Responsible Supply Chains of Minerals from Conflict-Affected and High-Risk Areas (2011); §§1502–1503 of the Dodd – Frank Wall Street Reform and Consumer Protection Act, Pub.L. 111–203, H.R. 4173 [regulates disclosures on conflict materials in or near the Democratic Republic of the Congo (DRC)].

36 U.N. Doc. E/CN.4/Sub.2/2003/12/Rev.2 (2003). Article 14 of the Draft Norms requires MNCs to act in accordance with national laws, regulations and policies relating to the preservation of the environment of their host countries. They must conduct their activities in accordance with relevant international agreements, principles, and standards in a manner that guarantees sustainable development.

37 U.N. Code of Conduct on Transnational Corporations, 23 I.L.M. 626 (1984).

38 Andrew Crane, Dirk Matten, et al., *Business Ethics: Managing Corporate Citizenship and Sustainability in the Age of Globalization* (2019) 232.

39 Special Representative of the Secretary-General on the Issue of Human Rights and Transnational Corporations and Other Business Enterprises, *Guiding Principles on Business and Human Rights: Implementing the United Nations “Protect, Respect and Remedy” Framework*, U.N. Doc. A/HRC/17/31 (21 March 2011).

40 See Human Rights Resolution 2005/69, “Human Rights and Transnational Corporations and Other Business Enterprises” Chap. XVII, E/CN.4/2005/L.10/Add.17 (20 April 2005).

41 Guiding Principles, above (n 1).

42 Ibid.

43 See Irene Pietropaoli, *Business, Human Rights and Transitional Justice* (2020).

44 Guiding Principles, above (n 1).
45 See B. Hamm, "The Struggle for Legitimacy in Business and Human Rights Regulation: A Consideration of the Processes Leading to the UN Guiding Principles and an International Treaty" (2021) *Human Rights Review* <https://doi.org/10.1007/s12142-020-00612-y; https://link.springer.com/article/10.1007/s12142-020-00612-y#citeas>
46 Human Rights Council, A/HRC/8/5, "Protect, Respect and Remedy: A Framework for Business and Human Rights" Report of the Special Representative of the Secretary-General on the Issue of Human Rights and Transnational Corporations and Other Business Enterprises (7 April 2008) para 7. ["A/HRC/8/5"].
47 Olawuyi (n 11) 7.
48 Florian Wettstein, "Normativity, Ethics, and the UN Guiding Principles on Business and Human Rights: A Critical Assessment" (2015) 14(2) *Journal of Human Rights* 170 [opposing Ruggie's "*do no harm*" proviso and arguing for positive duty on corporations to respect human rights]; Surya Deva, & David Bilchitz (eds.), *Human Rights Obligations of Business: Beyond the Corporate Responsibility to Respect?* (2013) [advocating for a broader understanding of corporate human rights responsibility]; Anna Grear, & Burns H. Weston, "The Betrayal of Human Rights and the Urgency of Universal Corporate Accountability: Reflections on a Post-Kiobel Lawscape" (2015) 15 *Human Rights Law Review* 40 [noting that the juridical order is too ideologically skewed to guarantee the kind of human rights justice hoped for globally].
49 Bruce Harvey, "Community Complaints, Disputes and Grievance Guidance" *Rio Tinto* (1 June 2011) <www.qal.com.au/media/9257/community-complaints-disputes-grievance-guidance-2011-2014.pdf> accessed 9 May 2021.
50 *Kiobel v. Royal Dutch Petroleum Co.*, 133 S.Ct. 1659 (2013).
51 Daily Trust, "Nigeria: Mobil, NNPC to Pay N82bn Damages to Akwa Ibom Communities Hit By Oil Spill" *Daily Trust* (21 June 2021) <https://dailytrust.com/mobil-nnpc-to-pay-n82bn-damages-to-akwa-ibom-communities-hit-by-oil-spill> accessed 30 June 2021.
52 Stanley Reed, "Shell and Eni to Be Tried Over $1.3 Billion Nigerian Oil Deal" *New York Times* (20 December 2017). Other cases of human rights violations which have ended in the courts include *Wiwa et al v. Royal Dutch Petroleum Company and Shell Transport and Trading Company PLC* (2002) 226 F. 3d 88 [out-of-court settlement]; *Larry Bowoto et al. v. Chevron Texaco Corp. et al* (2004) 312. F. Supp.2d 1229 [Plaintiffs' claims denied]; Bodo community oil spill (Shell agreed to a £ 55 million out-of-court settlement in January 2015 and an agreement to clean-up the oil pollution).
53 Alex Enumah, "Court Orders Mobil, NNPC to Pay A'Ibom Communities N82bn" *This Day* (22 June 2021) <www.thisdaylive.com/index.php/2021/06/22/court-orders-mobil-nnpc-to-pay-aibom-communities-n82bn/>.
54 Most, if not all MNCs have ethical statements indicating that they uphold human rights principles and standards. However, most statements are only good on paper. Their conduct and practice indicate otherwise.
55 V. Yilanci, M. Aslan, & O. Ozgur, "Disaggregated Analysis of the Curse of Natural Resources in Most Natural Resource-Abundant Countries" (2021) 71 *Resources Policy* 102017.
56 Ibid.
57 Samuel E. Wills, Lemma W. Senbet, et al., "Sovereign Wealth Funds and Natural Resource Management in Africa" (2016) *Journal of African Economies* ii3.
58 William B. Hurlbut, "Overcoming Poverty and Inequality in South Africa: An Assessment of Drivers, Constraints and Opportunities" (The World Bank, March 2018) 42.
59 Goal 16 seeks to "promote peaceful and inclusive societies for sustainable development, provide access to justice for all and build effective, accountable and inclusive institutions at all levels". See Transforming Our World: The 2030 Agenda for Sustainable Development <https://sdgs.un.org/2030agenda> accessed 18 September 2020.
60 For example, France: Corporate Duty of Vigilance Law.
61 GPs 1 and 2 clearly spell out the role of States and business in the business and human rights agenda.

2 Nature and scope of business and human rights challenges in Africa

2.1 Introduction

This chapter examines business and human rights challenges from an African perspective. It provides an overview of classical cases of business and human rights violations in Africa, highlighting their importance and the necessity for a heightened scrutiny and punitive measures for irresponsible corporate practices in Africa. The chapter further unpacks Africa's approach to the business and human rights (BHR) discourse. There is the tendency to believe that African states have outsourced the control and responsibility over multinational companies (MNCs) to home states. From a third world approach to international law perspective, this chapter considers the challenges of regulating MNCs in Africa noting the exclusionary, discriminatory, and inequitable characteristics of current global order that is stacked against Africa.

2.2 A third world approach to business and human rights in Africa

According to the 2017 resource governance index, several African countries score very low in terms of rule of law, control of corruption, and political stability.[1] For instance, Nigeria has the largest oil and gas reserves in sub-Saharan Africa,[2] and 188 trillion cubic feet of gas.[3] Not only is it the largest population on the continent, but its revenue earning sector, mainly from oil and gas is gravely managed. On the other hand, South Africa scores well in an enabling legal and institutional environment, government efficiency, and accountability.[4] While South Africa is sub-Saharan Africa's largest gold producer, it has the highest gini coefficient in the region.[5] However, disclosure rules on environmental impact assessments, mitigation management plans and licensing remains a challenge.[6]

The contemporary discourse on BHRs overlooks the African legal and political landscape. For example, the business and human rights debate is primarily anchored on corporate respect for human rights. This is predicated on the notion that a truly democratic society with dogmatic political system will safeguard corporate responsibility. However, African states still grapple with democratic constitutionalism that fails to acknowledge legal responsibility for non-state actors

DOI: 10.4324/9781003290124-4

and provide quality access to remedies for victims of human rights violations. The exponential increase in the legal, political, and institutional role of multinational companies (MNCs) and financial institutions has created a disequilibrium in dealing with African states over development projects. The remarkable power and influence of these non-state actors create a disproportionate relationship and the reduction in the socio legal, economic, and political negotiating power of African states. To complicate this relationship, most African states legal systems are weak, non-existent, or inadequate. This obfuscates the state duty to protect human rights as recourse to remedial action falls on a broken or weak legal system. Furthermore, despite the ubiquitous nature of the African human rights system, African states remain vulnerable to corporate human rights abuses. This requires an Afro-centric (third world) strategic approach rather than Euro-centric human rights mechanisms to address issues that hinder Africa's development.

This chapter reframes the business and human rights discourse from an African legal and political landscape.[7] It examines case studies, demonstrating how existing human rights mechanisms neglect to make MNCs account for irresponsible human right practices in the continent. In doing this, it considers the extent to which the inequality between the Global South and Global North has skewed the business and human rights narrative in favour of developed economies. For example, existing business and human rights discourse has not seriously considered the historical systems of colonisation, apartheid, and imperialism which aided the exploitation of weaker economies by MNCs. Furthermore, the entrenched state interests have prevented the realization of positive outcomes in the development of states resources.

Undoubtedly, most African states have established capacity and experience working with and obtaining capital for the development of their resources. In the process, state apparatus does negotiate corporatist pact with local communities, union workers, that have included several concessions to labour. While these states, to some extent, have the capacity, experience, and legal instruments to manage a positive sum coordination and obtained concessions from capital, the question is the political equation, context or will that have defied rationality. For example, the largest political party in South Africa – the Africa National Congress (ANC) – has become a highly organised rent-seeking machine that has failed to ensure that the development of mining is to the benefit of the citizens, and has especially become a lucrative source of rent. As will be discussed subsequently,[8] the challenge from a business and human rights perspective is that rents from these resources do not get ploughed back into social development and environmental protection, which has consequently left the country in the lower rung of a developmental state. Across Africa, extraction of resources which would have sustained the economies, have only continued to fuel ethnic tensions, civil wars, remonstrations, and reducing states to more predatory than developmental. Given the colonial history and third world approach to these challenges, this book argues that the mobilisation legacy of the anti- apartheid, nationalists' movements, and the strength of civil societies have encouraged a deep consideration of local level variation and approach to sustainable development. Consequently, irrespective of the national level pact with MNCs, local level actors will continue to have a key role to play in securing concessions from development and project proponents.

2.3 Country case studies

Most countries in Sub-Saharan Africa gained their independence through intense liberation struggles. In the process of doing this, two main challenges affected their developmental outcomes. First, at the time most of the countries discovered their natural resources, they had just gained independence. Hence, development of the "unexpected" resources raised significant governance challenges.[9] Rather than growth, the dividends of the resources turned the states into an autocratic system, – thereby weakening their fragile democracies. Second, the enormous investments in extractive projects placed a fiscal liability on these states. This resulted in slow growth and development, further depriving the states of the needed financial sustenance to embark on most of the extractive resource projects.[10] The following cases exemplifies these challenges.

2.3.1 Niger-Delta: the Ogoni experience

In 1970, Nigeria nationalised most sectors of the economy, including its oil industry,[11] and operates a Joint Venture Agreement with other foreign companies.[12] Moreover, constitutionally, oil derivatives accrue to states on a 13% basis. Much of the proceeds go to the federal government. One community that has been hugely impacted by resource exploitation in the Niger-Delta region of Nigeria, and which is extensively discussed in the literature, is the Ogoni community. This community drew much attention to their plight through the proactive engagement of "social movements like the Movement for the Survival of the Ogoni People (MOSOP)."[13]

The Ogonis are an ingenious and versatile indigenous group in Nigeria.[14] They have suffered various human rights violations since oil was discovered in the region.[15] For decades, oil spillage became a natural occurrence, partly due to the deleterious activities of Royal Dutch/Shell Company.[16] The United Nations Environment Programme (UNEP), in its assessment of numerous sites in Ogoni, discovered that several years of oil exploration in Ogoni land has resulted into "oil spillage, oil slicks, gas flaring and waste discharge – the once alluvial soil of the Niger-Delta is no longer viable for agricultural use due to widespread land degradation."[17]

Ken Saro-Wiwa, a well-known environmentalist, "led MOSOP in a non-violent crusade against" resource exploitation – especially by Shell (Nigeria). In October 1990, MOSOP presented the "Ogoni Bill of Rights, a document which provided for the "political and economic emancipation of the Ogoni people."[18] The Bill of Rights was designed to ensure that the Ogoni's gain ownership of their resources and land. Throughout the period of political turmoil, Saro-Wiwa alleged that MNCs and the Nigerian government were pursuing "environmental wars and genocidal attacks against the Ogoni and indeed all the peoples of the Niger-Delta."[19] Furious by the dauntless determinations of the Ogoni citizens led by MOSOP, the then military government continuously invaded the community –

resulting in deaths and general disempowerment of the Ogoni people. In 1995, Ken Saro-Wiwa was accused of involvement in the murder of four Ogoni leaders. He was then "sentenced to death by hanging, by a special military tribunal."[20]

Shell's activities in Nigeria are an example of how monstrous MNCs have become when they operate in weak jurisdictions like Nigeria. Shell and other extractive companies continue to pay huge fines for corrupt practices, oil spillage, and environmental degradation.[21] Apart from being banned from operating in Ogoniland since the Saro-Wiwa incident, Shell continues to exploit Nigeria's oil preserve. Shell has been part of Nigeria since independence.[22] The company aids and abets the Nigerian state in human rights violations through the hiring of state security forces to rape women, kill protesters, and to protect its assets. These security forces could have been used to protect oil pipelines to avoid pipeline sabotage – which MNCs are quick to blame on local residents when there is an oil spillage. Ironically, some of the "witnesses who testified against Saro-Wiwa" subsequently confessed that they had actually been bribed by Shell to testify falsely.[23] Several corporate liability human rights lawsuits were brought before Nigerian courts to hold Shell (and other MNCs: Chevron, Agip, Elf) culpable for human rights violations in Nigeria. These violations revolve around land grabbing, oil spillage, torture, and inhumane treatment in relation to the activities of the MNCs. In *Wiwa v. Royal Dutch Petroleum Co.*,[24] Shell agreed to a $15.5 million (N4.7 billion) "out-of-court settlement in a case brought by relatives of nine environmentalists – including Ken Saro-Wiwa."[25] In *Bowoto v. Chevron Texaco Corp.*,[26] it was alleged that Chevron committed serious human rights violations in Nigeria when it utilised the Nigerian military to shoot at and kill some non-violent protesters at its facilities – who were protesting economic sabotage and environmental degradation caused by Chevron. In *Bodo Community v. Shell Petroleum Development Company of Nigeria* (The Bomu-Bonny Oil Pipeline Litigation),[27] Shell agreed to an out-of-court settlement of £55 million (N 21 billion) due to oil spillage from Shell's pipelines – which left the Bodo and Gokana peoples and communities devastated. In *Okpabi v Royal Dutch Shell Plc*,[28] the question was whether the claimants have a disputable case against a UK domiciled parent company of Shell Nigeria. The Claimants had sought damages from the English court due to serious and ongoing environmental pollution caused by oil spills which could be traced to Shell's facilities in their community. The Supreme Court held that the claimant's case, which was not doubted or shown to be "demonstrably untrue", established the fact that "there were real issues to be tried" before the UK court.[29] In granting jurisdiction over the case, the question is not one of control but the degree of management responsibility over the subsidiary in the relevant activity, and the "extent to which the parent did take over."[30]

2.3.2 The Marikana incident (South Africa)

In 2012, Lonmin, a British company, sacked 12,000 miners after a prolonged strike over wages and a failure to adhere to labour standards.[31] This action then "led to sporadic strikes across the South African mining sector."[32] Apart from the needed wage increase, the local community had been despoiled through the activities of Lonmin: youth unemployment was high, and the miners were contracting silicosis and tuberculosis.[33] The subsequent strike action resulted in the death of 34 miners who were shot dead by the South African police on 16 August 2012. These deaths have been likened to the 1960 "Sharpeville Massacre."[34] The Marikana incident has shown that where not fully managed, development of extractive resources could further impoverish the citizens.[35]

Similarly, in Re: *South African Apartheid Litigation*,[36] a group of black South Africans brought claims against the US companies Ford Motors and IBM, for allegedly conducting business that helped perpetuate racial apartheid. The Second US Circuit Court of Appeals held that the parent companies could not be held accountable for the actions of their South African subsidiaries during the time the apartheid regime was in power. On appeal, the US Supreme Court, deferring to the lower court, further limited the contexts in which aliens could hold companies accountable in US courts – for their participation in, or complicity with, human rights abuse abroad.[37] In *Nkala & others v. Harmony Gold Mining Company Ltd & Others*,[38] the applicants were underground mineworkers who contracted silicosis or tuberculosis and died because of contracting these deadly diseases while working in the gold mines. They brought a class action against gold mining companies. The Johannesburg High Court granted the class action in the interest of justice. The Court further noted that the class action will also be to the advantage of the mining companies, as the "liability of each mining company will be determined at the second stage" of the trials, rather than at the initial stage where the entire case could have been dismissed, preventing dependants of the deceased mineworkers from proving their claims against each mine company.[39]

2.3.3 Lake Turkana Wind Power Project (Kenya)

Kenya recently launched the Lake Turkana Wind Power Project (LTWP), a project run by LTWP Company Ltd, and regarded as the largest wind power energy project in Africa.[40] Located on the shores of Lake Turkana in Sarima Valley, Marsabit County,[41] the people who inhabit this area are largely pastoralists who depend on their livestock for fishing.[42]

LTWP conducted its environmental and social impact assessment (ESIA) in 2006 and 2011.[43] The Assessment failed to recognize the existence of indigenous peoples in the project area,[44] neither did it contain a policy statement on the human rights impact of its project. The project recognizes that the local community have a special attachment to their ancestral land, and their communal identity is inherently associated with their territory and the resources there.[45] Such development projects that fail to address land displacement issues has the potential of becoming an investment risk as local communities could revolt against such projects.

Indeed, there are economic benefits to the project, including low-cost power and employment opportunities. However, it has caused adverse social and physical effect on the local communities. LTWP anticipated that the project would cause physical displacement on wind farm site due to construction hazards that may be harmful to the community, tourists, and the pastoralists.[46] To mitigate this, Kenya constructed a seasonal water catchment dam which enticed the pastoralists not to utilise the Sirima encampment area during the construction period. Thus, the indigenous groups who are remotely connected to the project had to travel long distance to carve out a living.[47] The large swathe of land demarcated for this project deprived the indigenous people and their livestock of any means of livelihood.[48] Closely related to this is the fact that LTWP failed to deliver high skilled jobs it promised, neither was there any conduct of free prior informed consent of the indigenous groups.[49]

Conflicts that arose from the projects are understandably about access and control of the project benefits. Although, there have been conflicts among the communities over cattle raiding, the wind project exacerbated the conflict. These intractable conflicts led to the case of *Mohamud Iltarakwa Kochale & others v. Lake Turkana Wind Power Ltd & others*.[50] In this case, the residents of Laisamis Constituency and Karare Ward of Marsabit County made an application against LTWP, Marsabit County, the Attorney-General, Chief Land Registrar, and the National Land Commission at the Environment and Land Court at Meru. The Application sought for an injunction restraining the Respondents from selling, transferring, and dealing in the land that had been leased to LTWP for the wind power project. They alleged that the Respondents illegally and in an unprocedural manner allocated about 150,000 acres of the land belonging to the applicants, in a flawed process, thereby depriving the applicants of their community land and utilising it for seasonal, cultural, and cyclic use as well as pasture for their livestock.[51] They further contended that there was no public consultation, notice of the proposal for setting apart, no reservations from the residents of Laisamis Constituency and Karare Ward, and no form of compensation or alternative settlement offered to the applicants in clear violation of the Kenyan Constitution and the Trust Land Act.[52] They also alleged that LTWP carried out a self-serving Environmental and Social Impact assessment of the Project without involving the residents and without evaluating the potential adverse impacts of the project to the economic, social, cultural, and physical wellbeing of the local community and holistic wellbeing of the indigenous community. Consequently, this resulted into land wastage, dereliction, and permanent alteration of their pastoral land to their irreparable detriment.[53]

Initially, the Court declined to grant an injunction. Rather, it encouraged the parties to negotiate an out of court settlement, directing the Marsabit County Assembly to constitute a panel to resolve the issue. In the meantime, Marsabit County and LTWP undertook to grant the residents access to Lake Turkana and the site. The parties failed to reach an out of court settlement and went back to Court despite the completion of the LTWP project.

The court had to consider the issue of competing rights of the indigenous communities, private entities, rights of the public as well as rights of the future generation. Given the complexity, length of time and nature of the suit, the court referred the matter to the Chief Justice for the constitution of a bench in terms of Article 165 (4) of the Constitution. A bench was constituted, and the matter is still pending in court. The determination of this case will have a ripple effect on responsibility of non-state actors for human rights violations.

2.4 The role of the African Union

The African Union has engaged in a process of developing an AU Policy Framework on Business and Human Rights.[54] The Policy Framework strengthens the need for implementation of the UN Guiding Principles on Business and Human Rights in Africa. There are two core objectives of the draft Policy. First, it seeks to foster a culture of corporate human rights respect. Second, it seeks to serve as a tool for states in the development of NAPS on BHRs.[55] It recognises that non state actors have positively and negatively impacted Africa's development, especially the human and peoples' rights on the continent.[56] Thus, it enjoins African states to speedily realise the right to development, especially for the marginalised groups in high-risk zones. Furthermore, the Policy Framework mandates the integration of human rights risk impact assessments at project negotiation and contract drafting, ensuring that accountability of MNCs remains crucial in project analysis and assessment. It also guarantees the protection of human rights defenders working on business and human rights.[57]

The Policy Framework is divided into three sections. Section one is introductory and gives the background, rationale, and objectives of the Policy Framework. This section recognizes that while businesses contribute immensely to the development of the continent, some of their activities have occasioned human rights challenges. The impacts of these activities have not only negatively affected peoples' right to development, but they have also made specific groups such as women, children, the elderly, migrants, and persons with disabilities – vulnerable. Seven cardinal principles are highlighted, namely, responsibility, accountability, African shared values, the human rights-based approach; local ownership; participation and inclusiveness; and non-discrimination. Section two deals with the foundational pillars or indicative elements of the Policy, namely, State duty to protect human and peoples' rights, business responsibility to respect human and people's rights, and access to judicial remedies. Section 3 examines resource mobilization, relevant actors, and mechanisms for implementation.[58]

To fulfil their duty to protect human and peoples' rights, the Policy Framework enjoins States to pursue fourteen indicative elements to realise their duty obligations.[59] The policy further incorporates seven benchmarks against which to assess the compliance of states with the duty to protect human rights. To realise the responsibility to respect human rights, eight imperatives are outlined in the Policy. First, businesses must develop and adopt policy statements to respect human and peoples' rights standards. Second, businesses are to conduct human rights due diligence. This needs to be in line with relevant standards at global and regional level. Third, businesses should have due regard to relevant standards at global and regional level in the delivery of public services, notably, in situations where such services are outsourced to them. Fourth, displacement should be prevented and consultation with communities should be advanced. Fifth, there is also a need for local communities to benefit from proceeds of business activities through fair and equitable benefit sharing. Sixth, businesses are to ensure that their activities do not contribute to environmental degradation which affects the right to the environment guaranteed in article 24 of the African Charter on human and peoples' rights. Seventh, businesses are to ensure that they strengthen due diligence and respect for international humanitarian law through self-regulatory mechanisms in (post) conflict situations, where there are no effective governance structures for the furtherance of human rights. Eight, businesses are to ensure that they set up effective remediation processes to address adverse human rights impacts and in this regard: adopt case-specific measures, track efficiency of response, engage external monitory mechanisms, and publish human rights performance. Finally, businesses are to register for tax purposes and transparency of revenue flows. The policy further incorporates six benchmarks against which to assess the compliance of states with the duty to protect human rights. On access to remedies, the Policy Framework advances a wide range of measures in the furtherance of adequate remediation – judicial and non-judicial, state-based, and non-state based. Thus, states and businesses are required to ensure access to remedies. States are obliged to establish and strengthen state-based judicial and non-judicial mechanisms; institutionalise and support non-state-based grievance mechanisms; and provide access to effective remedies.

While the Policy Framework enjoins States to have national laws and action plans on business and human rights, it is yet to be adopted by the continental body. Hopefully, the draft Policy will be ratified by the continental body and a roadmap for its implementation achieved by Member States.[60]

2.5 Africa's trade regime and human rights implications

The meaningful phenomenon of trade agreements emboldens the close-knit cooperation between signatories to such agreement. Trade agreements establish not only a meaningful attempt to order international economic relations but a means towards facilitating multilateral trade established under the World Trade Organization (WTO).[61] The essence of any regional trade agreement is to ensure that such region develops and grows geometrically.[62] A fundamental part of that growth trajectory is a consideration of human rights principles in trade agreements that seeks to facilitate regional growth.

The African Continental Free Trade Area Agreement (AfCFTA) was created as a conglomeration of two or more customs territories. The aim was to formulate a free trade agreement initially with the resultant benefit of transmuting into a customs union.[63] Facilitating trade flows within the sub region will no doubt contribute to the economic integration of the region.[64]

Pursuant to the Lagos Plan of Action signed in 1980,[65] the AU set forth to create the African Economic Community through a free trade area, customs union, and a common market amongst the 55 African Member States.[66] This was aimed at achieving greater cohesion and economic integration within the continent. The recent of these initiatives is the AfCFTA,[67] an agreement to make intra-African trade easier and competitive through the minimization of tariff and non-tariff barriers and gradual elimination of ninety percent tariffs within a period of five to 15 years, based on developing and least-developed country classification. The core objectives of AfCFTA are to eradicate tariffs and non-tariff barriers to trade in goods, trade liberalization in services, achieve a collaborative policy approach on investment, intellectual property rights, and competition policy, and an effective dispute resolution mechanism.[68]

While AfCFTA recognizes the importance of human rights for the development of international trade and economic cooperation,[69] it does not contain any specific provision on human rights implications of the trade agreement. Elimination of tariff and non-tariff barriers and trade liberalization can have significant impact on the socio-economic activities of African traders, especially informal cross-border trade. Informal economy sustains most African economy, at the same time, women and other vulnerable groups could particularly face lack of access to credit and economic opportunities as a result of agricultural trade liberalization. These could impede the realization of Africa's democratic and sustainable development goals fully encapsulated in its Agenda 2063. AfCFTA is pivotal to the realization of this Agenda, an inclusive social and economic development, democratic governance, peace, and security Agenda, premised on seven core aspirations of the AU.[70]

At its recently concluded meeting, the Heads of African Regional Economic Communities (RECs) stressed the importance of the role and commitment of RECs to Africa's economic transformation process, which would facilitate the effective implementation of the AfCFTA Agreement.[71] Unfortunately, the meeting did not consider human rights as relevant to effective realisation of the Agreement. Rather, it highlighted the establishment of an expanded Continental Task Force on AfCFTA, involvement of RECs, in particular Customs Unions that are not recognized by the African Union,[72] in the discussions on the AfCFTA in view of the recognition of Customs Unions within the overall framework of the Agreement, and the need for the private sector to be an active participant to the AfCFTA processes and not an observer.[73]

Understandably, economic integration and trade agreements do not always lead to desirable and sustainable outcomes.[74] Integrating human rights protection into trade agreements is essential to realizing the benefits from productivity and free flow of goods and services for the upliftment of the citizens. Where not properly implemented, AfCFA could impact diverse groups unjustly due to prevailing shapes of "discrimination, unequal access to resources" and lack of opportunities.[75] Furthermore, if the transformative agenda of AfCFTA is to be realized and a sustainable socio-economic development is to be achieved, human rights language must be integrated in AfCFTA as a pathway to implementing business and human rights norms through trade. One area human rights can be achieved is through relaxation of rules with digital trade. While some countries have adopted data localization policies, other countries have data protection laws or restrict cross border data transfers, especially through electronic means.[76] Adaptation of human rights to digital trade will ensure that "stakeholders whose inclusion and participation" is fundamental towards trade objectives, are identified, and therefore able to obtain the benefits of digital trade.[77] When States and businesses restrict data flows, they decrease access to information, which invariably weakens economic growth, efficiency, and invention locally and internationally.[78] Consequently, a human rights and business provision is needed in AfCFTA.

Article XXIV of *General Agreement on Tariffs and Trade* (GATT), 1947[79] proscribes two conditions that must be met before trade agreements can be consummated.[80] First is that the duties maintained in each of the member states at the formation of the Free Trade Agreement (FTA) are not "on the whole" higher than the duties existing in the same member states prior to the formation of the FTA; and second, an FTA liberalizes "substantially all the trade" between its members.[81] Trade liberalization under AfCFTA must be consummated in a way that integrates protection of vulnerable members of the society, especially women, cross border traders, who are key participants in the informal agricultural economy – a fundamental aspect of food security in Africa. For example, agricultural imports can be subsidized, and a Simplified Trade Regime (STR) developed to facilitate movement of goods and sustain cross border traders especially women and youths utilizing the already existing framework of RECs. While the AfCFTA focuses on trade liberalization and tariff reductions, it must create a synergy between trade and the enabling peaceful environment that guarantees free flow of trade. A human rights protection will guarantee that flow.

The key elements for achieving an efficient trade policy includes trade liberalisation, reduction of red tape, ensuring transparent customs procedures as well as institutionalising economic justice and entrenching human rights with particular reference to realising sustainable development as encapsulated in Agenda 2063. A human rights approach will circumvent the unintended consequences of trade and investment agreements, flags potential contribution of trade agreements to inequality and economic injustice, and guarantees that investment agreements incorporate participation of all members of the society, including local communities in realising the potentials and benefits of these agreements. Undoubtedly, deepening regional integration benefits the continent. However, a human rights approach, hopefully to be considered in the second and third Protocols currently undergoing negotiations, will prevent adverse economic impacts for the less privileged members of the society, who are often key stakeholders in realising the trade objectives states launch into. For instance, trade agreements can create more opportunities, while at the same time aggravate prevailing disparities and impair women's economic and social status.[82]

2.6 Conclusion

Due to Africa's dependence on its natural resources as a source of finance, there are likely to be key BHR concerns revolving around land, environment, the participation of local communities as well as benefit sharing arrangements.[83] The above issues require an integration of business and human rights principles in project planning and management. These cases show the stark realities of a regime of corporate impunity for human rights violations in weak zones, high risk countries.[84] There is recurring evidence that MNCs do not have systems in place to conduct their activities in a systemic way by incorporating key stakeholders in a manner that respects their human rights. MNCs do not respect local laws – especially given that the enforcement mechanisms and political will are unavailable. Firms may operate in highly challenging contexts and often prefer to enter contractual relationships with local business partners in the region that share their values and ideals. This has led to heightened levels of tension and distrust between the local community and the MNCs. The whole essence of socially responsible projects is to use the profits from natural resource extraction to develop the host community. MNCs are quick to accuse their host communities of sabotage, but on the other hand, local communities assert that the companies harm the environment through their activities and do not engage in any form of CSR. The assumption therefore is if these MNCs are accepted as joint stakeholders in the development theory, these communities may well in turn willingly offer security services for the firm's installations. This situation is an indication of the gap between globalisation and governance. This gap has created economic nationalism further complicated by the COVID-19 pandemic. The result is a highly fragile global production and manufacturing value chain. The AfCFTA must creatively and innovatively adapt human rights to trade liberalization, strengthen manufacturing capacity, drive value chain creation, and empower the participants at the local informal economy. The pertinent question is how the continent can leverage its vast resources to produce goods, at the same time guarantee social and economic inclusion of key stakeholders – women and youth in realizing trade objectives.

The next chapter discusses the theoretical approaches to corporate governance which, if effectively applied, will lead to a commendable and efficient management of development projects.

Notes

1 Natural Resource Governance Institute, "Nigeria Oil and Gas" (2017) <www.resourcegovernanceindex.org/country-profiles/NGA/oil-gas?years=2017> accessed 5 July 2021.
2 Organization of the Petroleum Exporting Countries (OPEC), *2020 OPEC Annual Statistical Bulletin* <https://asb.opec.org> accessed 5 July 2021.
3 U.S. Energy Information Administration (EIA), *Analysis: Energy Sector Highlights* <www.eia.gov/international/overview/country/NGA> accessed 5 July 2021.
4 Natural Resource Governance Institute, "South Africa Mining" (2017) <www.resourcegovernanceindex.org/country-profiles/ZAF/mining?years=2017> accessed 6 July 2021.
5 Ibid.
6 Ibid.
7 J. Gathii, "The Promise of International Law: A Third World View" Guest Lecture at the 2020 Virtual Annual Meeting of the American Society of International Law, 25 June 2020. [Arguing that third world countries can contribute to the practice of international law and should not merely be recipients of western contributions to the subject].
8 See Chapter 8.
9 Gavin Hilson, "Corporate Social Responsibility in the Extractive Industry: Experiences from Developing Countries" (2012) 37 *Resources Policy* 132.
10 Ibid. 133.

11 The Nigerian Enterprises Promotion Decree, 1979 created greater opportunity for Nigerians to own, manage, and control the productive enterprises in the country.
12 The Indigenization policy failed to utilize the capabilities or readiness of the private sector to optimally perform in the productive sector of the economy. See Chibuzo S.A. Ogbuagu, "The Nigerian Indigenization Policy: Nationalism or Pragmatism?" (1983) *African Affairs* 242. [Arguing that the indigenization policy was based on a strong feeling of political and economic nationalism. As a result, economic efficiency may in some cases be sacrificed in the drive to replace foreign nationals with indigenous Nigerians in the economic sector. Thus, the indigenization programme was highly politicized]. See further Eka Ikpe, "Developmental Post-Conflict Reconstruction in Postindependence *Nigeria: Lessons from Asian Developmental States*" (2020) *Journal of Peacebuilding & Development* 1.
13 Kevin Mckague, "Shell, Nigeria, and the Ogoni: Prospects for Reconciliation and Sustainable Development" <www.kevinmckague.com/wp-content/uploads/2017/08/Shell-Nigeria-and-the-Ogoni.pdf> accessed 5 July 2021; Z. Mai-Bornu, "The Nature of Leadership within the Ogoni and Ijaw Movements" (2020) *Political Violence and Oil in Africa* 129. See further "Movement for the Survival of the Ogoni People (MOSOP)" <www.mosop.org> accessed 29 April 2021.
14 O. Abe, "Utilization of Natural Resources in Nigeria: Human Rights Considerations" (2014) *India Quarterly: A J. Int'l Affairs* 5.
15 Ibid.
16 Ibid.
17 UNEP Report, "Environmental Assessment of Ogoniland" (2011) <https://postconflict.unep.ch/publications/OEA/UNEP_OEA.pdf> accessed 6 January 2021.
18 Abe, above (n 14) 6.
19 Ibid.
20 Ibid. For a detailed explication of the literature of and the impact of oil contamination in *Ogoniland*, see Olof Lindén, & Pålsson Jonas, "Oil Contamination in Ogoniland, Niger Delta" (2013) 42(6) *Ambio* 685–701; C.B. Obida, et al., "Counting the Cost of the Niger Delta's Largest Oil Spills: Satellite Remote Sensing Reveals Extensive Environmental Damage with >1 Million People in the Impact Zone" (2021) 775 *Science of the Total Environment* 145854; K. Sam, & N. Zabbey, "Contaminated Land and Wetland Remediation in Nigeria: Opportunities for Sustainable Livelihood Creation" (2018) 639 *Science of the Total Environment* 1560; H.P. Faga, & U. Philip, "Oil Exploration, Environmental Degradation, and Future Generations in the Niger Delta: Options for Enforcement of Intergenerational Rights and Sustainable Development through Legal and Judicial Activism" (2019) 34 *Journal of Environmental Law and Litigation* 185; Barisere Rachel Konne, "Inadequate Monitoring and Enforcement in the Nigerian Oil Industry: The Case of Shell and Ogoniland" (2014) 47 *Cornell International Law Journal* 181.
21 Daily Trust, "Mobil, NNPC to Pay N82bn Damages to Akwa Ibom Communities Hit by Oil Spill" *Daily Trust* (21 June 2021) <https://dailytrust.com/mobil-nnpc-to-pay-n82bn-damages-to-akwa-ibom-communities-hit-by-oil-spill>.
22 See Justine Nolan, "Business and Human Rights in Context" in Dorothée Baumann-Pauly & Justine Nolan (eds.) *Business and Human Rights: From Principles to Practice* (2016) 25.
23 Abe, above (n 13) 6. See further Eveline Lubbes, & Andy Rowell, "NGOs and BBC Targeted by Shell PR Machine in Wake of Saro-Wiwa Death" *The Guardian* (9 November 2010) <www.theguardian.com/business/2010/nov/09/shell-pr-saro-wiwa-nigeria> accessed 30 April 2021.
24 226 F.3d 88 (2d Cir. 2000), cert. denied, 532 U.S. 941.
25 Abe, above (n 14) 6.
26 312 F. Supp. 2d 1229 (N.D. Cal. 2004).
27 [2014] EWHC 1973 (TCC).

28 [2021] UKSC 3. [This case bothers on negligence and duty of care owed by a parent company to a subsidiary].
29 Ibid.
30 Ibid. See also *Kiobel v. Royal Dutch Petroleum*, 621 F.3d 111, 120 (2d Cir. 2010).
31 For a detailed discussion of the Marikana incident, see Edward Webster, "Marikana and Beyond: New Dynamics in Strikes in South Africa" (2017) 8(2) *Global Labour Journal* 139; M. Power, & M. Gwanyanya, "Massacre at Marikana" (2017) 25 *Int'l Journal on Human Rights* 61; Bonita Meyersfield, "Empty Promises and the Myth of Mining: Does Mining Lead to Pro-Poor Development?" (2017) *Business and Human Rights Journal* 37.
32 Abe, above (n 14) 139.
33 See SAPA, "Lonmin an Example of Exploitation" *Business Report* (17 August 2012) <www.iol.co.za/business-report/companies/lonmin-an-example-of-exploitation-1365221> accessed 10 January 2021.
34 Power, & Gwanyanya (above n 30) 62. See Marikana Commission of Inquiry, *Report on Matters of Public, National and International Concern Arising Out of the Tragic Incidents at the Lonmin Mine in Marikana, in the North-West Province* (2015) <www.gov.za/sites/default/files/gcis_document/201506/38978gen6993.pdf> accessed 30 April 2020. Lonmin, aware of the reports of intimidation and violence and being fully aware of their inability to protect their employees, urged the employees to go to work and after the killings of security personnel by the strikers, failed to inform employees of the dangers of coming to work and failed to withdraw their call to work during the strike.
35 Meyersfield, above (n 30) 34.
36 *Khulumani v. Barclay National Bank Ltd* 504 F.3d 254 (2nd Cir. 2007). In the original case, several complaints were filed in 2002 against numerous MNCs. The cases were consolidated in the Southern District of New York and dismissed by the district court in 2004.
37 See also See *Ntsebeza v. Ford Motor Co.*, 15–1020 (12 February 2016). See *Kiobel v Royal Dutch Petroleum Co.*, 133 S. Ct. 1659 (2013).
38 [2016] 2 All SA 233.
39 Ibid. see further C. Abrahams, "The South African Experience: Litigating Remedies" (2021) *Business and Human Rights Journal* 1.
40 Anmar Frangoul, "The Biggest Wind Farm in Africa Is Officially Up and Running" *CNBC* (22 July 2019) <www.cnbc.com/2019/07/22/the-biggest-wind-farm-in-africa-is-officially-up-and-running.html> accessed 22 June 2021.
41 The African Development Bank Group (AfDB) granted EUR436 million in senior credit facilities towards the project cost, while the consortium of companies includes KP&P Africa, British Aldwych International (largest shareholder), Danish Vestas Wind Systems and Sandpiper Ltd. Development funds came from Danish Investment Fund for Developing Countries (IFU), Finnfund and KLP Norfund Investments A/S. see further: ADB, "African Development Bank Helps Power Wind of Change in Kenya" <www.afdb.org/en/news-and-events/african-development-bank-helps-power-wind-change-kenya-28239> accessed 5 July 2021.
42 Zoe Cormack, "Kenya's Huge Wind Power Project Might Be Great for the Environment But Not for Local Communities" *Quartz* (3 September 2019) <https://qz.com/africa/1700925/kenyas-huge-wind-power-project-in-turkana-hurts-local-people/> accessed 29 January 2021.
43 Updated Environmental and Social Impact Assessment Summary, Lake Turkana Wind Power Project, Kenya (2011) <www.eib.org/attachments/registers/53222536.pdf> accessed 5 July 2021 [Updated ESIA].
44 Kanyinke Sena, "Renewable Energy Projects and the Rights of Marginalised/Indigenous Communities in Kenya" IWGIA: Report 21 (2015) <www.iwgia.org/images/publications/0725_REPORT21.pdf> accessed 5 July 2021.
45 Sena, Ibid.

46 Updated ESIA (n 42) 12.
47 Ilse Renkens, "The Impact of Renewable Energy Projects on Indigenous Communities in Kenya" IWGIA Report 28 (2019) <www.iwgia.org/images/publications/new-publications/IWGIA_report_28_The_impact_of_renewable_energy_projects_on_Indigenous_communities_in_Kenya_Dec_2019.pdf> accessed 29 July 2021.
48 A similar situation with the Ogoni case earlier discussed.
49 Renkens (n 46) 7.
50 [2016] eKLR.
51 Ibid.
52 Ibid. para 74.
53 Ibid. para 2.
54 African Union, "Validation Workshop of the African Union Policy on Business and Human Rights" <https://africa-eu-partnership.org/sites/default/files/documents/joint_au-eu_press_release_on_stakeholders_validation_workshop_au-hrb_mar.pdf> accessed 29 May 2021.
55 AU Policy Framework on Business and Human Rights (Draft).
56 Ibid.
57 Ibid.
58 Ibid. See further Oyeniyi Abe, "A Study on the State of Business and Human Rights in Africa and Potentials for Adopting the African Union Draft Policy Framework on Business and Human Rights" FES/AUPAPS Commissioned Report (April 2022).
59 These indicative elements include: adopting national laws, policies, and strategies for regulating human rights related activities of businesses; synergise national laws and policies with BHRs principles and the Draft policy; create an enabling environment to implement and enforce the recommendations and decisions of judicial and non-judicial mechanisms at national and regional levels concerning the human and peoples' rights impacts of the businesses that operate on their territories; encourage a human and peoples' rights culture among the businesses that operate on their territories through support for training programmes and activities; mandate periodic human rights reporting on how businesses address adverse human rights impact in their spheres of operation; integrate human and peoples' rights risk management into investment contracts that could generate social, economic, or environmental risks; conclude bilateral and multilateral agreements that adopt human rights with the home states of the transnational companies; engage with businesses which operate in conflict zones to avoid, identify, assess, mitigate, and redress human and peoples' rights related risks; enhance human rights practice within SOEs, business transactions by the state and agencies linked to the State; protect peoples' rights and the rights of local communities; establish an effective tax regime and administration capable of collecting due taxes from the relevant businesses to be deployed toward the realisation of the human and peoples' rights of the relevant population(s); acknowledge the importance of informal sector businesses for the economic development of the state, and thus for the realization of human rights; deter conflict of interest among state officials and business leaders that may affect the realisation of the duty to protect human and peoples' rights; and encourage the protection of human and peoples' rights defenders working on ensuring that businesses respect human and peoples' rights.
60 A Summary of the draft African Union Policy Framework on Business and Human Rights.
61 J.-A. Crawford, & R.V. Fiorentino, *The Changing Landscape of Regional Trade Agreements* (Geneva, Switzerland: World Trade Organization Publications, 2005).
62 O. Abe, "Deepening Regional Integration and Organizing World Trade" (2014) 4(1) *International Journal of Public Law and Policy* 71.
63 Article XXIV (8) of GATT further provides that: "A customs union shall be understood to mean the substitution of a single customs territory for two or more customs territories, so that duties and other restrictive regulations of commerce . . . are eliminated with respect to

substantially all the trade between the constituent territories of the union or at least with respect to substantially all the trade in products originating in such territories . . . A free-trade area shall be understood to mean a group of two or more customs territories in which the duties and other restrictive regulations of commerce . . . are eliminated on substantially all the trade between the constituent territories in products originating in such territories."

64 Abe (n 62) 72.

65 See the Treaty Establishing the African Economic Community, Lagos Plan of Action for the Economic Development of Africa 1980–2000 4 (1980); Adopted on 3 June 1991; entered into force on 12 May 1994.

66 See O. Abe, & S. Taye, "The "Flexibility" Standard in the African Union and its Ramification for the Implementation of the African Continental Free Trade Area (AfCFTA) Agreement" (2020) *Global Trade and Customs Journal* 81.

67 Ibid.

68 See Article 4 of AfCFTA.

69 Preamble to the Agreement.

70 African Union, "Our Aspirations for the Africa WeWwant" <https://au.int/en/agenda2063/aspirations>. Agenda 2063 emphasizes human rights approach to governance and democratic principles. It affirms poverty reduction, socio economic and third generational rights, as well as sustainable development of Africa's natural resources.

71 AfCFTA Secretariat, "First (1st) Coordination Meeting of the Heads of Regional Economic Communities (RECs) on the Implementation of the African Continental Free Trade Area (AfCFTA)" AfCFTA/RECs/1/REPORT/FINAL (20 September 2021).

72 African Union does not recognise SACU, CEMAC and UEMOA.

73 Ibid.

74 UNECA, "The Continental Free Trade Area (CFTA) in Africa: A Human Rights Perspective" 11.

75 Ibid. 12.

76 Lukman Abdulrauf, & Oyeniyi Abe, "The (Potential) Economic Impact of Data Localisation Policies on Nigeria's Regional Trade Obligations" Policy Brief 04, Mandela Institute, University of Witwatersrand, South Africa.

77 TRALAC, "Digital Trade in Africa Implications for Inclusion and Human Rights" <www.tralac.org/documents/news/2893-digital-trade-in-africa-implications-for-inclusion-and-human-rights-executive-summary-and-policy-recommendations-july-2019/file.html>.

78 Abdulrauf and Abe (n 76).

79 *General Agreement on Tariffs and Trade*, 30 October 1947, 58 U.N.T.S. 187, Can. T.S. 1947 No. 27 (entered into force 1 January 1948) [GATT]. Available online at: <www.wto.org/english/docs_e/legal_e/gatt47_e.pdf>.

80 See further Abe (n 62) 78.

81 Article XXIV of GATT.

82 See K. Higgins, "Gender and Free Trade Agreements: Best Practices and Policy Guidance" Research Report, The North-South Institute (2013) <www.nsi-ins.ca/wp-content/uploads/2013/03/2013-Gender-and-FTAs-Best-Practices-and-Policy-Guidance.pdf>.

83 Workshop on "Business and Human Rights: Addressing Human Rights Impacts of Business in Eastern and Southern Africa" Workshop Report (10 & 11 April 2018) <www.somo.nl/wp-content/uploads/2018/10/workshop-report_final.pdf> accessed 6 July 2021.

84 Incidents like this have also happened in other parts of the world. The Bhopal toxic gas leakage at the Bhopal chemical plant in India led to the death of about 10,000 people within a three day period [see Surya Deva, "Bhopal: The Saga Continues 31 Years On" in Dorothée Baumann-Pauly & Justine Nolan (eds.) *Business and Human Rights: From Principles to Practice* (2016) 41]; On 24 April, 2013, there was an accident at the Rana Plaza factory, Dhaka, Bangladesh, where a garment factory collapsed leading to the death of about 1,129 people [S. Deva, *Regulating Corporate Human Rights Violations: Humanizing Business* (2012) 25].

3 Corporate governance paradigms and regulatory framework

3.1 Introduction

Chapter 1 highlighted the need to implement business and human rights (BHRs) principles in the wake of increasingly belligerent corporate activities in Africa. This chapter surveys the applicable theories and regimes underpinning corporate social responsibility (CSR) in Africa. In doing so, it deals with several complicated matters relating to the competing theories of CSR. First, it contextualizes the discourse by ascertaining the parallels between BHRs and CSR. It then reviews the diverse theories that have been put forward to clarify whether BHRs challenges are within the purview of corporate entities, especially with regards to the shareholder-centric approach of companies. This chapter is anchored on a key variable: implementation of BHRs principles will accommodate the needs of those who are impacted most by the activities of the development companies. This approach will also provide a basis for granting social legitimacy to development projects.

3.2 Theoretical basis for implementing business and human rights principles

The concept of corporate social responsibility (CSR) has progressed since the 19th century,[1] and continues to do so, shaped in part by the dynamics of globalisation and the demands of economic liberty.[2] While the debate on Business and Human Rights (BHR) continues to increase, CSR has reduced the rigid state-centric role in human rights matters and has created revolutionary responsibilities for corporate organisations. These responsibilities stem from the financial implications of carrying out socially responsible projects. Companies are thus obliged to perform CSR – whether they like it or not. In addition, the enforcement of CSR initiatives has been influenced by the Westphalian regime which recognizes states as the only bodies that can enforce rights under international law.

BHR seems to have conflated states' role as duty bearers with that of corporate human rights responsibility. Wettstein argues that CSR cannot be linked to BHR without focusing on its connection to the "pre-existing obligation of states."[3] This is the core intention of the UNGPs. Wettstein's reasoning resonates with the contention

DOI: 10.4324/9781003290124-5

that states are now integrated with companies under the BHR regime – a responsibility they never shared with corporations under the CSR regime. While CSR requirements focus on the social responsibilities of companies, the UNGPs expand the responsibilities of states and companies more cohesively. This is instructive for several reasons. Hitherto, there were set boundaries between states and businesses under CSR discussions. States were not fully concerned about developments in the CSR field. Under the BHR regime, states are now more fully integrated and involved in BHR issues. Therefore, the BHR debate has helped heighten the role of states in implementing CSR paradigms. This is evident in some states developing National Action Plans (NAP) detailing the roadmap for implementing the UNGPs.[4]

BHR and CSR are two sides of a flip coin, each working together to enhance corporate responsibility for human rights. The real challenge under BHR is to develop a framework or model for corporate accountability, and at the same time identify distinct roles and responsibilities of States. What this chapter therefore seeks to do is to identify the best approach under the BHR and CSR paradigms – and use it as a basis to advance the argument for the implementation of the UNGPs. Ironically, development (especially extractive) companies operating in Africa comply with the regulatory laws of their home states (Global North countries), while most African states grapple with enforcing human rights principles applicable to corporate entities.

Just as corporations are being inundated with various challenges – so also has the implementation of BHRs principles become challenging for developing states. By design, BHRs principles entails a regime of constructing social infrastructure, giving back to host communities, value added for businesses, "holding business accountable and sharing collective responsibility."[5]

Corporations are designed to make a profit – which entails pursuing social ends, notwithstanding voluntarily. Meanwhile, a "myopic focus on profit over human welfare" often drives MNCs to be involved in crimes against humanity.[6] When this economic rationale is applied to their activities – companies often consider that any consideration of human rights compliance cannot offset the resources and time it would take them to deal with other multifaceted matters underscoring BHRs. In the European Union (EU), CSR raises three significant innovations: First, firms raise their standards higher and go beyond those set by legal or regulatory requirements – and by implication set a higher benchmark of social development, environmental protection and regard for human rights.[7] In so doing, they are "giving back to host communities." Second, CSR regulates the relationship between the corporation and its stakeholders.[8] Third, CSR ensures that the Board of the corporation raises the standard set for their fiduciary duties.[9] Amid global transformation, climate change, and terrorism – to mention just a few challenges – how will corporations, while focusing on profit maximisation, make a lasting and positive impact on their host communities? Should firms see BHRs as an investment or as a cost? If states are committed to mitigating adverse risks associated with corporate-made disasters through BHRs – what role should the corporate entities themselves play considering that irresponsible and distrustful behavior can undermine a company's core business interests.[10]

The discussion on the theoretical basis for BHR is incomplete without briefly mentioning the role of NGOs. NGOs have from time immemorial, and continue to be, the champions of BHRs.[11] The initial approach was to wage war against poor living and working conditions, low wages, health and safety violations, and the right to form trade unions. Unfortunately, however, these issues still linger. The complexity in resolving these problems is complicated by labour standards in supply chains – as reflected in the Rana Plaza incident (Bangladesh). Firms want to maximise profits with the lowest personnel costs. They are also mindful that poor working conditions could have serious implications for the reputation of their firms. This creates a dilemma and to resolve this dilemma the UNGPs seek to offer improved normative clearness and convergence on corporate respect for human rights. The effect of this clarity is to offer new and positive paradigms for the corporate conduct and approach towards human rights compliance. For instance, in Chapter 1, it was stated that the UNGPs have now become sources of reference for corporate human rights policies.[12] The UNGPs are also influencing legislation,[13] and offering prototypes in terms of the access of victims to judicial remedies[14] – thereby balancing corporate profit maximisation and societal expectations of being socially responsible. Integrating human rights into business becomes imperative for granting the social licence to operate (SLO). A company that desires local community legitimisation, therefore recognises this imperative and constructs appropriate human rights policies and compliance. Creating a shared responsibility or approach between BHR and CSR, is important to identify this legitimisation. Social legitimacy of development projects is instrumental in fostering the corporate-community relationship, which is needed to actualise the objectives of the UNGPs. But how can a company earn this social legitimacy or integrate human rights into its business? The next section critically examines the theories of corporate governance and adopts a realistic model.

3.3 Competing theories of corporate governance

This section examines the main dominant theories of corporate governance approach to business and human rights principles. The discussions here are based on two assumptions: first, firms have sufficient legal personality to bear legal rights and duties; and second, despite tremendous BHRs initiatives by MNCs, local communities do not feel sufficient positive impact of development projects compared to the high socio-economic and environmental costs of such projects.[15] Drawing examples from development projects, cases, and the literature, this section argues for a well-adjusted methodology among government (in the form of policies and directives) and extractive companies (in the form of BHRs initiatives) – and pays particular attention to responsibility and development results in the extractive industry. After all, corporate obligation to respect human rights stems from the obligations arising under domestic corporate law and international human rights instruments.

3.3.1 Social change as a system of corporate transformation

This section discusses social change theory and how its understanding can help transform systemic conduct of corporate entities in relation to respect for human rights.

Social change emphasises the directions of structural changes, effects, and consequences from a particular group.[16] Jenson conceives of social change as "modification in ways of doing and thinking of people."[17] Lundberg and others define social change as "any modification in established . . . standards of conduct."[18] Social change may therefore be holistically construed as "an alteration in the cultural, structural, population, or ecological characteristics of a social system such as a society."[19] Social change theory allows us to conceive monumental processes of transformation across historical and contemporary timelines. Thus, where there is a variation in the *status quo* due to alterations in geographical spread, cultural values, or ideologies, social change is said to have taken place. Through the processes of social change there are evident changes in the values and social norms that bring people together to help create social order. Thus, social change can be driven by cultural, religious, economic, legal, or technological forces.[20]

The debate on the imperatives of corporate "duty" to respect human rights is driven by cultural, religious (for example, local communities resisting land grabs by extractive companies due to their spiritual ties to the land), economic, and legal aspects of social change. Thus, corporate responsibility to respect human rights goes beyond the mere duty to be involved in socially responsible projects. This responsibility demands a conscious attempt by companies to inject BHRs into board management and programmes – so that over time it becomes an unassailable part of corporate culture. In such a scenario, social change is said to have taken place. Consequently, social norms could become law over time if compliance with the UNGPs is strategically done – evolving into "corporate culture."[21] This culture will involve a conflation of voluntary and legal regimes with cultural and socio-economic forces within a social field.

The social change model guarantees the implementation of the UNGPs in a certain way. Basically, social norms do not necessarily demand legislative enforcement. These norms grant MNCs the needed social license to extract natural resources. Therefore, the implementation of the UNGPs emerge from corporate adaptation to the demands of socio-economic forces. Most allegations against corporations have stemmed from their inability to keep up with social change and to adapt to social behaviour. It is easy for companies to publish reports on CSR – but how do they ensure that they adapt to social change? Often, there are no systems in place to support the claim of human rights compliance. The theory of change has been developed to ensure that companies adapt to social change. The next section briefly discusses the imperative of adaptation to change.

A. Business respect for human rights

Businesses have a candid aspiration to comprehend the value of respecting human rights. A theory of social change helps companies to identify what is needed, strengths and weaknesses of the information they have access to and improve their overall decision-making processes. Thus, companies have to identify those human rights risk evident from their operations and prioritize the greatest need that needs intervention.

Companies have to proactively think methodically about the essential obligations and conditions to accomplish a preferred outcome. Understandably, addressing human rights risk in complex environments, such as the extractive industries, requires a consideration of some factors and actors eventually inducing results. Hence, the question is whether social change within a company can ultimately reduce the difficulty and capricious transformations in social, political setting in which human rights are realized.[22]

It is critical that business managers put in place governance systems that embed rights respecting culture. A regime of human rights respect within an organization should be a shared value approach of members, so that over time, it becomes an organizational way of life even when board management changes. The standards and principles that sustain a rights-respecting culture align with reliable business culture. Companies must therefore be able to demonstrate "authenticity of commitment" to its code of conduct, sustainability report or other human rights statements; "responsibility and accountability" that evidence duty of the people to respect human rights; "respect and empathy" where stakeholders understand the importance respecting local community rights; and "openness and learning" to embrace understandings about human rights risks.[23]

3.3.2 Shareholder value principle

Theorists under this philosophy ground their belief in the understanding that corporate organisations are juristic persons – formed to make profits for the benefit of shareholders. They do not believe that the firm exists to serve the purpose of other constituencies, including the community in which that corporation may operate.[24] In his seminal work on "Capitalism and Freedom," Friedman stated that:

> There is one and only one social responsibility – to use its resources and engaging in activities designed to increase its profits as long as it stays within the rules of the game, which is to say, engages in free and open competition *without deception or fraud.*[25]
>
> (emphasis added)

Friedman further stated that:

> In a free enterprise, private-property system, a corporate executive is an employee of the owners of the business. He has direct responsibility to his employers. That responsibility is to conduct the business in accordance with their desires, which generally will be to make as much money as possible *while conforming to the basic rules of the society*, both those embodied in law and those *embodied in ethical custom.*[26]
>
> (emphasis added)

Friedman's idea about CSR fails to consider that a particular code of conduct can metamorphose into a treaty, if it has become a set of accepted norms of behaviour in the international community. When a CSR becomes a treaty, CSR becomes mandatory. Can it then be concluded that firms are solely there to make profits, going by the same Friedman directive that "firms must comply with law set up for that purpose"? If Friedman had seen CSR as an investment rather than a cost, he would have appreciated that events change over the course of time. A business concern could change from producing artificial products to organic products and this has serious ethical considerations. Since firms must comply with the laws governing their activities at any point in time, the organic-producing company must place ethical considerations above profit maximisation – with serious implications for its CSR initiatives.[27] To therefore have the idea of CSR being set in stone as *just* profit making – defies all logic. In their bid to further entrench shareholder wealth maximisation, adherents of shareholder theory would deem as outright stealing, any attempt by managers to become involved in CSR. Since CSR has not been legally provided for, theorists believe that any deviation from the agreed Memorandum and Articles of Association of the Company must be submitted to the general meeting of the company for approval. Even then, they expect government to give legal backing to such a decision through legislation.[28] Obviously, BHR grew out of concerns of these theorists, who believe that CSR must be legally provided for in order to be recognised.

Shareholder theorists believe that the dictates of capitalism allow only strict legal compliance, without more, as the hallmarks of corporate governance. CSR on the other hand, takes business beyond the scope of legal provisions, recognising that the means to an end of profits involves many other stakeholders – particularly in the local community – whose recognition in the extractive resource industry goes a long way in the success story of any firm.

Much debate has occurred around Friedman's conception of the essence of a firm. However, a closer look at his statements above indicates that in as much as Friedman emphasises the essence of profit maximisation for a company – he supports the notion that this must be morally done in an ethical and a just way,[29] which is the essence of BHR. In a way, therefore, Friedman's idea delves into an aspect which BHR will, in later years, become associated with. If we all agree that the Board or CEO of a company is the moral agent of the company and thus has a moral obligation to make more money for the company in the right way – the issue of solely and narrowly categorising companies as money-making ventures would not arise. The decision-makers of a firm must be well informed of the activities of the firm and must take full responsibility for the decisions that affect that firm. This has led proponents of mandatory CSR to argue that even though the company makes profits for the shareholders, they owe it a moral duty to ensure that their company is involved in some form of socially responsible project.[30] This book does not agree with Friedman's philosophy, and it emphatically questions the logic behind "economic rationale" as the main reason behind activities in the extractive resource industry. Following the law and obeying ethical customs embedded in society are a *sine qua non* for sensible corporate practice.

The evolution of modernity and advances in technological innovations can no longer support the claim that corporations are founded solely for profit. Were this to be so, surely the founders of corporate organisations would not be involved in socially responsible projects all over the world? To claim – as Friedman's theory suggests – that the founders of corporate giants like Warren Buffet, Bill Gates, or Mark Zuckerberg who spend money on their philanthropic work, are robbing their company of profits meant for the company, is in fact uncharitable. If these "philanthropists" were employees, they would be paid salaries, bonuses and other emoluments. If upon their retirement, they decide to invest their life savings in issues that are of interest to them – how would that translate into "robbing Peter to pay Paul'? Corporate foundations are indeed set aside independently of the firm, and so do MNCs activate the "subsidiary corporate personality principle" to avoid culpability for human rights violations of a subsidiary company.

In response to Milton Friedman's comments in a 21st century public debate, Whole Foods CEO, John Mackey, denied that his company's commitment in its mission statement to donate 5% of net profits to philanthropic causes (approved unanimously by company owners) – amounted to philanthropic "theft" from the company's investors.[31] Indeed, corporate human rights initiatives improve individual and communal lives by creating value in many dimensions.

The narrow approach of Friedman to business can be better understood in the context in which it was presented. In the late 19th century, most of the countries that depended on and fought for control over natural resources were in the Global North. BHRs issues in the development and extractive industries were not a major issue to contend with. The huge investment, highly intensive labour, and other associated climate-change factors now associated with extractive resource development in the Global South were non-existent. Furthermore, there were major socio-economic uncertainties, and many people were not pleased with the way the global market was run, and also the legacy of interventionism and Keynesian economics pervaded the historical narrative. Thus, the dynamics of globalisation and different socio-economic, legal, and political landscapes of resource extraction, challenge the conclusion that the purpose of a company is solely to maximise profits. Today, the question that begs an answer is: of what benefit will companies be to society if their sole purpose is profit making, and in that process the environment is polluted, human lives are lost, and poverty increases? Globalisation and climate change are prompting stakeholders to broadly conceptualize the role of corporations, and at the same time avoid any conflict with the law. Certainly, societies have the right to demand that corporations consider moral factors in decision-making.

According to the agency theory, directors are the agents of the shareholders and are engaged to manage the company's affairs on behalf of the shareholders. As a result, only the shareholders can monitor and punish directors where they fail to dutifully exercise their powers and duties.[32] This is essentially the idea behind shareholder value principle (SVP) which attempts to bridge the gap between shareholder and stakeholder approach to corporate governance.

The SVP principle is grounded on productivity. Companies can induce wealth generation and foster "economic efficiency" in a more inclusive approach that values the construction of "long-term relationships."[33] In achieving shareholder wealth, the SVP recognizes the importance of realizing the success of the company by considering the necessity of maintaining relationships with wide range of stakeholders and the impact of their "operations on the community and the environment."[34] Evidently, corporate best practices and good conduct legitimizes corporate presence in Africa. This may not be achieved through mandatory or voluntary mechanisms, but through a combination of both approaches.[35]

3.3.3 Stakeholder theory

The modern concept of the stakeholder theory is associated with Robert E. Freeman.[36] His work was a challenge to Friedman's philosophy that shareholders should have priority over stakeholders. Interestingly, Freeman had just published his seminal book when the Bhopal (India) disaster happened. In his work, he contends there is a fiduciary duty between the management of the company and all its stakeholders, and therefore corporate management must prioritise its stakeholders. But who then are the stakeholders? According to Freeman, these "are those who have a stake in or claim on the firm";[37] those that can affect or be affected by a company's purpose, each seeking something different from the company. In the extractive sector, these stakeholders include the investors, civil society and host communities. Thus, Freeman would support the view that managers have a duty to their host community who are impacted by their activities.[38] Indeed, a consideration of the host community is vital to the granting of social legitimacy, and, by implication, the success of the firm. Certainly, the local communities, hosts to development projects, has an interest in the action and behaviour of the industry. Thus, managers must develop relationships, inspire their stakeholders, and create communities where everyone strives to give their best to deliver the value the firm promises.

Extractive companies must balance profit maximisation and create a positive impact on their immediate community. Such an impact can only be created where there is a receptive community. While the "stakeholders" feel a level of distrust towards the MNCs, they expect some economic activity in their community. The challenge is how to mitigate or reduce adverse human rights violations. This book adopts a stakeholder approach to refer to the local communities which host extractive projects. Stakeholder theory supports the desire to avoid, redress and mitigate human rights violation. The theory follows a simple logic: If the company does not meet the needs of the local community, it is highly likely that the community will revolt, and economic sustainability will be hampered.[39] Government will then be deprived of FDI, the local community will be deprived of white-collar jobs, and development will not take place in that community. In the long term, the stakeholders lose out in the power play of profit maximisation. Therefore, to ensure social legitimacy, the "stakeholder" (local community) must be given a high priority and must be deferred to in certain key decisions involving project planning, and execution and implementation – through a transparent and open process. It is not only conscionable for the MNCs to do this – it is in their best interest.

Understandably, profits are a critical feature of a business enterprise, but concern for profits is the result rather than the driver in the process of value creation.[40] When viewed in this context as a normative theory, the stakeholder theory asserts that, regardless of whether or not stakeholder management leads to improved financial performance, managers should direct the business for the benefit of all stakeholders. The corporation and its managers have special obligations to ensure that the shareholders receive a "fair" return on their investment; but the corporation also has special obligations to other stakeholders, which go beyond those required by law. In cases where these interests' conflict, the demands, and interests of some stakeholders, particularly host communities, must be safeguarded.[41]

Principles 3, 10, 16, 18, 20, 21, 28, 29, and 31 support the foregoing argument by making copious references to "affected stakeholder," which in the context of this book would be referred to as the "local community." These Principles emphasize the whole essence of a rights-based approach to extractive resource governance. For instance, the UNGPs require companies to communicate their human rights impact to stakeholders. This is particularly so in the context of extractive resources where the operating environment poses a substantial risk to human rights. The commentary to GP 10 states that the UNGPs could serve as a foundation for accumulative positive effect – that stipulates the separate "roles and responsibilities of all relevant stakeholders." It also requires states to encourage or incentivize corporate reporting.[42] Therefore, the UNGPs have integrated BHR principles, creating functions for states and corporations in a bid to facilitate a regime of corporate respect for human rights. They further enjoin the companies to engage in meaningful consultation with the local community (see UNGP 18(b)). Consultation obviates many challenges. It reduces tension with host communities, facilitates social legitimacy, builds community trust in development companies in the face of dwindling resources, and prioritizes respect for ethical behaviour and local community initiatives.[43]

It is an imperative for companies to be socially responsible. Without the support of its stakeholders, the continued existence of a firm is in doubt – given the connection between economics and social activity. Business is all about the voluntary and mutual exchange of goods and services. If people remain the dominant factor in the market chain, firms must constructively ensure that their services have a positive impact on the people.[44]

The local communities are the single dominant stakeholder in the BHRs debate. Otherwise, how does one quantify the damages or pay the community whose social and physical infrastructure have been destroyed by development projects.[45] It is difficult to understand how MNCs perform creditably well in developed countries – but complicit in human rights risks in Africa. It is not only normative to be socially responsive – but also it is morally just and equitable to be so.

Scholars have grappled with the question of whether moral status can be accorded to corporations in the same way as persons.[46] It is not the intention of this book to add to that debate. However, suffice to say, corporations could be criminally prosecuted for their wrongdoings – distinct from the officers of the company. For instance, when a court decides to dissolve a company, this terminates the company, much like sentencing a human being to death for murder. Concluding, therefore, as Werhane did, that because companies do not have hands, legs, and ears, and therefore cannot be literally punished, but humans as primary moral agents – would be a misunderstanding of the corporate entity as a social construct.[47]

The UNGPs are normative principles stating the respective roles and responsibilities for states and businesses. These are several principles which specify societal expectations from states in general, and companies in particular. If the host communities allow the companies to operate, the firms should be able to reciprocate a good gesture in terms of making the communities better than they met it. Companies must evaluate and respond to why community support is low, and how it can be improved. For instance, when communities are distraught about service delivery, which is under the purview of states, they resort to violence against the MNCs. Sustaining relationships must therefore be contingent on delivering value to stakeholders in a shared valued manner.

Freeman's work clearly affirms that local communities and development companies are moral agents which are obliged to respect each other's dignity and autonomy.[48] This book follows this paradigm. Firms are obliged to treat their stakeholders with the utmost of dignity and respect and must remediate any claim relating to human rights violation(s).[49] This responsibility on the part of firms does not preclude the need for host communities to be accountable; responsibility applies both ways. Development projects benefit the host communities as much as they do all of society. The implementation of the UNGPs will be achieved on the platform of reciprocal rights and duties. Certainly, communities have a sense of relationship mentoring when stakeholders engage in a respectful way. After all, firms are the socio-legal, and economic products of the community.

3.4 Stakeholder value approach

The stakeholder theory has had its fair share of criticism. Some claim that the theory destroys business accountability since "a business that is accountable to all is accountable to none."[50] Granted, raising one stakeholder above another may limit accountability and develop favouritism in decision-making. However, the doctrine of checks and balances is there to monitor the Board and management of the company and to prevent them from deviating from the BHRs initiative bestowed on a stakeholder group. In articulating the purpose of the firm, the Board must determine the extent of the relationship between management and a key stakeholder, in order to achieve that purpose. Both political and managerial will are needed on the part of states and the firm, to build lasting relationships between the firm and the host community. This creates a shared value system between the corporation and the community. Profit maximization is the result, and community building through BHRs is the driver that will propel the realization of this result.

Accordingly, a company's culture should promote integrity and openness, value diversity, and be responsive to the views of shareholders and wider stakeholders.

To succeed in the long term, MNCs need to build and maintain successful relationships with a wide range of stakeholders. These relationships will be successful and enduring if they are based on respect, trust, and mutual benefit. For example, if Eket community in Nigeria grants Shell Nigeria Ltd the right to construct development project in their community, Shell should not expose the community to continuous gas flaring with the resultant effect of toxic pollutants, and environmental pollution. If Shell decides to leave Eket for some reasons, there is the expectation that Shell must inform Eket and any remedial or mitigating procedures are put in place to solve any intractable problem. Shell as a corporate citizen should not mismanage the relationship with its community, otherwise, it would have only succeeded in violating the social contract that binds it with that community. Consequently, in their decision-making process, MNCs should not think in terms of short-term gains alone, but to consider the long-term consequences of their decisions.[51]

3.5 The board structure of a firm: correlative rights and duties between corporations and local communities

A firm act through its members in a General Meeting, its Board of Directors, or through its officers and agents.[52] The General Meeting or the Board directs issues and determines socially responsible projects to be undertaken by the company. Since the business of the company is managed by the Board, the Board has wide-ranging executive powers. For instance, they may deviate from the resolution of the members of the company in a General Meeting. The condition for doing this, however, is that the Board must act in good faith and with due diligence. Such acts carried out by the Board are still sometimes subject to the Memorandum and Articles of the Company.

The responsibility of the Board goes a long way in terms of apportioning blame for human rights violations. Sometimes conflicts arise as the Board struggles to work in the interests of the organisation, while at the same time engaging in CSR. MNCs often operate in conflict zones with the attendant effects of youth restiveness, militancy, and environmental pollution. As a result, subsistence activities like farming and fishing tend to become impossible or extremely difficult for the communities to undertake. A rising concern has been the predicted effect of global warming, flooding of coastlines, severe storms, a rise in sea levels, and departure from normal agricultural conditions.[53] However, how do these concerns affect the Board? Where the Board decides not to use their power in a socially responsible manner, they will probably lose it.

Firms act on the collective will of persons – whose sole responsibility is to work in the best interests of the firm. In light of this, this book takes the position that under the stakeholder theory the firm works in the best interests of those who will be greatly impacted by their activities – and in the context of this work these are the host communities to development projects. The mutuality or reciprocity of these responsibilities or duties between corporation and host community is not in doubt. Thus, as much as the Board is directly responsible to the firm through a corporate structure, it indirectly expects that the structure works in the best interests of their stakeholders (the host community) – otherwise the loss of social legitimacy could have serious implications for the firm itself. This book offers four propositions to demonstrate the correlative rights and duties between firms and stakeholders.

3.5.1 *Social license validates the responsibility and power of firms*

MNCs may have the necessary legal license to operate, but they often lack the social licence to operate (SLO). This was the basis for tension and conflict in the Shell (Nigeria) and Marikana (South Africa) incidents. Obtaining SLO is instrumental to the continued existence of MNCs – due to the potential for the adverse infringement of human rights in host communities. To achieve SLO, companies must engage and partner with their host communities in designing and implementing extractive and development projects. A key area in which this can be achieved is testing their projects in terms of a human rights impact assessment – in line with UNGP 18. The inability to obtain SLO leads to tension and conflict, which destroys the community-corporate trust, which is a veritable foundation for the granting of SLO. Furthermore, MNCs wield remarkable power over developing countries, especially when such control extends to human rights compliance, extractive resources, and community development.[54] Considering that some MNCs are richer and more powerful than states, this proposition yields value.[55] The local community must take part in project design, execution, and implementation. This creates an avenue for social trust and amity between the community and the firm.

3.5.2 *Transparency and accountability are sine-qua-non for obtaining social licence to operate*

Principles 21 and 31 require firms to present the human rights impact in a transparent and accountable way, to all of those who will be impacted by their activities. Though the GPs state that companies should provide this information when stakeholders raise concerns about the human rights impact – companies should not wait until they are asked to provide information. Responsibility demands doing what is needful, without being prompted to do so. When a community is unaware of a series of issues like efforts in remediating oil spillage, contracts between states and investors – heightened tensions and distrust set in. The shrouded secrecy of development contracts and various legal requirements breed environmental disasters, which have resulted in conflicts and battles in Nigeria's Niger-Delta. Open channels of communication ensure transparency and accountability. The UNGPs also state that the information can be provided through various means such as case studies and statistics. These avenues provide the basis for social legitimacy.

3.5.3 Cost-benefit analysis and environmental impact assessments prevent unmitigated violation of human rights

The idea that firms are created solely for profit defies logic considering the benefits or impact of profit maximisation on the community. Most countries ensure that firms establish and consider the extent to which any activity to be authorised by any level of government could affect the environment.[56] Thus, firms are obliged to study the potential, substantial, organic, and socio-economic effects of a proposed development project on the immediate and more distant environment. These effects must be identified, examined, and foreseen.[57] The responsible use and exploitation of natural resources is necessary – considering the "social costs and benefits of a proposed activity," sustainable productivity of the ecosystem, and preventing degradation of the environment.[58]

3.5.4 Firms as moral agents owe society social service responsibility

This proposition is at the core of this book. Firms must be encouraged to do much more than what the law strictly provides, as far as BHRs is concerned. This underscores the debate over the mandatory versus voluntary status of the UNGPs. When oil spillage occurs or environmental degradation arises, MNCs are always quick to attribute it to sabotage. However, these companies have the expertise to prevent, mitigate, and address human rights violations, and also to prevent further sabotage. Furthermore, where the fault cannot be traced to the firm, firms should still be involved in solving social problems related to their activities. Shell's inability to remediate oil spillage led to the environmental degradation of Ogoni land. It is not only for the good of the community, but also in the interests of the company for it to be involved in socially responsible projects.[59]

BHRs as a public value is in the interest of the public good. Companies need public value to sustain their businesses. When their services are not appreciated or held in public veneration, they lose social legitimacy. This is more so when firms solve social problems and support human rights.

3.6 Sustainable approach to business and human rights principles

BHRs has fused state responsibility as the duty bearer with that of a corporate function in terms of respecting human rights. Hence, BHRs compliance demands that States and corporations integrate for effective governance. This chapter has focused on the integration of state and business functions – to submit that a stakeholder theory putting local communities which are host to extractive projects on a high pedestal, is instrumental and functional for the discourse in this book. Thus, a pathway for implementing BHRs principles is replicated in the social responsibility of the companies to do much more than what is actually stated in the law, while states should create incentives for entering such BHRs commitments. Indeed, states, firms, and the local community can form a synergic relationship.

After all, issues of climate change, environmental pollution, business, and human rights affect all strata of society. One way this social responsibility can be achieved is in the idea of corporate reporting. For instance, Zerk cites the "comply or explain" approach in the Johannesburg Stock Exchange Listing Rules. Firms are obliged to report annually the extent of their compliance with designated corporate governance standards in the form of an "if not, why not" basis – as an example of a corporate disclosure regulation exerting "pressure on companies to be more socially responsible."[60]

The notion of human rights as it applies to corporations continues to evolve. As MNCs continue to grow significantly in developing countries, so also are human rights challenges evolving.[61] Human rights abuse has not declined – rather it has continued to grow exponentially. MNCs are either complacent in terms of recognising international human rights principles or are complicit in human rights violations. States, on the other hand, are weak in enforcing their laws, especially when it comes to MNCs – for fear of losing FDI. Firms that desire longevity and social legitimacy will work towards increasing an internal and external relationship, in order to provide value for the company. After all, what goes on in the internal structure of a firm can affect external conditionality.[62] Once the needs of local communities are met, the needs of the shareholders will already have been met. If it is the contention that corporate law is shareholder-centric, companies cannot meet the expectations of these shareholders if they do not have the enabling environment to operate. Shareholders expect profits which are only possible if companies are fully functional. Where there is tension and conflict in their areas of operation, it is difficult to meet corporate objectives. One of the pathways to sustaining BHRs debate is to incentivise social responsibility projects.

3.6.1 Incentivizing socially responsible projects

Where firms value accepted norms, reputational concerns about the future may create incentives for them to enforce the norms. However, to create a robust relationship, the duty of being socially responsible should not fall on the companies alone. States and local communities have a role to play. On the part of the states, incentivising and compliance programmes can be designed for companies to promote human rights compliance. The basis for incentives is found in the commentary to GP 3, which provides that states are to encourage companies who communicate their human rights impact through incentives – which "could include provisions to give weight to such self-reporting in the event of any judicial or administrative proceeding."[63]

African states can demand that MNCs have an ethics and compliance programme to comply with the UNGPs. This could be drafted into the Companies Act or similar regulations. Where companies violate those programmes, this could form the basis for criminal prosecution. Indirectly, BHRs compliance would form part of corporate culture – as no company wants to be prosecuted, be it for civil or criminal crimes.[64] However, mere non-compliance should not be the basis for prosecution. At the first instance, companies should be given the opportunity to remedy any harm caused by their activities, and this is where the incentives come in.[65] The 2008 economic crunch heightened unethical and irresponsible behaviour in MNCs, and it is difficult for the government to ensure and promote compliance when it is not doing its part to protect human rights. Besides, a compliance programme cannot stop gas flaring with the attendant environmental pollution when that is a cheaper option for the company than other operational processes. Thus, compliance with human rights norms should not affect profit making. Therefore, government – in creating these incentives[66] – must use the UNGPs as benchmarks for assessing the human rights performance of companies.

The goal of incentivising is to establish a sustained corporate culture that would, over time, enable firms to comply with laws without being forced to do so. Although a visible, financial, incentive-based approach would aid compliance with ethical norms, the incentive need not be only financially based. It could also take the form of annual awards and a medal, and also television documentaries highlighting how the company is responding to the corporate-community relationship. This would promote an organisational culture of self-regulation, and companies would be enthusiastic and eager to conform with the law.

Undeniably, culture plays a substantial role in the life of an organisation. Firms can only operate optimally in resource-rich areas if they have social legitimacy. By so doing, companies avoid distracting court cases, punitive fines, and the distrust of the host community; court cases take up a significant part of the firm's time and progress. In Nigeria, for instance, court cases involving MNCs drag on for decades – compelling some plaintiffs to seek help in foreign jurisdictions. During this period, firms are uncertain about their stance: huge fines may be imposed, reputational damage occurs, and managers' job security may be at risk. These issues seriously divert the company's attention.[67] Providing incentives for compliance therefore helps organisations detect illegality on time.[68] It is also a sustainable way of ensuring the social responsibility of firms.

3.7 Conclusion

Local communities epitomize an important group that has an interest in how development projects affect their sustenance. The inability of MNCs to recognize this salient fact led to the Shell (Nigeria), Marikana (South Africa), and Lake Turkana Windmill project (Kenya) incidents. The tragedies of these events clearly revealed major gaps in the way companies observe human rights principles. To avoid these tragedies, MNCs should consider the inclusion of these stakeholders in the Board as this enhances the reputation of the firm and creates an environment of trust.

Since all stakeholders do not have the same effect on an organization, this chapter established that in the hierarchy of stakeholders, especially in development and extractive projects, the local communities should have a heightened stake in development benefits. This approach is a better way for thinking about creating value for host communities – by paying attention to the community's demands. Social responsibilities of business therefore must be seen from the standpoint of the practical creation of social values – which will create a positive business impact on their immediate communities. The stakeholder value theory starts with an idea of purpose and tries to create value for a narrow group of people. Business creates value in a responsible way when it connects with the local community and civil society who are instrumental in meeting societal demands. This approach takes care of the community and at the same time can still make money for shareholders.

Notes

1 Ved P. Nanda, & Ralph Lake (eds.), *The Law of Transnational Business Transactions* (2014) 19.
2 S. Bhaduri, & E. Selarka, "Corporate Governance and Corporate Social Responsibility: Introduction" in S. Bhaduri & E. Selarka (eds.) *Corporate Governance and Corporate Social Responsibility of Indian Companies* (2016) 1; A.M. Safwat, "Corporate Social Responsibility: Rewriting the Relationship between Business and Society" (2015) 4(1) *International Journal of Social Sciences* 85.
3 Florian Wettstein, "From Side Show to Main Act: Can Business and Human Rights Save Corporate Responsibility?" in Dorothée Baumann-Pauly & Justine Nolan (eds.) *Business and Human Rights: From Principles to Practice* (2016) 99.
4 Ibid.
5 Bryan Horrigan, *Corporate Social Responsibility in the 21st Century, Debates, Models and Practices across Government, Law and Business* (2010) 34.
6 With reference to Shell (Nigeria); Bhopal (India); Marikana (South Africa), see chapter 1.2. See also *Doe v. Nestle USA* No. 10–56739 D.C. No. 2:05-CV-05133- SVW-JTL, where the US Court of Appeals concluded that "the plaintiffs' allegations satisfied the more stringent 'purpose' standard by suggesting that a narrow-minded focus on profit over human welfare drove the defendants to act with the purpose of obtaining the cheapest cocoa possible, even if it meant facilitating child slavery."
7 Green Paper, "Promoting a European Framework for Corporate Social Responsibility" DOC/01/9 (18 July 2001) 4.
8 Terje I. Vaaland, & Morten Heide, "Managing Corporate Social Responsibility: Lessons from the Oil Industry" (2008) 3(2) *Corporate Communications: An International Journal* 212–225. [arguing that CSR implies building and maintaining relationships with society through interplay between actors, resources, and activities].
9 Green Paper (above n 7) 35.
10 Z. Larson, "The Sullivan Principles: South Africa, Apartheid, and Globalization" (2020) 44(3) *Diplomatic History* 479.
11 Nadia Bernaz, & Irene Pietropaoli, "The Role of Non-Governmental Organizations in the Business and Human Rights Treaty Negotiations" (2017) 9(2) *Journal of Human Rights Practice* 287.
12 See Chapter 1.2. Barrick Gold's human rights management approach states that: "We have zero tolerance for human rights violations . . . our commitment to respect human rights is . . . informed by the expectations of the UN Guiding Principles on Business and Human Rights (UNGPs) . . ." See Barrick Gold, "Human Rights Management Approach" <www.barrick.com/English/sustainability/human-rights/default.aspx> accessed 30 April 2021.
13 See French "Duty of Vigilance" Law; EU Directive 2014/95/EU of the European Parliament and of the Council of 22 October 2014 amending Directive 2013/34/EU as regards disclosure of non-financial and diversity information by certain large undertakings and groups, OJ 2014 No. L 330, in force 6 December 2014.
14 *Choc v Hudbay Minerals Inc*, 2013 ONSC 1414. *Okpabi and others v. Royal Dutch Shell Plc and others* [2021] 1 WLR 1294. Royal Dutch Shell Plc and another (Respondents).

15 O. Egbon, U. Idemudia, & K. Amaeshi, "Shell Nigeria's Global Memorandum of Understanding and Corporate-Community Accountability Relations: A Critical Appraisal" (2018) 31(1) *Accounting, Auditing & Accountability Journal* 51; U. Idemudia, "Corporate Social Responsibility and the Rentier Nigerian State: Rethinking the Role of Government and the Possibility of Corporate Social Development in the Niger Delta" (2010) *Canadian Journal of Development Studies* 131. [explaining that there have been over 5,000 oil spills between 2000 and 2004 as well as a massive oil spill in November 2012].

16 Marc Parés, Sonia Ospina, & Joan Subirats, *Social Innovation and Democratic Leadership: Communities and Social Change from Below* (2017).

17 Shelly Shah, "Theories of Social Change: Meaning, Nature and Processes" <www.sociologydiscussion.com/sociology/theories-of-social-change-meaning-nature-and-processes/2364> accessed 6 May 2021.

18 Ibid.

19 A.G. Johnson, *The Blackwell Dictionary of Sociology: A User's Guide to Sociological Language* (2000) 285.

20 A.O. Agugua, "Theories of Social Change and Development in Africa" in S. Oloruntoba & T. Falola (eds.) *The Palgrave Handbook of African Politics, Governance and Development* (2018) 104.

21 In most European countries today, smoking outside has been banned by regulation, subject to the enactment of a law. Social change occurred when the society instinctively supported moves to curb the smoking menace. See Meera Senthilingam, "What Finland's Plan to Be Tobacco-Free Can Teach the World" *CNN Health* (26 January 2017) <https://edition.cnn.com/2017/01/26/health/finland-tobacco-free-plan/> accessed 6 May 2021 [Finland begins plans to end smoking in 2040].

22 See further: Shift, "Evaluating Business Respect for Human Rights: A Theory of Change Methodology to Develop Meaningful Indicators" <https://shiftproject.org/resource/evaluating-business-respect-for-human-rights-a-theory-of-change-methodology-to-develop-meaningful-indicators/> accessed 10 July 2021.

23 J.F. Sherman, "Rights Respecting Corporate Culture" <https://shiftproject.org/wp-content/uploads/2019/09/VRP_Culture_Respect%20for%20Human%20Rights_Sherman.pdf> accessed 10 July 2021.

24 See Samuel Mansell, "Shareholder Theory and Kant's "Duty of Beneficence"" (2013) 3 *Journal of Business Ethics* 583–599. [noting the possibility within the ethical framework of shareholder theory for managers to directly pursue the happiness of non-shareholders]

25 Milton Friedman, *Capitalism and Freedom* (1982) 133.

26 Milton Friedman, "The Social Responsibility of Business Is to Increase Its Profits" *New York Times* (13 September 1970) 126. See also Frederick Hayek, "The Corporation in a Democratic Society: In Whose Interest Ought it and Will It Be Run?" in Melvin Anshen & George Bach (eds.) *Management in the Corporation* (1985) 100 [corporations should not use their resources for specific ends other than those of a long-run maximization of the return on the capital placed under their control].

27 See further John Mackey, & Rajendra Sisodia, *Conscious Capitalism: Liberating the Heroic Spirit of Business* (2013). John Mackey is the co-founder of Whole Foods, the largest organic food manufacturing company in the US. He pioneered the concept of conscious businesses where he believes that business should strive to benefit people and the environment.

28 Friedman, above (n 26).

29 See Justine Nolan, "Business and Human Rights in Context" in Dorothee Baumann-Pauly & Justine Nolan (eds.) *Business and Human Rights: From Principles to Practice* (2016) 21.

30 See Florian Wettstein, "Waiting for the Mountain to Move: The Role of Multinational Corporations in the Quest for Global Justice" (2013) *Notizie di Politeia* 13; Surya Deva

& David Bilchitz (eds.) *Human Rights Obligations of Business: Beyond the Corporate Responsibility to Respect?* (2013).
31 M. Friedman, J. Mackey, & T.J. Rodgers, "Rethinking the Social Responsibility of Business" <https://reason.com/2005/10/01/rethinking-the-social-responsi-2/> accessed 10 July 2021.
32 Andrew Keay, "Tackling the Issue of the Corporate Objective: An Analysis of the United Kingdom's "Enlightened Shareholder Value Approach"" (2007) 29(4) *Sydney Law Review* 577. See further, K. Levillain, & B. Segrestin, "From Primacy to Purpose Commitment: How Emerging Profit-with-Purpose Corporations Open New Corporate Governance Avenues" (2019) 37(5) *European Management Journal* 637; See also J.J. Du Plesis, A. Hargovan, & J. Harris (eds.), *Principles of Contemporary Corporate Governance* (2018) 23.
33 Ibid.
34 Ibid. at 580.
35 See for example, South Africa's King Code on Corporate Governance <www.iodsa.co.za/page/kingIII> accessed 8 July 2021, which is a voluntary mechanism. However, compliance with the Code is a requirement for companies to be listed on the Johannesburg Stock Exchange, and hence the Codes are indirectly mandatory. The Code also co-exists with the Companies Act – making it imperative for the Board and the company to comply with it.
36 See Robert E. Freeman, *Strategic Management: A Stakeholder Approach* (1984) 144.
37 Robert E. Freeman, "A Stakeholder Theory of the Modern Corporation" *Perspectives in Business Ethics* (2001) 144.
38 Ibid. at 59.
39 M. Fia, & L Sacconi, "Justice and Corporate Governance: New Insights from Rawlsian Social Contract and Sen's Capabilities Approach" (2019) 160 *Journal of Business Ethics* 937. [CSR operates where those who run a firm have responsibilities towards all the firm's stakeholders].
40 R. Freeman, A. Wicks, & B. Parmar, "Stakeholder Theory and 'the Corporate Objective Revisited'" (2004) 15(3) *Organization Science* 364; G.J. Lemoine, C.A. Hartnell, & H. Leroy, "Taking Stock of Moral Approaches to Leadership: An Integrative Review of Ethical, Authentic, and Servant Leadership" (2019) 13(1) *Academy of Management Annals* 148.
41 See further: B. Best, S. Moffett, & R. McAdam, "Stakeholder Salience in Public Sector Value Co-Creation" (2019) 21(11) *Public Management Review* 1707.
42 See Commentary to UNGP 10.
43 On 5 November 2015, a tailings dam collapsed in Brazil releasing huge wastes and industrial chemicals. About 17 people died as a result and several million lives were impacted. Subsequently, an agreement was reached by Samarco Mining S.A (the company operating the dam) and the Brazilian government. The court suspended the settlement agreement because there was not only minimal consultation with the communities impacted by the incident, but there was also no public participation and transparency in arriving at an agreed sum. See further Baskut Tuncak, "Lessons from the Samarco Disaster" (2017) *Business and Human Rights Journal* 161.
44 Heather Elms, Michael E. Johnson-Cramer, & Shawn L. Berman, "Bounding the World's Miseries: Corporate Responsibility and Freemans Stakeholder Theory" in Robert A. Phillips (ed.) *Stakeholder Theory: Impact and Prospects* (2011) 11.
45 M.L. Barnett, I. Henriques, & B. Husted, "Beyond Good Intentions: Designing CSR Initiatives for Greater Social Impact" (2020) 46(6) *Journal of Management* 937. [CSR initiatives must foster specific social and environmental objectives].
46 Patricia Werhane, "Corporate Moral Agency and the Responsibility to Respect Human Rights in the UN Guiding Principles: Do Corporations Have Moral Rights?" (2016) *Business and Human Rights Journal* 7.

47 V. Valentinov, & M. Pérez-Valls, "A Conception of Moral Wayfinding for Business Managers: The Obligation for a Sustainable Corporation" (2021) 284 *Journal of Cleaner Production* 124771; J.S. Harrison, R.A. Phillips, & R.E. Freeman, "On the 2019 Business Roundtable Statement on the Purpose of a Corporation" (2019) 46(7) *Journal of Management* 1223.

48 R.E. Freeman, & S.D. Dmytriyev, "Stakeholder Theory and the Resource-Based View of the Firm" (2021) XX(X) *Journal of Management* 1.

49 M. Woermann, & S. Engelbrecht, "The Ubuntu Challenge to Business: From Stakeholders to Relation Holders" (2019) 157 *Journal of Business Ethics* 27.

50 Robert Phillips, R. Edward Freeman, & Andrew C. Wicks, "What Stakeholder Theory Is Not" (2003) 13(4) *Business Ethics Quarterly* 479–502.

51 Keay (n 32 above).

52 See section 63 of the Companies and Allied Matters Act, Nigeria.

53 MNCs operating in Nigeria enhance the greenhouse effect due to massive gas flaring. Until this natural gas is effectively cupped, processed, and sold as domestic gas, addressing global warming may remain a mirage.

54 See UNGPs 11 and 13.

55 See further J. Ruggie, "Multinationals as Global Institutions: Power, Authority and Relative Autonomy" (2017) *Regulation and Governance* 9, 13. [Noting that MNCs have become a global institution in terms of their power, authority, and relative autonomy].

56 See section 1 of the Environmental Impact Assessment Act of 1992, Nigeria; See also Damilola Olawuyi, *The Principles of Nigerian Environmental Law* (2015) 208.

57 See Principle 19.

58 See *Oronto Douglas v Shell Petroleum Development Company*, Unreported suit No: FHC/L/C/573/931. See further sections 2(2) and 7 of the Environmental Impact Assessment Act of 1992, Nigeria.

59 See generally D. Jijelava, & F. Vanclay, "How a Large Project Was Halted by the Lack of a Social Licence to Operate: Testing the Applicability of the Thomson and Boutilier Model" (2018) 73 *Environmental Impact Assessment* 31; Keith Davis, "Five Propositions for Social Responsibility" (1975) 18(3) *Business Horizons* XVIII.

60 Jennifer A. Zerk, *Multinationals and Corporate Social Responsibility: Limitations and Opportunities in International Law* (2011) 36.

61 The 2013 Raza Plana incident.

62 See *Revlon, Inc. v. MacAndrews & Forbes Holdings, Inc.*, 506 A. 2d 173, 182 (Del. 1986) [Directors can consider other constituencies: employees, community interests, only when doing so provides benefit to shareholders as well].

63 See commentary to GP 3.

64 See further Maurice E. Stucke, "In Search of Effective Ethic and Compliance Programme" (2014) 39(4) *Journal of Corporation Law*; Peter Henning, "Lessons from the Glaxo Case in China" *New York Times* (29 July 2013) [companies have invested massively in compliance programs to avoid wrongdoing].

65 In the United States, Section 101 (c) (2) of the Sarbanes Oxley Act (2002) mandates public disclosure of compliance programme. Directors of companies are now obliged to ensure truthful reportage of the firm's compliance efforts.

66 Such as tax breaks.

67 F. Vanclay, & P. Hanna, "Conceptualizing Company Response to Community Protest: Principles to Achieve a Social License to Operate" (2019) 8(6) *Land* 101.

68 See Wouter P.J. Wils, "Antitrust Compliance Programmes and Optimal Antitrust Enforcement" (2013) 1(1) *J. Antitrust Enforcement* 52.

Part II

Human rights-based approach to business and human rights in Africa

4 Corporate duty to respect human rights

4.1 Introduction

This book has anchored its arguments on the premise that businesses must not only consider their profitability and growth – but also the interests of their immediate environment. They must weigh the impact of their activities on their host communities. To date, the international legal order does not offer a robust regime for corporate liability. The result is a conflict between human rights principles under international law and under national laws. It is even more complex when such rules or laws are of normative value, making liability difficult to become domesticated. To avoid the challenges of implementation of human rights standards, the UNGPs can be integrated into various rules, regulations, and memoranda to produce an indirect effect. While this chapter discusses the fundamental key elements of corporate duty to respect human rights: corporate human rights due diligence, and corporate human rights impact assessment, Chapter 5 examines the important contributions of the elements of a rights-based approach to development projects.[1] The discussion in this chapter assumes that businesses have sufficient legal personality to bear legal rights and duties.[2]

4.2 Corporate Human Rights Due Diligence (HRDD)

In clarifying the concept of corporate HRDD, Ruggie and Sherman distinguish between "standard of conduct to discharge a responsibility" and a "process to manage human rights risks."[3] The authors explicitly state that businesses are obliged to go beyond the law in preventing and addressing any involvement in adverse human rights impact. As a result, companies obtain a social license from their host communities. The corporate responsibility to respect human rights applies regardless of any efforts by the state. The essence of HRDD is to "understand the specific impacts on specific people, given a specific context," and hence it is not just checking the assets and liabilities of a firm – but is an attempt to unravel any actual or potential human rights violations over the whole duration of a project. Therefore, corporate HRDD seeks to assess actual and potential human rights impacts, integrate and act upon the findings, track responses, and communicate how the impacts are addressed.[4] This process obviates the need for companies to show that they respect human rights.

DOI: 10.4324/9781003290124-7

According to Taylor, due diligence is the solution to the intractable problem of corporate responsibility – especially when companies source "metals and minerals from war zones where serious human rights abuses and armed conflicts were rampant."[5] States are required to warn corporations operating in conflict-prone zones of the risk of being involved in gross human rights abuses. Furthermore, corporations are obliged to have "policies and programmes" in place in order to be able to meet their human rights responsibility. These policies and programmes, which must be in accordance with their size and circumstances, include HRDD practices that identify, address, and mitigate adverse human rights impacts.[6] But how can companies identify and mitigate adverse human rights abuses? Principle 17 gives direction on what must be contained in a HRDD. It specifies that companies should integrate findings from the HRDD into their human rights policy and must communicate how human rights impacts are addressed. HRDD must cover adverse human rights impact of the business activities, the nature and context of the company's operations, and must be an ongoing exercise – considering that the risks associated with human rights may change as the corporations change practice.[7]

Even with the best of intentions, corporations in the extractive and energy industries have the potential to be involved in human rights violations. Hence, when HRDD identifies an intentional or unintentional violation, it must actively remediate such impacts on rights holders: the host communities. When firms integrate HRDD into their programmes, they can easily defend themselves against legal claims, as there would be an opportunity to indicate there was every reasonable precaution to prevent human rights violations.

Although, showing good cause for HRDD does not absolve the company of any allegation of human rights abuses – it does show serious commitment to the ideals of human rights, as typified under the UNGPs.[8] Therefore, HRDD should run through the life cycle of a project, especially in situations where social tensions are rampant. For example, the underlying basis for corporate involvement in adverse human rights impacts stems from the extent of such a company's participation in the human rights infringement. The questions that determine this are, did the company: cause the impact; contribute to the impact; and is it directly linked to its actions, products, or services without contributing to the infringement. In effectively answering these questions, corporate HRDD must include consultation with those who are at heightened risk of being affected by the corporate conduct. This would include assessing "specific impacts on specific people, given a specific context of operations."[9]

The various ways that project proponents have failed to conduct HRDD and remediate the adverse impacts of their activities are evident in human rights impact such as oil pollution, gas flaring, and climate change effects. In the Nigerian case of *Jonah Gbemre (for himself and as representing Iwherekan Community in Delta State, Nigeria) v Shell Petroleum Development Company, NNPC & Attorney General of the Federation*,[10] the applicant's claim was that due to the first respondent's activities in their community, their right to a clean, poison-free, and healthy environment had been violated. Furthermore, the applicant claimed that the first respondent's continuous gas flaring in the applicant's local community constituted a violation of their fundamental rights to life and dignity of the human person, respectively, which are guaranteed by sections 33(1) and 34(1) of the Nigerian Constitution and which are reinforced by articles 4, 16, and 24 of the African Charter on Human and Peoples Rights (Ratification and Enforcement) Act.[11] The court was unsparing in its condemnation of the respondents. It held that the continuous flaring of gas by Shell in the *Iwherekan* community was a gross violation of the applicants" right to life and dignity of the human person which are provided for under the Constitution. The court further ordered the applicants to cease gas flaring. The court also ordered the Attorney-General, who never made an appearance throughout the proceedings, to begin the process of amending the relevant sections of the Associated Gas Re-Injection Act, 1979,[12] and the Regulations made pursuant to the Act – so that they are compatible with Chapter 4 of the Constitution.[13]

Rather than comply with this judgment and cease gas flaring, the state frustrated every attempt at enforcement of the judgment. Initially, upon the expiration of the order of stay of execution, the applicants appeared in court – but not the defendants or their representatives. Subsequently it was revealed that the trial judge had been removed and transferred to a High Court in northern Nigeria. The case file also went missing. Secondly, when Shell and NNPC appealed on the grounds of jurisdiction, the court staff – without putting the applicant or his lawyer on notice – deceitfully adjourned the case. Even when the presiding judge promised to investigate the matter and discipline the person responsible, the matter was never heard in public.[14] This is proof that in weakly governed jurisdictions, bureaucracy and administrative bottlenecks often prevent litigants from achieving justice in national courts. In the European Union (EU), legislation requires corporate due diligence.[15] States are required under EU law to subject their due diligence conduct to necessity, proportionality, and legislation.[16] In some other jurisdictions due diligence requirements have been translated into law.[17]

HRDD must focus on what impact the company is making on its host community. For instance, Nike or Adidas might decide to build a children's playground as part of their corporate social responsibility (CSR). The question then is – why are they doing this? This is simply because they are potential consumers and not because of human rights impacts. Therefore, CSR is different from corporate respect for human rights under the business and human rights paradigm. Furthermore, there is a difference between ordinary due diligence and HRDD. For instance, in mergers and acquisitions, where one company buys the other, corporate lawyers check the debts, assets, and liabilities of each company. This is business due diligence, while HRDD is about impacts. What impact is that company having on its immediate environment? It could be on its host community, indigenous people, or even employees. Corporate HRDD therefore advances corporate engagement with issues that could otherwise affect the corporate image of the company.

Another argument is to develop incentives for corporations involved in due diligence. States, for instance, may reduce the costs of remedying environmental pollution as well as criminal liability for such pollution. States can also provide guidance to corporations through information materials explaining the importance of HRDD under the UNGPs. Corporate laws should incorporate reporting requirements for due diligence. The law should stipulate what constitutes adequate HRDD and that reporting of such HRDD is required. Mechanisms should be in place to verify such information given by the company – and could include the auditing of reports and adequate sanctions issued where there are false reports or information. Corporate lawyers should be trained on how to advise their corporate clients on human rights impacts. The courts should also be agents of social change – by creating stronger legal standards through their judgments.

The UNGPs offer a functional examination of the importance of corporate HRDD. First, HRDD will identify the major stakeholders who will be impacted by their activities: the local community. Second, it will identify all the human rights values that could potentially be violated: land displacement; air, land, and water pollution; and serious health implications (tuberculosis and silicosis). Third, HRDD will provide solutions to mitigate or reduce such potential or actual impact. In light of emerging threats occasioned by globalization, the business and human rights principles have created a standard for corporations to inculcate HRDD and impact assessment into their corporate culture. The next section discusses the promise and potential of a human rights impact assessment in addressing human rights risks.

4.3 Corporate Human Rights Impact Assessment (HRIA)

A rights-based approach identifies the need for a corporate human rights impact assessment (HRIA) in for determining, recognizing, and alleviating the potential adverse human rights impacts of development projects. In providing a model for implementing human rights standards, the HRIA structure builds rights development, practical, and real solutions to a corporate activity.[18]

Corporate HRIA faces significant challenges in Africa. This is further exacerbated by obstructive land rights, gender disparities, and lack of resources to ensure that victims of human rights violations adequately seek justice when development projects impact their existence.[19] Thus, national laws must be strengthened to require rights-based permissible infrastructure for energy and extractive projects, by integrating human rights standards into energy and extractive law and policy.

HRIA is a mechanism for examining policies, legislation, programs, and projects to identify and measure their effects on human rights.[20] As a pre-condition for granting licenses and leases, energy and extractive companies must investigate and determine the possible effect of their project on human rights. Their investigation must be able to identify specific human rights challenges, group of people their project might likely impact – women, children, and disabled, how such impacts could be prevented or mitigated. Detailed HRIA prevents adverse human rights impact of project.

It also offers businesses a practical basis for identifying sources of environmental degradation, climate injustice, human rights violations, and avenues for realising social license from their host communities. If diligently pursued, HRIA creates some form of affinity between the corporation and the host community as projects are seen as joint development initiatives rather than a state-investor approach to development. Furthermore, human rights are synchronized and incorporated into policies to enable society a pathway to participate in project design and implementation, including periodic review of the project where it may have derailed from the initial human rights approach.

Indeed, several legal and institutional obstacles prevent the actualisation of HRIA at the local level. Some of these challenges include "arbitrary land tenure systems, inadequacy or absence of climate change laws, exclusionary customary practices, and inadequate capacity impact vulnerable groups" ability to invoke human rights norms to seek redress when energy access projects threaten their ways of life."[21] African states must adopt proactive human rights legislation requiring the conduct of HRIAs in the design, financing, and implementation of their projects. Nigeria's Petroleum Industry Act (2021) requires an environmental management plan before a project commences. National legislation should go further by mandating HRIAs as an essential constituent of existing legislation on environmental impact assessment or human rights.[22] This will embolden local communities to demand for justice where development of energy and extractive projects are no longer sustainable.

Project proponents typically do not communicate whether any assessment has been done or whether they took human rights into consideration when planning their projects. Companies should be monitored to ensure they consistently prioritise and address human rights risks and proffer ways to avoid or mitigate the adverse results flowing from such risks. Although most extractive companies have codes of conduct which detail their social responsibility and impact assessments – much more than that is needed. Real-time tracking of efforts made in addressing and mitigating the impact and communicating these efforts to stakeholders must accompany the activity of extractive companies. Furthermore, involving the community in the design of a company grievance mechanism and building on community traditions shows respect for the community, and in the long-term secures a social licence and a community sense of ownership.[23]

Conducting HRDD and HRIA requires sufficient financial resources, especially on the part of monitoring responsibilities of states. State agencies and ministries have failed to sufficiently carry out their statutory obligations due to lack of funds. Consequently, NHRIs, whose sole responsibility is human rights, could be better funded to address the challenges in carrying out HRDD and HRIA.

4.4 Conclusion

This chapter discussed the rights-based approach to ensuring that companies implement human rights standards in their spheres of operations. In allocating responsibility for corporate duty, the chapter examined corporate human rights due diligence and human rights impact assessment as integral path of business sustainability, and a net effect that certifies social inclusion. Adopting these safeguards mirrors African states' desire to ensure that companies under their jurisdictions respect human rights. Critical to implementing these protections is the need to develop robust legal and institutional frameworks at that domestic level that captures inclusivity, transparency, and community development paradigms. Corporate responsibility should not be construed to mean that corporations do not have any legal duties under national laws. After all, social responsibility needs are paramount in areas where governance structures are porous.

Notes

1 Surya Deva, "Treating Human Rights Lightly: A Critique of the Consensus Rhetoric and the Language Employed by the Guiding Principles" in Surya Deva & David Bilchitz (eds.) *Human Rights Obligations of Business: Beyond the Corporate Responsibility to Respect?* (2013) 78 at 93 [arguing that the usage of responsibility as against "duty" is to denote "non-legal duties"].

2 Uwafiokun Idemudia, "Corporate Social Responsibility and the Rentier Nigerian State: Rethinking the Role of Government and the Possibility of Corporate Social Development in the Niger Delta" (2010) *Canadian Journal of Development Studies* 131. [Explaining that there have been over 5,000 oil spills between 2000 and 2004 as well as a massive oil spill in November 2012].

3 See J.G. Ruggie, & J.F. Sherman, "The Concept of "Due Diligence" in the UN Guiding Principles on Business and Human Rights: Reply to Professors Bonnitcha and Mccorquodale" (2017) 28(3) *European Journal of International Law* 921; N. Bueno, & C. Bright, "Implementing Human Rights Due Diligence through Corporate Civil Liability" (2020) 69(4) *International & Comparative Law Quarterly* 789–818. *Politics* 667–697.

4 See Principle 17.

5 T.L. Kirkebø, & M. Langford, "The Commitment Curve: Global Regulation of Business and Human Rights" (2018) 3(2) *Business and Human Rights Journal* 157.

6 See Principle 17.

7 Ibid. See further Principles 18–21.

8 See for instance Principles 17, 22 and commentary to Principle 19.

9 Commentary to Principle 18.

10 FHC/B/CS/S3/05. [A Federal High Court decision on the 14 November 2005 before Honourable Justice C.V. Nwokorie].

11 Cap A9, LFN, 2004. [African Charter].

12 The Petroleum Industry Act 2021 effectively repeals this Act.

13 Ibid.

14 G. Enogholase, "Benin Court Registrar Under Investigation" *Vanguard* (27 September 2006).

15 See Olga Martin-Ortega, "Human Rights Due Diligence for Corporations: From Voluntary Standards to Hard Law at Last?" (2013) 31 *Netherlands Quarterly of Human Rights* 44, 52.

16 See Regulation (EU) No 995/2010 of the European Parliament and of the Council of 20 October 2010; see further Directive 2013/34/EU of the European Parliament and of the Council, 26 June 2013, OJ L182/52 [Amended by Directive 2014/95/EU concerning disclosure of non-financial and diversity information by certain large undertakings and groups, 22 October 2014].

17 See Section 1502 of the US Dodd-Frank Act as it relates to certification of minerals from the Democratic Republic of the Congo; see the revisions to the OECD Guidelines (2011). See also the French Corporate Duty of Vigilance Law which impose due diligence obligations for parent and subsidiary companies.

18 D. Olawuyi, "Advancing Climate Justice in International Law: An Evaluation of the United Nations Human Rights-Based Approach" (2016) 11 *Florda A & M University Law Review* 1.

19 D. Olawuyi, "Energy (And Human Rights) for All: Addressing Human Rights Risks in Energy Access Projects" in R. Salter, C. Gonzalez, & E. Warner (eds.) *Energy Justice US and International Perspectives* (2018) 73.

20 World Bank, "Human Rights Impact Assessments: A Review of the Literature, Differences with Other Forms of Assessments and Relevance for Development" (2013) <https://documents1.worldbank.org/curated/en/834611524474505865/pdf/125557-WP-PUBLIC-HRIA-Web.pdf> accessed 23 August 2021.

21 Olawuyi (n 19) 78.

22 Ibid.

23 Institute for Business and Human Rights, Extractive Sector in Kenya, 76.

5 Integrating a rights-based approach to developmental projects

5.1 Introduction

Despite the existence of various corporate theories,[1] declarations, and policy document for corporate accountability for human rights violations, there is a lack of robust legal remedies and protection to address corporate induced human rights violations. The concerns arising from corporate conduct has remained contentious in most African countries. The absence of detailed operational guidelines, metrics, or indicators on what responsible corporations should do to advance business and human rights principles has remained a challenge. This chapter examines human rights-based approach to addressing corporate induced human rights abuse. It discusses the drivers for corporate accountability and how human rights-based approaches can be integrated to business and human rights standards and principles. The methodical and fundamental injustice host communities are subjected to has made any subsequent distribution of income from development projects contentious. The stymied growth in weakly governed countries arises from the lack of an ideological roadmap to develop critical industries in Africa.[2] This is due to poor political and socio-economic infrastructure, corruption, and weak or non-existent rule of law and law enforcement.[3]

5.2 A human rights-based approach to developmental governance

A human rights-based approach is necessary for a number of factors. First, Africa "hosts over two-thirds of the world's reserves of platinum, which are essential in the electronic industry."[4] Natural resources in Africa "constitutes a major share of exports and tax revenues."[5] These resources present both challenges and prospects for the countries concerned. The countries can leverage the resources to accelerate broad-based economic development, poverty reduction, and prosperity for all their citizens. However, harnessing the benefits of the resources have been problematic. Not only have these countries failed to reap the benefits of the resources, but the development of the resources has triggered violent conflicts, destroyed the environment, exacerbated inequalities across gender and geography, displaced communities, and undermined

DOI: 10.4324/9781003290124-8

democratic governance.[6] But there are also countries where effective management of the resources has produced sustainable and equitable human development.[7] It is generally believed that what makes the difference between these two categories of countries – is the design and implementation of a broad set of rules and regulations.[8] These include legal and institutional frameworks for the distribution of revenue from the resources; legal and institutional mechanisms that "foster transparency and accountability in the management" of revenues from the resources (Principle 21); mechanisms which address the social, human, and environmental impacts of extractive resource development (through the adaptation of the stakeholder theory) – especially in "indigenous peoples and local communities"; and policies and mechanisms that "ensure that human rights are well integrated" into the extractive sector.[9] Second, the rise of rights-based approaches to development projects has become part of a broader effort at integrating social, environmental, and human rights standards in projects and contracts. For example, the *2018 Framework Principles on Human Rights and the Environment*,[10] underscored the importance of state and non-state actors" respect to, and fulfilment of human rights that takes into cognizance a safe, clean, and sustainable environment.[11] The *African Union's 2012 Resolution on a Human Rights-Based Approach to Natural Resource Governance*,[12] was aimed at corporate actors to consider, prevent, and mitigate human rights impacts of their activities. The Resolution calls on government to "set up independent monitoring and accountability mechanisms that ensure that human rights are justiciable and extractive industries and investors legally accountable in the country hosting their activities and in the country of legal domicile."[13] Third, the role of corporations in addressing human rights impacts have assumed greater significance and urgency with the adoption of African Union's Agenda 2063.[14] Agenda 2063 is anchored on an inclusive social and economic development, democratic governance, peace, and security. One of the core aspirations of the Agenda is "an Africa of good governance, democracy, respect for human rights, justice and rule of law – aimed at entrenching respect for a culture of democratic values and human rights, improving the quality of governance and building strong institutions for a development state headed by development oriented and visionary leadership."[15] Adhering to business and human rights principles are a core part of this culture of respect for human rights, justice and rule of law.

These factors underscore the expectation of businesses to respect, promote, and fulfil human rights obligations in their spheres of operations. Understanding the connection between corporate conduct and human rights can help businesses cultivate receptive and consistent risk mitigation and adaptation strategies. However, while the UNGPs and several human rights instruments have provided for corporate responsibility to respect human rights, it still remains unclear how businesses can foresee and avoid egregious verse human rights impacts of development projects. A human rights-based approach enables responsible corporations to anticipate and prevent any adverse human rights impact. The next section unpacks key elements of this approach and how it can be integrated into corporate practice.

5.3 What is a human rights-based approach to developmental governance?

This section discusses the legal prospects of adopting the UNGPs as a framework through which human rights standards can be systemically integrated into development projects, legal regimes, and policies.[16]

Some countries have adopted the "rights-based approach" as a tool for "integrating human rights" into their decision making processes.[17] The Swedish government, for instance, went further to describe the HRBA as an efficient tool grounded in internationally accepted standards, which thereby provides a legal standard and a framework clarifying the State's duty to protect and realise human rights.[18] The HRBA thus have potential to identify the root causes of human rights violations and for creating a pathway to address those root causes. When applied consistently, they transform into state action over time – eventually becoming accepted general principles applied by non-state actors. This approach requires the inclusion of human rights considerations into state laws and project agreements.

Being a conceptual framework of the UN, the HRBA actualises human development by working to "redress discriminatory practices and unjust distributions of power that impede developmental progress."[19] A HRBA would incorporate the wishes and concerns of the local community, the poor and vulnerable people – in terms of siting development projects in their communities. Due to its very nature, the HRBA is a means of integrating human rights principles into other measures of planned institutional processes.[20]

HRBA cannot solve all socio-economic and political challenges facing a developing country, and this book agrees with this ideology. Rather, the arguments proffered here examines the emergence of business and human rights principles as a potential HRBA for addressing the human rights violations with particular reference to the host communities.

The UN did not provide any universal requirements for a HRBA.[21] However, human rights bodies have agreed on certain minimum qualities for recognition as a HRBA. First, it must fulfil human rights. Second, it must "identify rights-holders and their entitlements, and corresponding duty-bearers and their obligations."[22] Third, it must "work towards strengthening the capacities of rights-holders to make their claims – and those of duty-bearers to meet their obligations."[23] The *Human Rights-Based Approach to Development Cooperation Towards a Common Understanding Among UN Agencies* (the Common Understanding),[24] provides a template for ensuring that a HRBA is applied consistently in the meaning, nature, design, and implementation of such HRBA – and also applied consistently at all levels of governance.[25]

The state therefore shares a larger responsibility, compared to corporations, in implementing rules that establish human rights considerations as the basis for development. The Common Understanding requires states to further the realization of human rights instruments – thereby providing a foundation for applying the UNGPs to development projects. Certain elements are indispensable and unique to an approach deemed a HRBA. These are:

a) Assessment and analysis of the human rights claims of rights-holders and the corresponding human rights obligations of duty-bearers – as well as the immediate, underlying, and structural causes of the non-realization of rights.
b) Programmes assess the capacity of rights-holders to claim their rights and of duty-bearers to fulfil their obligations, and then develop strategies to build these capacities.
c) Programmes monitor and evaluate both outcomes and processes, guided by human rights standards and principles.
d) Programming is informed by the recommendations of international human rights bodies and mechanisms.[26]

Principle 1 of the UNGPs specifies that "states must protect against human rights violations within their territory." Thus, states, as duty bearers, must fulfil their obligations to enable rights-holders, and the local community, to claim their rights. The HRBA supports efforts aimed at addressing causes of rights violations at all developmental stages, and also how to address them. To achieve this, Pillar 1 re-emphasises the importance of states' duty to protect the human rights of its citizens against the belligerent activity of third parties. By integrating the UNGPs such as participation (Principle 18), access to justice (Pillar III), and access to information (Principles 8, 21, 31) into laws and policies regulating development projects – the UNGPs would be a preventive approach to human rights repressions occasioned by such projects.[27] Business and human rights principles also provide a basis for citizens to hold MNCs accountable for human rights violations.

Essentially, what this approach envisages is that existing labour, environmental, and corporate legislation would be reformed to make room for project-approval guidelines that will integrate human rights principles. This will give rights-holders the basis to seek redress when development projects violate their human rights or to seek a review of already approved projects. A rights-based approach consequently call attention to the obligation of the state to protect the human rights of its citizens through the adaptation of its laws, programmes and policies to align to the objectives of the UNGPs. But how can states adapt these human rights principles for domestic application? The next sections identify areas of convergence between states and businesses in incorporating a rights-based approach to development project.

5.4 Adaptation of HRBA to development projects

States' duty to protect human rights and corporate responsibility to respect human rights requires states and businesses to aggressively integrate human rights principles into investment and trade agreements, design and approval of development contracts, finance, and implementation of projects to avoid serious human rights impacts. Through the incorporation of business and human rights principles into corporate activities, businesses can satisfy their international and domestic obligations to respect human rights and operate sustainably. Businesses can anticipate and immediately address adverse human rights impacts in a holistic and rights-based method by adapting six interrelated business and human rights principles into their project design, and development processes. These principles are participation, accountability, and transparency, access to information, non-discrimination, and fairness.

5.4.1 Participation

One of the most important international human rights safeguards is the right of local communities to participate in decision-making processes. This book conceives participation as the right of the local or host community to take part in decision-making processes – with a view to influencing the outcomes.[28] Principle 18 provides that for businesses to gauge human rights risks, they must "identify and assess any actual or potential adverse human rights impacts" which they may have participated in. One avenue to assess this impact is by meaningful consultation with affected groups and other stakeholders. In these processes, businesses must consider the human rights impacts on vulnerable groups or populations that may be at a heightened risk of marginalization. Furthermore, businesses are also obliged to "integrate the findings from their impact assessments across relevant internal functions and processes and take appropriate action."[29]

The theoretical basis for participation advocates that local communities express their views and advance their position on projects that could impact on them, before those projects are approved.[30] In the context of development projects, participation improves effectiveness, justness, responsibility, and the "inclusion of local people who have been excluded by the command and control model."[31] Participation includes consultation and an opportunity for local communities to actively take part in a free and informed manner, that will create a meaningful and robust contribution to any project affecting their socio-political, cultural, and environmental rights.

The emergence of participatory mechanisms can be traced to the activism of civil rights organisations in the late 1990s, when the business and human rights debate began to gain traction.[32] The mechanism therefore emerged as a response to increasing challenges occasioned by globalisation, which has left a wide vacuum in governance.[33] The inability of those who are likely to be affected by a project, to take part in their democratic affairs, further left the challenge of achieving sustainable development.[34] It was also during this period that nations around the world started tilting towards the idea of liberal democracy.[35] The fall of communist Russia and its influence on eastern European countries paved the way for capitalism to thrive. In between these developments, the aspirations of the potentially affected public were however not factored into the push for economic liberalisation.[36] The result was that the state, far disconnected from the people, entered investment contracts on behalf of these people. These contracts did not take human rights concerns into consideration. Thus, the state, and by extension the companies, created economic values for themselves – in a way that did not produce values for society. As a result, societal needs and challenges could not be met[37] – thereby creating a period of social exclusion.

Various international human rights instruments support the idea of participatory development.[38] These calls for public participation ensure that host communities to extractive projects, which were previously on a low rung of the ladder, were now seen as strategic partners and not as "abstract concepts" in terms of ensuring positive extractive resource governance.[39] The opinions of local community members were therefore seen as being instrumental for having conflict-free, socio-cultural development of extractive communities. This is obvious in three ways. First, the MNCs are strangers to the host country, and even more so to the local community. Second, MNCs do not understand the political, socio-cultural, and spiritual attachment of the locals to their ancestral lands. Third, both government and MNCs do not understand the complexity and enormity of the problem at local level. The attendant skirmishes can be avoided if the local community takes part in development project decisions that facilitate social cohesion and social licence.

It is the expectation of society that income from development projects must benefit members of the society, particularly, the host communities where such resources are obtained. The questions that follow are: can it be said that the local communities are consulted before development projects are sited in their communities? Does there exist social contract between host communities and the states whose role is to distribute the social and economic benefits accordingly? For instance, the indigenization policy of Nigeria in the 1970s and the Broad-Based Economic Empowerment Act (Act 53 of 2003) of South Africa sought to empower local content in the areas of control of natural resources. Initially, the idea behind these policies was that stakes would be transferred from foreign company owned local subsidiaries to indigenous owners or to the state. These utopian policies would have gone a long way to eradicate environmental injustice and perceived structural imbalances. However, the failure of state machinery to defend and implement these laws aggressively took over much of their existence.

Participation gives the local community the basis to determine their own future and to take part in decisions affecting them. The core indices of participation are consultation, which includes an opportunity to actively take part in a free and informed manner – that will create a meaningful and robust contribution to any project affecting socio-political, cultural, and environmental rights. As a result, host communities play a vital role in reducing the conflicts, protests, and tensions which are usually associated with these projects, when they participate in project design and implementation.

Participation is the right of the public to "take part in" and "influence" decision making processes on activities and projects that may affect them.[40] This definition includes two vital elements: "taking part" and "influencing." Taking part simply means having the chance to freely express one's views without pressure and manipulation in an authentic deliberative process.[41] Influencing a decision is to have an effect on the final outcome of the deliberative process. As such, allowing the public to express an opinion is not the end; the public's opinion must be reflected in the actions and steps following the deliberative process.

The inclusion of local people in development projects increases the knowledge of policymakers and development professionals of the needs and desires of the local people. Thus, development professionals must listen to and learn from the very people they are trying to help. In the hierarchy of affected stakeholders, the local community ranks first. The marginalized and vulnerable must be at the epicentre of development projects. Thus, in the context of resource governance, development projects that have the input of the people, the local community, and which are pro-poor and conform to the ideals of environmental justice, would easily facilitate social licence and enjoy the legitimacy of the people. Participation can be premised on the following variables.

A. *The nature of participation*

Timely and adequate information on development projects must be provided to the affected local community. The adequacy of the contribution to such projects must be measured under a reasonable person's test. Local communities must take part in and be able to influence decisions that affect them – especially considering that most members of this community, typically being illiterate, may not be able to understand the technicalities of contractual language. Environmental treaties such as the Aarhus Convention provide some ideas on what constitutes adequate participation.[42] The Convention guarantees the "right of access to information, public participation in decision-making, and access to justice in environmental matters"[43] Article 7 provides that each Party to the Convention "shall make appropriate practical and/or other provisions for the public to participate during the preparation of plans and programmes relating to the environment, within a transparent and fair framework, having provided the necessary information to the public."[44] The Article also obliges each party to endeavour to provide opportunities for public participation in the preparation of policies relating to the environment.[45] What this means is that state parties are to provide for public participation before any decision on environmental matters can be made. African countries can draw significant lessons from the Aarhus Convention in the areas of public participation in decision-making, access to justice, and access to information.

Although the UNGPs do not mention participation – they provide for meaningful consultation with key stakeholders. For instance, to measure human rights risks or to engage in corporate human rights due diligence, corporations should assess their "actual or potential human rights impacts." This assessment involves "meaningful consultation with potentially affected groups." To fulfil the right to participate, local communities must be able to express their views freely and fairly – without any form of coercion, manipulation or use of force. This is the hallmark of a democratic society. The people know what is best for them and can decide how that transformative project can be best achieved. The right to participate can only be achieved in an open and inclusive decision-making process.

B. *Scope of participation*

For local communities to participate in extractive governance, corporate management will have to integrate members of the community into decision-making.[46]

This participation should be sought in a transparent and consultative manner, while stakeholders should be able to express their views fairly and fearlessly. Host communities are the most impacted by the harmful activities of MNCs. Involving the stakeholders legitimises the project to be carried out in their community and also creates social license for the firms. The mere fact that the host community has been given the necessary advantage of participating in decision-making, should not be an avenue used to delay development projects. The aim of broad-based participation is to avoid unnecessary hurdles and the politicization of the entire process. The community should not see it as an avenue to impede development. The objective should be a transparent solution which is anchored on a solid based, pragmatic approach.

In engaging meaningfully with the local community stakeholders, the commentary to Principle 18 obliges companies to consult their host communities directly – considering "language and other potential barriers to effective engagement." What are these barriers to effective engagement? Stakeholder engagement and meetings should be held in the community which will be hosting the project in question. The meetings should be conducted in the language understood by the community, and all scientific and technical terms must be explained. Logistical support (use of interpreters, for instance) should be provided to facilitate attendance by all community members. Furthermore, adequate care must be taken to ensure that vulnerable members of the society are well represented. Firms can obtain the opinion of the community beforehand (in the form of questionnaires, surveys) – to establish what the immediate needs of the society would be. For instance, on the relationship between local communities and extractive companies, it is important that the government support the process of engaging with the community before issuing legal license to operate. They should enquire from the local community if they can empower any company that wants to start operation in the particular local government. Communities should empower the government to enter into extractive contracts, not governments attempting to enter into contracts on behalf of the people.

Greater responsibility should be placed on government and firms to show that wide consultation took place with the local community, and that such communities were given adequate opportunities to take part in decision-making. Domestic policies must be focused on giving mandatory backing to this suggestion. The participation of local community is indispensable to understanding the local context. Citizens must lead their own development and build their own institutions. In effect, where companies have incorporated local community participation into their policies – there must be rewards. At the same time, sanctions should be meted out to those who have failed to comply with established human rights benchmarks.[47]

When participation fails, the community is left with no choice but to resist any projects that may be sited on their land. The ability to decide whether to allow extractive companies into their territory or to protect their land, rivers, and farms, is the bedrock of sustainable development. Environmental sustainability lays the foundation for environmental justice. Encouraging local community participation reduces conflicts in the resource zones. The recourse to participatory paradigms prevents the unilateral exercise of control, and, by extension, decisions by the central government in relation to control of natural resources.

C. How is participation occurring?

The foundation, method, scope, and consequence of the occurrence of participation are best typified by the codification of a new and growing concept of participatory development: the Free, Prior and Informed Consent (FPIC) – which provides a platform through which the right to participate can be realised.[48] The FPIC allows the local community to freely give or withhold consent to any decision that will affect their lands, territories, or livelihoods.[49] To be able to refuse or approve any developmental projects, a local community must be fully engaged with the extractive companies and government regarding decisions about the projects to be made. They also must also have access to this process in a form and language that is understood by them.[50]

The FPIC principle has its foundation in the ILO Convention 169.[51] The Convention was introduced to protect the rights of indigenous peoples – whose communities are endowed with natural resources. The Convention provides that indigenous peoples are entitled to free and informed consent before they are relocated from their land.[52] Progressively, businesses are beginning to recognize the importance of FPIC in development projects.[53] The African Mining Vision highlights the necessity for states to increase participation and "strengthen the capacity of local communities to make informed decisions."[54] The ECOWAS Mining Directive obliges businesses to obtain the FPIC of local communities prior to exploration of natural resources.[55] The concept has the potential of nurturing "equitable solutions and evolutionary development which may lead, in their turn, to co-management and decision-making" for businesses.[56] The goal of the concept is to collaborate with local populations and integrate them in decision-making processes.

The FPIC principle respects tribal peoples' cultural, political, and spiritual practices. As each community's challenges and circumstances vary – so also should this concept be adapted to each project. The general requirement should be that the concept should be applied from the time of project conceptualization, through to design, proposal, information, execution, and evaluation.[57] This principle outlines how stakeholders should relate with each other and gives priority to the local community. It is therefore safe to conclude that while FPIC lays the foundation, the UNGPs build on it. For FPIC to achieve remarkable success, there must be some mechanisms to determine what counts as FPIC. These must centre on the collaborative efforts of the entire community and must accommodate the concerns of the voiceless. As stated earlier, this collaboration must be free – that is honest, and devoid of any coercion, bias, intimidation, or manipulation. In doing this, traditional cultures and spiritual connection must be respected. The term "Prior" denotes that consent has been sought and obtained before the project was embarked upon. "Informed" means that the local community is aware of the full intent and scope of any project to be embarked upon, before giving their consent.[58] Any relevant information should be made known to the community prior to seeking their consent. "Consent" denotes that the information given was processed well by the local community.[59] Due to the nature of development projects, extractive projects in particular, consent once given can be withdrawn.[60] For instance, licenses can be granted on short term and subject to review. Host communities should form a critical part of the review process and their consent must be considered before government renews such licenses. This collaborative review process will prevent MNCs from fraudulently obtaining consent prior to the commencement of a project. The application of the FPIC would allow stakeholders to discuss the importance of the development project before embarking on the project. Where the project would be greatly inimical to the environment and the peoples that live therein, it should be discontinued.

Adoption of due diligence requirements will facilitate the implementation of a FPIC process. For example, businesses must evaluate or review their internal mechanisms to ensure that a prospective investment or project adheres to sustainable business practices and human rights standards.[61] This includes developing indicators, metrics, and sustainability plans which the company must adhere to before embarking on the development project or investment. Where investments will not contribute to the social, economic, and environmental sustainability of the host community, it must be discontinued. Likewise, where the social and environmental cost is excessive, the company can make an informed decision to proceed with the investment, especially where the benefits far outweigh the risks. An internal review mechanism strengthens corporate efforts to adopt human rights safeguards. Closely aligned to internal review mechanism is the adoption of human rights impact assessment (HRIA), prior to commencement of the project. HRIA can help businesses foresee, comprehend, and prevent adverse human rights impacts. In conducting HRIA, businesses will scope local content policies, laws, programmes to recognize and gauge the effect of their activities on human rights.[62] A combination of corporate due diligence and HRIA, critical elements of a rights-based approach, will enable companies to identify possible impact of their projects on human rights, and determine whether to proceed on the project.

The application of the FPIC is, however, fraught with many challenges. First, lack of awareness of its existence coupled with absence of legal requirements in most African states has complicated the ability of local communities to confront development projects that do not conform with this rights-based approach. Also, there should be mandatory provisions in environmental laws that safeguard the implementation of FPIC. Gaining the consent of the local community in project planning and execution would allow corporations to discuss the benefits and risks associated with the project, and the means to avoid or mitigate those risks.[63] Second, local communities must be given access to information in a language they understand, and they have a right to give and to withhold consent for any investment or development projects on their community. Principles 18 and 31 provide that barriers of access to non-judicial grievance mechanisms may include language difficulties. Consent can only be given to requests that are well understood.

An understanding of the FPIC will be beneficial for the prospects of implementing the UNGPs. African states must adopt a mandatory requirement for companies to ensure participation and adoption of the FPIC, as a requirement for the commencement of any project.[64] Sadly, however, most extractive projects do not comply with FPIC requirements. Since the discovery of oil, Nigeria has been struggling with curbing gas flaring.[65] The Kwale/Okpai Gas Plant, which started on-stream production in 1987, was designed to curb that gas flaring. The project, which was designed to reduce gas flaring from oil and gas explorations, involves a process whereby gas previously flared at the Kwale Oil-Gas Processing Plant (OGPP) is transported through a pipeline to the Okpai combined gas cycle turbine power plant – in order to generate electricity.[66] Despite its nobility, projects like this do not impact positively on the lives of the host communities. First, the federal government never consulted or informed the Kwale community about the project or its immediate impact on the community. Second, residents of the Kwale community, for instance, do not benefit from the electricity generated through the plant. Rather, the electricity goes directly into the national grid and is redistributed by the Nigerian government. Besides, the project suffers from a lack of transparency in its bidding, approval, and execution phases; a lack of stakeholder participation and free, informed consultation; and a lack of transparent environmental impact assessment, which should run throughout the project.[67] These human rights concerns continue to blur the social license of the MNCs and affect the legitimacy of the projects. As a result, host communities take to the streets in protests, disturb construction works, and petitions from environmentalists and NGOs become rampant.[68] Furthermore, the Kwale project is significant for one reason: it failed to comply with the FPIC of the Kwale community before the project started.

The South African silicosis cases earlier discussed reveals the inability of mines to provide an adequate and enabling environment for the mineworkers to work and to be informed of the impact of the project on their land and health.[69] In 2011, Jindal Africa (Pty) Ltd began the extraction of iron ore in the Makhasaneni area of South Africa. The residents of Makhasaneni area have the rights to use and access their land, which is protected under the Constitution and under the Interim Protection of Informal Land Rights Act (IPILRA).[70] However, Jindal did not consult with the residents of Makhasaneni on the mining activities – before exploring the ore. It was only when the mining vehicles arrived at the site that the residents heard about the project for the first time. Interestingly, the mining company contended that it was given the mining rights by the local traditional ruler, inkosi Thandazani Zulu, and by the nominal owner of the land (the Ingonyama Trust). The livestock and ancestral graves of some residents were damaged and water sources were contaminated.[71] There was also the story of an aged woman who owned land and had been cultivating it for about 20 years. She depended on the farm produce from the land to feed her eleven grandchildren and five other children. The mine – without FPIC notice – descended on her land and immediately commenced prospecting. Jindal not only failed to inform her of its intended actions, but also failed to remedy any environmental effect on the land.[72]

In the *Endorois* case,[73] the African Commission affirmed the FPIC principle. The indigenous Endorois peoples had been removed from their ancestral land by the Kenyan government in order to create a natural park – without prior consultation and adequate compensation.[74] The Endorois people are traditional pastoralists who had lived in or around Lake Bogoria in Kenya from time immemorial.[75] The case relates to their eviction from their ancestral and traditional land, in order to pave the way for a state-run reserve and tourist destination. The Kenyan courts refused to hear the case, and hence the Endorois people approached the African Commission on Human and Peoples' Rights – which held that the Kenyan government had infringed on the human rights of the Endorois people by evicting them from their land, and had paid them little or no compensation.[76] This was a violation of the Endorois peoples' rights to property, development, health, culture, religion, and natural resources.[77] The Commission therefore ordered Kenya to restore the indigenous people to their historical and traditional land, and also to adequately compensate them.[78]

The *Endorois* case admits two presumptions. First, the state is more interested in investment contracts than the impact of such investments on the local community. In this case, Lake Bogoria where the Endorois people lived, had great potential for tourism due to its population of flamingos and abundant flora and fauna. However, the Endorois people claimed that the lake was a symbol of their religion and culture and was also a traditional burial site for their ancestors. Second, the state does not consult the local community before embarking on any government developmental initiatives – especially concerning natural resources which are a growing source of income for most African nations. For instance, the Endorois people claimed that they fruitlessly tried to persuade the Kenyan government to reverse its policy on Lake Bogoria, and were also rebuffed by the local authorities and agencies in charge of wildlife. This case therefore illustrates the importance of the FPIC rule in project development. The Kenyan government deprived its citizens of adequate compensation or substitute grazing land, refused the Endorois people any form of participation and consultation before their land was usurped, and did not comply with the FPIC principle.

The African Commission held that the Kenyan government was under an obligation to obtain the FPIC of the whole community – since the project had major implications for their lives.[79] What flows from the Endorois decision, and which is instructive for the Nigerian situation, is that in the context of natural resources, for any extractive project or development that could significantly affect the host community – the state and MNCs must not only consult the host community, but must also obtain their FPIC in line with the religion, customs and traditions of the community. The African Commission also confirmed a rights-based approach to extractive resource governance in a 2012 resolution.[80] The Commission held that the state must take all necessary measures to ensure participation – including the FPIC of communities which are host to extractive projects – in decision-making processes related to extractive resource governance.[81]

In *African Commission on Human and Peoples' Rights v. Kenya*,[82] two NGOs, Centre for Minority Rights Development (CEMIRIDE), and Minority Rights

Group International (MRGI), acting on behalf of the Ogiek Community of the Mau Forest brought an action before the African Commission on Human and Peoples' Rights (African Commission). In October 2009, Kenyan Forestry Service (KFS), issued a 30-day eviction notice to the Ogiek Community and other settlers of the Mau Forest, asking them to leave the forest.[83] The "public interest justification" for evicting the Ogieks was for the preservation of the natural ecosystem. The government claimed that the forest is a reserved water catchment zone, and therefore part of government land.[84] The African Commission initially ordered the KFS to suspend the implementation of the eviction notice.[85] The Commission considered the socio-economic and political survival of the Ogiek Community should the eviction notice be carried out. However, KFS failed to observe this order. Considering the grave human rights violations in this case, the African Commission referred the matter to the African Court on Human and Peoples' Right (African Court) for adjudication.

The Ogieks are an indigenous community in Kenya, who have been living in the Mau Forest complex for generations. They are predominantly hunter-gatherers and their way of life and survival depend on the Forest which is their ancestral land. Their survival, in part, depends on unhindered access to and use of their traditional land and natural resources.[86] The attachment to land and natural resources is one of the inviolable rights of indigenous communities. The Ogieks people contended that they were not involved in the decision leading to their eviction. This non-consultation is a continuation of the historical injustices suffered by the Ogieks.[87] The Ogieks therefore allege a violation of articles 1 (obligation of member states), 2 (right to freedom from discrimination), 4 (right to life), 8 (right to freedom of conscience), 14 (right to property), 17(2) (right to take part in cultural life) and (3) (promotion and protection of traditional values), 21 (right to free disposal of wealth and natural resources), and 22 (right to economic, social, and cultural development) of the African Charter on Human and Peoples' Rights. The Applicants therefore prayed the court to stop their eviction; recognize the Ogieks' historic land;[88] and be compensated by the Kenyan government for all the loss the Ogieks have suffered through the loss of their property, natural resources and freedom to practice their religion and culture.[89]

The court unanimously held that the Kenyan government violated Articles 1, 2, 8, 14 17(2) and (3), 21 and 22 of the African Charter. It also ordered the Kenyan government to take all appropriate measures within a reasonable time frame to remedy all the violations established.[90] In particular, the Court held that evicting the Ogieks people from their ancestral lands, without due prior consultation and against their will violated the Ogieks peoples' right to land under Article 14 of the African Charter.[91] The judgment recognises Ogieks' status as a distinct tribe under Article 2 of the African Charter; it also recognises the connection between the indigenous peoples and the spiritual attachment their land. Hence, the eviction notice would deprive the Ogieks a right to practice their religion and will also limit their freedom to engage in cultural activities and practices – a clear violation of Articles 8 and Article 17 (2) and (3) of the African Charter.[92] The Court further held that by the governments action, the Ogieks are prevented from enjoying the abundance of food produced by their ancestral land, thus constituting a violation of Article 21.[93]

This case advances two principles. First, it was not in dispute that the Ogieks have never been consulted on matters relating to the Mau Forest or on their eviction. Active consultation prevents community revolt. The eviction would have negatively impacted the socio-economic and cultural development of the Ogiek people. Second, one of the hallmarks of determining indigeneity is whether there have been changes in the way of life or cultural tendencies of the indigenous peoples. The Court noted that while some features of indigenous culture, for instance, dressing, could change over time, the intrinsic traditional values rooted in their "self-identification and shared mentality often remain unchanged."[94] In this case, the cultural traits of the Ogieks peoples had been kept intact over the years despite infiltration of their culture as a result of civilization and modernisation.

5.4.2 Accountability and transparency

Accountability occurs where businesses experience consequences for their negative performance or actions. Accountability is essential for businesses and for society. Businesses must be able to establish that a project has been developed in agreement with human rights rules and standards. Transparency on the other hand connotes openness, and candid communication with the local community on all aspects of the investment project or activity.

Accountability and transparency are key elements of a rights-based approach to – which guarantees the potential implementation of the UNGPs. Principle 1 stipulates that states have a duty to protect and promote human rights. One of the ways to achieve this protection is by providing for adequate accountability and also through legal transparency. Furthermore, the commentary to Principle 21 provides that the obligation to respect human rights requires companies to have programmes and policies through which they can demonstrate human rights compliance. Indeed, this obligation requires companies to communicate those policies and provide "a measure of transparency and accountability" to individuals or the local community. Principle 31 further provides that states and non-state actors should keep parties to a grievance informed about the progress of such grievance. This information could be in the form of case studies, indicators, or more exhaustive information about the management of certain cases. Accountability is established where there are concrete human rights review, monitoring of compliance, and fulfilment of human rights rules in the company.[95]

Measuring human rights observance provides a clear and precise indication of progress made, when previously it had been lacking. Rules and safeguards help to prevent human rights violations. Transparency and accountability are at the core of development projects in Africa. A transparent and accountable business practice which is consistent with human rights, will measure the impact of laws and policies on human rights compliance. For example, all environmental laws must provide for compliance mechanisms that monitor the actualisation of human rights. Absence of transparency and accountability has led to concerns about the role of states, development partners, especially, International Financial Institutions, to implement strong and mandatory human rights standards that must be met before projects are funded. For example, despite Nigeria's plethora of laws regulating the resource industry, there has been weak implementation of those laws. Besides, these laws do not provide for adequate monitoring, and do not insist on human rights compliance information. This laxity fails to hold MNCs accountable for human rights violations in the extractive industry.

Businesses must adopt internal compliance mechanisms to measure and evaluate human rights outcomes within the company and throughout the entire business supply chain. This includes adopting clear human rights standards in project plan, employee training, third party contracts, delivery, closure, and post construction activity. Failure to monitor projects' compliance with set objectives and approved accountability measures could have severe ramifications for the company. In *Akpan v Shell Petroleum Development Company of Nigeria Ltd & Royal Dutch Shell Plc*,[96] two major oil spills from Shell Petroleum Development Company's (SPDC) oil wells between 2006 and 2007 were the source of contention before the courts. These oil wells were situated in the plaintiff's village and vicinity. For some years, the oil wells were not used for production as they were mainly exploratory wells. They were subsequently abandoned. In August 2006, large volumes of oil spilled from these wells. These spillages were reported to SPDC which made efforts, together with its employees and government agencies, to contain and secure the oil spills. However, the host communities prevented access to the well. After careful negotiations with the host community, an SPDC employee finally gained access and stopped the spill in 2007. The well had spilled about 629 barrels of oil, and the cause of the spill was linked to tampering with the wellhead. Indeed, oil leaks can be attributed to sabotage or obsolete equipment used by operators. One of the main reasons for sabotage is to indirectly receive compensation from MNCs. Another factor could be to steal oil. Between 2008 and 2009, SPDC contracted two companies to perform remediation work (using the RENA method) in the plaintiff's village, and, in particular, near to the oil wells.[97]

Despite SPDC's efforts, however, the plaintiff claimed that the company – being the well operator – failed, refused, or neglected to properly secure the wellhead, thereby resulting in an oil spill which damaged the plaintiff's farm and land in the vicinity. The plaintiff therefore brought various claims against SPDC, including: liability for the torts of negligence, nuisance and liability for damages under the common law rule in *Rylands v Fletcher*, which has been codified into Nigerian law.[98] The plaintiff believed that he should be compensated by SPDC for the damage he had suffered and continues to suffer, as a result of the alleged various torts by SPDC.[99] SPDC, on the other hand, claimed that the wellhead was damaged by sabotage.

Under Nigerian law, a finding of sabotage as the cause of an oil spill, by a court, does not lead to the liability of the operator.[100] Based on the Dutch conflict of law rules, the Dutch District Court applied Nigerian law and found that the two oil spills of 2006 and 2007 were caused by sabotage triggered by third parties. As a result of this finding, the court held that SPDC was not liable for damage caused by the two oil spills,[101] since, under Nigerian law, an operator cannot be liable for sabotage caused by third parties. The court relied on the common-law rule in *Rylands v Fletcher*, which has been codified under the OPA. Thus, liability for the consequences of the occurrence of an oil spill will be determined by the parties that caused it. If the damage had been caused by SPDC's negligence, the company would have been liable, but it was not liable if the damage had been caused by the plaintiff or third parties. The court found that under Nigerian law there is no general duty of care to prevent third parties from inflicting damage on others.[102] Thus, upon a finding of sabotage as the cause of spillage, SPDC will not be liable – since it had no control over the acts of third parties. In effect, Nigerian law did not provide for a "general legal obligation for pipeline operators to prevent sabotage."[103]

On liability for the tort of negligence and duty of care of SPDC against the plaintiff, the court established that under Nigerian law, SPDC would be liable for the act of negligence if it neglected to "protect, maintain or repair any work structure executed under its license."[104] Unfortunately, however, there are no cases under Nigerian law where an MNCs was found liable for damage due to an oil spill arising from the tort of negligence, which attributed negligence to situations where the company had violated a general duty of care to prevent sabotage of its oil wells by third parties.[105] Despite the court's findings on sabotage, it held that SPDC failed to properly secure the oil wells in question. In the opinion of the court, SPDC should have "foreseen this obvious risk of sabotage,"[106] and taken "preventive measures against any risk'[107] occasioned by not properly protecting an equipment it had abandoned for years. The conclusion, therefore, was that SPDC committed a specific tort of negligence against Akpan by insufficiently securing the wellhead of its installation before the oil spills happened, and which destroyed Akpan's farms.[108] This inadequate protection was the main reason for the sabotage – done in a less strenuous manner by third parties – which led to the oil spills. SPDC was thus found liable for the damage Akpan suffered as a result of these spills. While SPDC was not responsible for any active conduct in this case, it was liable for the specific tort of negligence against Akpan.

On appeal,[109] the Hague Court of Appeals held that Shell Nigeria was liable for damages caused by oil spills in Cases A to D and ordered payment of damages to the claimants. It also ordered SPDC and RDS (parent and subsidiary) to install a leak detection system (LDS) in the pipeline central to Cases A and B.[110] In Cases E and F, the court have an interlocutory ruling that the spills were caused by sabotage. However, the court requested additional information from the parties on the extent of the damage and subsequent clean-up actions. *In SPDC v Ijaw Aborigines of Bayelsa State*,[111] the Federal High Court, Port Harcourt ordered Shell to pay the sum of $1.5 billion to the Ijaw Aborigines of Bayelsa State, having found that Shell violated the right to environment under article 24 of the African Charter on Human and Peoples' Rights. On appeal,[112] the Supreme Court found for Shell and remitted the case back to the Federal High Court for determination of the substantive suit.

These cases represent a major push towards corporate accountability and a positive attempt at bringing MNCs who operate under a culture of impunity, to answer for their negligence and excesses. SPDC had the financial capability and clout to correctly remediate the contamination of the lands and fishponds that belonged to the claimants in accordance with Nigerian law – but failed to do so. Nigerian courts should develop a proactive approach to upholding the sanctity of human dignity of those affected by the activities of the MNCs – by ensuring that court judgments are complied with. To date, Nigerian case law built on a tort of negligence has no precedent in which an extractive company was held liable for damages due to oil spillage, gas flaring or environmental pollution – because the MNCs had violated a general duty of care to prevent sabotage of its oil installations by third parties. Where Nigerian courts found that sabotage in oil spillage occurred, the MNCs were not held liable. The Nigerian Supreme Court missed the opportunity to remedy this situation in *Shell Petroleum Development Company of Nigeria Limited v Tiebo & Ors*.[113] In this case, the court did not consider the company's negligence, even though it was the company's equipment that caused the oil spill. Rather, the court dwelt extensively on the award of general and special damages to the plaintiff. The Nigerian parliament should immediately enact laws that would provide for a general legal obligation for MNCs to prevent sabotage. This is the essence of the business and human rights debate. Unless there is a foreseeable risk, MNCs are obliged to remedy any adverse human rights impact occasioned by its activities, even where such impact was caused by third parties.[114] Furthermore, there is no legal obligation under Nigerian law for a parent company to stop its subsidiaries from causing injury to individuals or third parties – except in a few circumstances that were not applicable in the present case.[115]

In *Shell v Isaiah*,[116] the respondents claimed compensation from the appellants for the damage and loss to the marine and domestic life of the respondents. The damage was caused by the appellant's oil exploration activities which resulted in oil spillage and pollution on the respondent's land. The case was wrongly filed at the State High Court instead of the Federal High Court. As a result, the Supreme Court declined to award compensation because the lower court that had awarded compensation, had no jurisdiction to do so in the first place. Likewise, in *Ogaile v Shell*,[117] the plaintiff's case was on the scientific proof of oil spillage on the plaintiff's land.[118] The court dismissed the plaintiff's claim because it believed that the testimony of the expert witness called by Shell to establish Shell's defence, was more convincing than that of the expert witness called by the plaintiff to establish Shell's liability.

The implication of the Akpan case, in particular, for the business and human rights regime, is that under Nigerian law, MNCs do not have a general duty of care towards their host communities – where sabotage occurs. Remarkably, Akpan's case contrasts sharply with the *Gbemre* case. In the *Gbemre* case, the court held that Shell violated the human rights of the plaintiff and his community by actively engaging in gas flaring for an extended period. However, in Akpan's case, Shell was not involved in any active misconduct – but was merely negligent. The court was however wrong to have found that Shell cannot be held responsible for sabotage it did not take part in. Failure to properly protect its facilities can lead to damaging outcomes for the community. As the Dutch court rightly found, under

Nigerian law, MNCs have no general duty of care towards host communities to extractive projects – to be able to prevent sabotage of their facilities and oil wells. Despite the frequent occurrence of sabotage as a cause of oil spillage, as evident in this case, Nigerian law does not provide a cause of action whereby the installation of an oil pipeline, oil wells or any oil facility, creates a hazardous situation that will give rise to a general duty of care. MNCs have both horizontal and vertical relationships with the local community – an important stakeholder in the BHR paradigm. In Akpan's case, the burden of proof lies heavily on the company to prove that the local community did not cause the oil spillage as a result of sabotage. This case, founded on a horizontal relationship because there was no nexus between the company and the saboteurs to warrant a breach of a duty of care, has illustrated the reluctance of the Nigerian courts to hold that an act of sabotage by third parties can lead to an infringement of human rights. Greater responsibility lies with the company to protect its facilities against any form of destruction or damage. To prevent sabotage, MNCs should engage closely with the local communities in relation to the security and protection of their facilities. This is the essence of a social licence. Fostering a closer relationship with the local communities will enhance business activities and both the MNCs and the communities stand to benefit.

Corporate accountability stems from the inability to prevent projects that completely violate the human rights of host communities. To avoid this, a compliance mechanism should be established within the company to forestall any potential projects that do not meet the accountability threshold discussed in this book. Perhaps the impact assessment, which should run through the project cycle, becomes instructive here. This assessment can quickly identify potential violations and mitigate against them. Furthermore, independent institutions are essential for accountability in terms of project review and implementation – to ensure that guidelines and laws are complied with. It is easy for national governments and project proponents to lay claim to transparency and human rights protection during the design and execution of an extractive project. Some even go as far as providing policy statements on websites. These should, however, not take the place of formal compliance mechanisms under a BHR regime – for measuring and monitoring human rights compliance before and during the execution of extractive projects.[119]

Transparency and accountability go beyond mere statements on websites and reports and should include reviewing and monitoring the methods and approaches of complying with such statements. Without adequate monitoring and accountability mechanisms under the UNGPs – a project designed to achieve a laudable goal can produce monstrous repercussions for the public. It is therefore imperative for the state to establish institutions that will monitor and investigate allegations of human rights abuses. Any institution established by the state to investigate allegations of human rights abuse must be independent of government or any form of political control. The institutions that will monitor and investigate allegations of human rights abuses must also indicate that MNCs have satisfied the requirements for human rights compliance before a project commences.

5.4.3 Access to information

Principle 21 mandates companies to communicate externally the ways in which they address their human rights impacts – especially in such circumstances where the local community demands to know the communal impact of their projects. The communication of such information must be accessible to intended audiences.[120] The rights of the local community to demand answers to questions about developments in their community should not be constrained. International instruments guarantee the right of people to receive information. Article 9 of the African Charter on Human and Peoples' Rights provides that every individual shall have the right to receive information. Access to information guarantees transparency and holds decision-makers accountable. Any restriction on the right to information creates room for manipulation of the participatory process.

Corporate reporting is a fundamental tool in safeguarding accountability and effective communication. Most developmental projects are shrouded in so much secrecy that host communities remonstrate against such potentially projects. Local communities are entitled to certain key and basic information on how a project will benefit and affect them. They can, however, only make this informed decision if they are part of the decision-making process. Corporate reporting must include all the necessary details (and those not even considered necessary) of a project. Although the accuracy or honesty in such a report by corporate entities remains debatable – the utility in reporting shows transparency and accountability. The question though, is what constitutes adequate information?[121]

The adequacy of information must be assessed by reference to the amount of information publicly available, disclosure of new information, and also the ease of access to that information. The nature of the project also determines the adequacy of that information. In Nigeria, the Freedom of Information Act seems to provide an avenue for local communities to seek information on resource extraction projects in their communities.[122] The operation of this Act has however been hindered by the reluctance of government to grant requests made by people. In *Nigerian Contract Monitoring Coalition v Power Holding Company of Nigeria (PHCN)*,[123] a coalition of civil society organisations sought an order to compel the PHCN and the Attorney General of Nigeria to provide it with procurement information relating to Bid N. NGP-D2 – for the supply of 300 units of 11 KV, 500A On-Load Sectionalisers for installation at the High Voltage Distribution System (HVDS) networks in Abuja, Lagos, and also Oyo States. In the suit brought under a representative capacity by an NGO – Public and Private Development Center (PPDC) – under the Freedom of Information Act, the coalition asked the PHCN to provide information on the contract sum, the conditions of the contract, payment terms, and the number of required sectionalisers in each of the HVDS networks. It also sought information on impact assessment, documents relating to the design and specification requirements, and also other documents. PHCN had initially refused to provide any of the records and documents. However, a judgment of the Federal High Court in Abuja compelled PHCN to release the information, which showed lack of regard to due process in the award of the contract.[124] The long and tortuous road to litigation could have been avoided if PHCN had acceded to the initial request to release the information. Release of information, as in this case, allows civil society to monitor the award and execution of a contract. Access to information continues to remain a challenge in Nigeria, where management of investment projects are shrouded in secrecy. Lack of openness, transparency, and information, all deprive the community of the opportunity to participate in matters that concern them.

MNCs must develop a culture of information dissemination. They must constantly make public to the local residents and the country at large, detailed information about their activities. Corporate reporting and ease of access to information enables the local community to assess projects, comprehend their potential human rights impact and are prepared to mitigate any adverse human rights violations. Denials of access to relevant documents and information breed mistrust and a lack of faith in the process. Firms must publish information regarding environmental and other climate change effects whenever it occurs and detailing why it occurred and the efforts made to mitigate the occurrence. Presently, no law requires MNCs to publish information on these effects, and particularly on their greenhouse gas emissions and the acid rain pollutants they generate. It is the right of the people to know the causes and effects of the degradation of their environment. Furthermore, it is essential for everybody to know which mineral/petroleum rights have been allocated in a country, what the successful applications are, and which applications or auctions were unsuccessful. Furthermore, society has the right to know who owns the concessions, and who owns the contracts for the development of oil and mineral resources in any given country. This is essential for resource management. People should be able to know who has ultimate control over concessions or natural resource contracts. However, the public is typically not even aware of such contracts. Making information on extractive resource projects accessible, will boost transparency. Considering the huge investments in development projects, it is imperative that information on all activities be disclosed – including information on the social, political, cultural, and environmental impacts of the project.

5.4.4 Non-discrimination and fairness

Development companies must show that their consultation covers a wide range of local community stakeholders. Vulnerable and marginalised members must be included in the decision-making process of a project by being given equal access in terms of attending and participating in meetings.[125] They must also be provided with language interpreters and access to healthcare and free transportation during the consultation process. Considering that development projects are sited in rural communities, the principle of non-discrimination becomes imperative. Businesses should not contribute to discriminatory allocation of advantages from project development in a way that violates basic human decency. For example, businesses can address discriminatory policies that are propelled by state policies by tracking the "effectiveness of their response."[126] The objective is to ensure that negative outcomes from development projects do not impact vulnerable members of the society.

Safeguarding non-discriminatory policies entails design of corporate internal mechanisms in the design, development, and selection of project locations. There is a growing necessity for businesses to an internal tracking system to assess risks of development projects and its impact on gender, poor, youth, and the disabled. Project development should give due consideration to local community religious practices, ethnic colouration, age differences, and other human rights concerns within the community.

5.5 Conclusion

A human rights-based approach prevents egregious conduct of business practices. The expectation of businesses to protect, respect, and fulfil human rights is a growing and essential requirement for corporate obligation within the business and human rights debate. Businesses are obliged to ensure that they operate sustainably by investing in clean energy, mitigate adverse effects of climate change projects, heighten their reporting mechanisms, and promote transparent project development. Businesses can also guarantee social license to operate when then proactively conducting a human rights impact assessment, environmental impact assessment, and corporate due diligence. Combating serious environmental and developmental threat requires urgent and timely action through instruments that impose tough sanctions on project proponents that violates human rights. The determination of those sanctions leads to the third pillar of the UNGPs: Access to Remedies, which is discussed in the next chapter.

Notes

1 Relevant corporate theories have been identified in Chapter 3.
2 See E.F. Pomeranz, & R.C. Stedman, "Measuring Good Governance: Piloting an Instrument for Evaluating Good Governance Principles" (2020) 22(3) *Journal of Environmental Policy & Planning* 428–440 [Transparency, less corruption, accountability are *sine-qua-non* to effective and efficient management].
3 Ibid.
4 African Development Bank Information Note, *Natural Resource Management and Structural Transformation in Africa* (2013) 156.
5 UNECA Africa Union Commission Issue Paper E/ECA/COE/31/3 and AU/CAMEF/EXP/3(VII) *Unleashing Africa's Potential as a Pole of Global Growth* (2012).
6 Hany Gamil Besada, Franklyn Lisk, & Philip Martin, "Regulating Extraction in Africa: Towards a Framework for Accountability in the Global South" (2015) 2(1) *Governance in Africa* 1.
7 Ibid. Botswana is a prime example of how best to use natural resources to expedite economic growth and development. It enforced a policy to process its mined diamonds locally and has created a strong private sector aimed at transforming its development path towards achieving sustainable outcomes.
8 Daniel Béland, Bonnie Campbell, Mylène Coderre, & Privilege Haang'andu, "Policy Change and Paradigm Shifts in Sub-Saharan Africa: Implementing the Africa Mining Vision" (2021) *Canadian Journal of African Studies* <https://doi.org/10.1080/00083968.2021.1886955>. See also Bonnie Campbell, "Corporate Social Responsibility and

Issues of Legitimacy and Development: Reflections on the Mining Sector in Africa" in N. Andrews & J. Grant (eds.) *Corporate Social Responsibility and Canada's Role in Africa's Extractive Sectors* (2020) 245–264.

9 Ibid. See also Michael Ross, *The Oil Curse: How Petroleum Wealth Shapes the Development of Nations* (2012) [arguing that extractive resource dependence insulates political leaders from transparency and accountability-a core manifestation of the "resource curse"– with an observable correlation between resource abundance and political corruption].

10 UN Human Rights Special Procedures, Framework Principles of Human Rights and the Environment (UN Doc. A/HRC/37/59).

11 See Principles 1 and 2.

12 Resolution on a Human Rights-Based Approach to Natural Resources Governance, African Commission on Human and Peoples' Rights, ACHPR/Res.224(LI)2012 <www.achpr.org/sessions/resolutions?id=243> accessed 30 June 2021.

13 Ibid.

14 African Union, "Our Aspirations for the Africa We Want" <https://au.int/en/agenda2063/aspirations> accessed 29 June 2021.

15 Ibid.

16 "The Human Rights Based Approach to Development Cooperation: Towards a Common Understanding among UN Agencies" <https://unsdg.un.org/sites/default/files/6959-The_Human_Rights_Based_Approach_to_Development_Cooperation_Towards_a_Common_Understanding_among_UN.pdf> accessed 29 June 2021. [HRBA].

17 Australian Human Rights Commission, "Human Rights Based Approaches" <https://humanrights.gov.au/our-work/rights-and-freedoms/human-rights-based-approaches> accessed 26 June 2021.

18 A. Frankovits, & P. Earle, "Working Together: The Human Rights Based Approach to Development Cooperation Stockholm Workshop 16–19 October 2000" <https://research-direct.westernsydney.edu.au/islandora/object/uws:11676> accessed 26 June 2021.

19 HRBA, above (n 16).

20 Jacob Boesen, & Hans Otto Sano, "The Implications and Value Added of a Human Rights Based Approach" in Bard Andreassen & Stephen P. Marks (eds.) *Development as a Human Right: Legal, Political and Economic Dimensions* (2010) 82.

21 HRBA, above (n 16).

22 Ibid.

23 Ibid.

24 Ibid.

25 Ibid.

26 Ibid.

27 D. Olawuyi, *The Human Rights-Based Approach to Carbon Finance* (2016) 253.

28 Olawuyi (above n 27) 1–25.

29 Principle 19.

30 See further Stephan Hügel, & Anna R. Davies, "Public Participation, Engagement, and Climate Change Adaptation: A Review of the Research Literature" (2020) 11(4) *WIREs Climate Change* 1.

31 Volker Mauerhofer, "Public Participation in Environmental Matters: Compendium, Challenges and Chances Globally" (2016) 52 *Land Use Policy* 481 [noting that participation in environmental matters covers decision-making, access to information and justice].

32 The 1984 Bhopal toxic chemical spill (India), various Shell atrocities in Niger-Delta (Nigeria), Nike confessing to facilitating worker exploitation (Indonesia). Interestingly, these incidents still happen till date, the 2013 collapse of the Rana Plaza building (Bangladesh) is a clear example.

33 Ruggie claims that "conflict zones can function as essentially law-free zones where corporate-related human rights abuses are subject only to self-restraint and the occasional lawsuit in another country based on statutes with extraterritorial reach. This

created the biggest gap between globalization and governance," see J. Ruggie, *Business and Human Rights* (2013) 33.

34 G.I. Priyadarisini, "Environmental Policies in India towards Achieving Sustainable Development" (2016) *IQSR J Humanities & Soc. Science* 58.

35 Ibid.

36 See Peter Seele, & Irina Lock, "Instrumental and/or Deliberative? A Typology of CSR Communication Tools" (2015) *J Business Ethics* 401.

37 Michael E. Porter, & Mark R. Kramer, "Creating Shared Value" *Harvard Business Review* (2011) 89.

38 See article 1 of the UN Declaration on the Right to Development, adopted 4 December 1986, UN Doc. A/RES/41/128 at 186; article 13 of the African Charter.

39 Zarina Patel, "Environmental Justice in South Africa: Tools and Trade-Offs" (2009) *J Social Dynamics* 94; see also Nzalalemba Kubanza, Dillip Das, & Danny Simatele, "Some Happy, Others Sad: Exploring Environmental Justice in Solid Waste Management in Kinshasa, the Democratic Republic of Congo"(2017) *J Local Environment* 595. [Finding that waste products end up in the poorest and least powerful communities in DRC and arguing for a politico-cultural mechanism on remedying these inequalities].

40 Olawuyi (above n 27) 25.

41 Ibid.

42 See the Convention on Access to Information, Public Participation in Decision-Making and Access to Justice in Environmental Matters, at Aarhus, Denmark, on 25 June 1998 (Aarhus Convention).

43 Ibid. at article 1.

44 Ibid. at article 7.

45 Ibid.

46 In Germany, workers have the right to participate in management of the companies at which they work. See Germanys Co-determination Act, 1976. See further E. McGaughey, "The Codetermination Bargains: The History of German Corporate and Labour Law" LSE Legal Studies Working Paper No. 10/2015 (2015). This book argues that representatives of host communities should take part in board meetings of extractive companies planning to start a development project.

47 See Environmental Justice Atlas, "Hydraulic Fracking in the Karoo, South Africa" <https://ejatlas.org/conflict/hydraulic-fracturing-fracking-in-the-karoo-south-africa> accessed 11 May 2021. [Community objecting to shale gas fracking].

48 Frank Vanclay, & Philippe Hanna, "Conceptualizing Company Response to Community Protest: Principles to Achieve a Social License to Operate" (2019) 8(6) *Land* 101; Adrienne Mckeehan, & Theresa Buppert, "Free, Prior and Informed Consent: Empowering Communities for People-Focused Conservation" (2014) 35(3) *Harvard International Review* 48; Phillippe Hanna, & Frank Vanclay, "Human Rights, Indigenous Peoples and the Concept of Free, Prior and Informed Consent" (2013) 31(2) *Impact Assessment and Project Appraisal* 146.

49 Mckeehan, & Buppert, above (n 48) 48.

50 Deanna Kemp, & John Owen, "Corporate Readiness and the Human Rights Risks of Applying FPIC in the Global Mining" (2017) *Business and Human Rights Journal* 164. [Noting that FPIC must be adapted to local context and corporate ability to support the principle].

51 (ILO No. 169) (1989), Convention on Indigenous and Tribal Peoples in Independent Countries – 169/1989. Adopted in 1989 and entered force in 1991. This is a legally binding instrument that deals with indigenous and tribal people's rights.

52 Ibid. See further sections 6 (consultation must take place), 7, 16, and 22 of the Convention; see also articles 1, 12, 19 (states shall consult and cooperate in good faith with the indigenous peoples concerned though their own representative institutions in order to obtain Free, Prior and Informed consent before adopting and implementing legislative

or administrative measures that may affect them), 20 and 27 of the UN Declaration on the Rights of Indigenous Peoples, UN Doc/A/61/L.67 (2007).

53 See Shell, *Sustainability Report* (2016) 49, where Shell recognizes FPIC as "interpreted by the International Financial Corporate Performance Standards, as a safeguard for indigenous peoples' rights."

54 *African Mining Vision* (2009) 33–34.

55 See article 16(3) of the ECOWAS Directive on the Harmonization of Guiding Principles and Policies in the Mining Sector (2009).

56 See Permanent Forum on Indigenous Issues, Report of the International Workshop on Methodologies regarding Free, Prior and Informed Consent and Indigenous Peoples, UN Doc E/C.19/2005/3 (17 February 2005), para 42.

57 See also Report of the International Workshop on Methodologies Regarding Free Prior and Informed Consent E/C.19/2005/3, endorsed by the United Nations Permanent Forum on Indigenous Issues (UNPFII) at its Fourth Session in 2005).

58 Hanna, & Vanclay (above n 48).

59 Ibid.

60 Sometimes, extractive companies can manipulate local residents through financial incentives so as to get their consent to a project. Where this is discovered subsequently, it can form a basis for withdrawing consent.

61 OECD, "Responsible Business Conduct for Institutional Investors" <https://mneguidelines.oecd.org/RBC-for-Institutional-Investors.pdf> accessed 28 June 2021.

62 J. Harrison, "The Use of Impact Assessments by Governments and Businesses: Questioning Purpose and Utility" in N. Götzmann (ed.) *Handbook on Human Rights Impact Assessment* (2019) 424.

63 Olawuyi (n 27) 294.

64 See further Articles 1(1), 2(3), 8(2) of the UN Declaration on the Right to Development [right to vote and to participate in public affairs, and constitutive – rights to freedom of expression, of assembly and of association. Right to participate in cultural life and in family life. Rights of participation for vulnerable groups: women, children, minorities, indigenous peoples, peoples with disabilities, and migrant workers].

65 See Okorowo C. Agochi, "Gas Flaring in the Niger Delta Nigeria: An Act of Inhumanity to Man and His Environment" (2014) *Int'l J Social, Behavioural, Educational, Economic, Business and Industrial Engineering* 2346. [Nigeria flares more natural gas associated with oil extraction than any other country on the planet, with estimates suggesting that of the 3.5 billion cubic feet of Associated Gas (AG) produced annually 2.5 billion cubic feet, or about 70% is wasted via flaring. This equals about 25% of the UK's total natural gas consumption and is equivalent of the entire African continent's gas consumption. Most of these flares burn 24 hours a day and some have been doing so for over 50 years. Communities near these flares are deprived of even the comfort of night's natural darkness]; See also "Kwale Community Projects" <www.napims.com/Kwale.html> accessed 16 July 2021.

66 Olawuyi (n 27) 78. Presently, the Kwale/Okpai gas project runs through eight communities. The host communities are: Oleh, Irri, Idheze, Kwale, Beneku, Aboh, Abalagada, and Okpa.

67 Ibid. 79.

68 See Environmental Justice Atlas, "Kwale-Okpai CDM Project, Nigeria" <https://ejatlas.org/conflict/kwale-okpai-cdm-project-nigeria> accessed 26 July 2021.

69 See *Bongani Nkala & 68 ors v. Harmony Gold Mining Company & 31 ors*, Consolidated Case Number: 48226/12. See further chapter 3.5.3.

70 See Tabelo Timse, "King's Trust Sells People Out to Mining" *Mail & Guardian* (5 June 2015) <https://mg.co.za/article/2015-06-04-kings-trust-sells-people-out-to-mining/> accessed 9 July 2021.

71 Ibid.

72 Ibid.

73 *Centre for Minority Rights Development & Others v Kenya* (2009) AHRLR 75 (ACHPR 2009).

74 Ibid. at 291.
75 Ibid.
76 Ibid.
77 Ibid.
78 Ibid.
79 Ibid. at 226.
80 Resolution on a Human Rights-Based Approach to Natural Resources Governance (n 12).
81 Ibid.
82 Application No. 006/2012 (Judgment delivered on 26 May 2017, Arusha, Tanzania).
83 Ibid. 3.
84 Ibid.
85 Ibid. 2.
86 Ibid. 32.
87 Ibid. 3.
88 Ibid. 9.
89 Ibid.
90 Ibid. 68.
91 Ibid. 38.
92 Ibid. 57.
93 Ibid. 61.
94 Ibid. 57.
95 See further Nadia Bernaz, *Business and Human Rights History, Law and Policy: Bridging the Accountability Gap* (2016); Michael Riegner, "Regionalizing Business and Human Rights: Corporate Accountability in the European, African and Inter-American Human Rights Systems" (2020) 93 (1) *Journal of International Peace and Organization* 1; Cedric Ryngaert, "Accountability for Corporate Human Rights Abuses: Lessons from the Possible Exercise of Dutch National Criminal Jurisdiction over Multinational Corporations" (2018) 29(1) *Criminal Law Forum*.
96 C/09/337050 / HA ZA 09–1580 (2013) ['Akpan']. Other cases with similar facts of oil spillage destroying farmlands which were decided by the Dutch Court but not successful are: *Oguru & ors v. SPDC*, C/09/330891 / HA ZA 09–0579(2013); *Dooh v. SPDC*, C/09/337058 / HA ZA 09–1581 (2013). In Oguru's case, however, the court held that mandating Shell Plc, the degrader of the environment to remediate the environmental pollution and prepare an adequate contingency plan for future responses to oil spills will benefit not only the communities involved in the suit but the environment and society in general, it ruled that the claims of the plaintiffs must fail due to inability to proof beyond reasonable doubt the tort of negligence.
97 Ibid. RENA stands for "Remediation by Enhanced Natural Attenuation through land farming process."
98 See section 11 (5) (c) of the Oil Pipelines Act, 1956. [OPA].
99 Ibid. 6.
100 OPA (n 98).
101 Akpan (n 96) 20.
102 Ibid. 21.
103 See further Christine Kaufmann, "Holding Multinational Corporations Accountable for Human Rights Violations: Litigation Outside the United States" in Dorothée Baumann-Pauly & Justine Nolan (eds.) *Business and Human Rights: From Principles to Practice* (2016) 270.
104 See section 11 (5) (b) of the OPA.
105 Akpan (n 96) 21.
106 Ibid. 23.
107 Ibid.
108 Ibid. 28.

109 See the case of *Four Nigerian Farmers and Milieudefensie v. Shell*, C/09/330891 / HA ZA 09–0579 (zaak b) [https://uitspraken.rechtspraak.nl/inziendocument?id=ECLI:NL:GHDHA:2021:132]. Akpan's case was appealed with three other cases involving the same legal issues, different claimants, and slightly different facts. See further *Milieudefensie v Royal Dutch Shell plc (1) and Shell Petroleum Development Company of Nigeria Ltd* (E), and *Shell Petroleum Company of Nigeria Ltd v Akpan*: Cases A and B (https://uitspraken.rechtspraak.nl/inziendocument?id=ECLI:NL:GHDHA:2021:132&showbutton=true), Cases C and D (https://uitspraken.rechtspraak.nl/inziendocument?id=ECLI:NL:GHDHA:2021:133&showbutton=true), cases E and F (https://uitspraken.rechtspraak.nl/inziendocument?id=ECLI:NL:GHDHA:2021:134&showbutton=true&) accessed 25 August 2021.

110 Ibid.

111 On 24 February 2006, Justice O J. Okeke sitting at the Federal High Court, Yenagoa Division delivered judgment.

112 See *Pere Ajunwa (on behalf of Ijaw Aborigines) v Shell Nigeria*, SC 290/2007.

113 (2005) 9 NWLR (Pt. 931) 439.

114 See Principle 22.

115 In *Tel-Oren v Libyan Arab Republic*, 726 F.2d 774 (DC Cir. 1984), the plaintiffs sued the Palestine Liberation Organization for terrorist related attacks in Israel. The court dismissed the case but no reason for dismissal was given. Justice Bork concluded that the plaintiff lacked the *locus standi* to sue since international law did not provide for a "right to sue." The US congress responded to Justice Bork's conclusion by passing the Torture Victim Protection Act, 28 USC §1350, which grants aliens the "right to sue" for torture and extrajudicial killing under foreign law.

116 (1997) 6 NWLR [Pt. 508] 236.

117 (1997) 1 NWLR [Pt. 480] 148.

118 See section 15 of the Oil Pipelines Act, 1956.

119 See article 15 of the Aarhus Convention which established a non-confrontational and non-judicial Compliance Committee.

120 See Principle 21 (a).

121 See also article 19 of the Universal Declaration on Human Rights [right to seek, receive and impart information].

122 See section 1 of the Freedom of Information Act, 2011.

123 Suit No: FHC/ABJ/CS/582/2012.

124 Ibid.

125 See further EGM/EPDM /2005/REPORT, "Equal Participation of Women and Men in Decision-Making Processes, with Particular Emphasis on Political Participation and Leadership" Report of the Expert Group Meeting, Addis-Ababa, Ethiopia, 24–27 October 2005 <www.un.org/womenwatch/daw/egm/eql-men/FinalReport.pdf> accessed 24 August 2021.

126 Principle 20.

6 Access to effective judicial and non-judicial remedies

6.1 Introduction

Principle 25 of the UNGPs provides that states have a duty to take measures – including judicial, administrative, and legislative measures – to protect the public against human rights violations by businesses. Businesses, on their part, have a heightened obligation to comply with all applicable laws, including human rights standards.[1] This chapter examines the judicial and non-judicial process of obtaining remedy. It highlights states and corporate responsibility to guarantee effective remedial mechanisms for victims of corporate induced human rights violations. The importance of non-judicial grievance mechanisms to remedy corporate-related human rights violations is the hallmark of the business and human rights debate.[2]

6.2 Legitimacy and the question of access

To avoid adverse human rights impacts, businesses must proactively comply with human rights standards and principles, with reference to deterrence, precaution, mitigation efforts, and sustainable approach to business practice. Prevention is preferable to mitigatory efforts.

Principle 22 provides that "where business enterprises identify that they have caused or contributed to adverse impacts, they should provide for or cooperate in their remediation through legitimate processes." Thus, where businesses discover they have caused environmental degradation, contributed to gas flaring, and depleted natures resources, they must remedy this egregious conduct through legitimate means. Most African countries have laws that demands companies remedy any adverse human rights impact of their activities. This includes clean-up efforts, cooperation with state agencies to document pollution and compensation for victims of corporate actions. Extractive activities have the potential of rendering an area unusable or devalue a community. For example, unsuccessful mine closure and rehabilitation strategies are intractable challenges for mines in sub-Saharan Africa. Sustainable decommissioning of mines and integrated mine closures are dynamic and iterative processes that enhances environmental, social, and economic development of the project and community.[3] Consequently, businesses must advance complete and broad strategies and procedures that contemplate all

DOI: 10.4324/9781003290124-9

ecological, communal, and economic risks in their projects and activities so as to encourage decent social and environmental outcomes.

Access to remedies is a fundamental component of the business and human rights debate. Not only must victims of corporate induced human rights violations have access to effective remedial mechanism, but businesses must also integrate access as part of their due diligence process. Efficient judicial mechanisms are central to the question of access to remedy. For instance, corporate internal (and external) grievance mechanisms offer a veritable source for complaints to be immediately addressed before there is breakdown of relationship between companies and their host communities. These grievance mechanisms will be an avenue to get feedback about their activities.

Some countries mandate businesses to contribute to an environment restoration fund before the commencement of any project, to safeguard any corporate obligations towards the host community or other unforeseen events, including human rights impact.[4] The failure of corporate actors to comply with environmental laws and restoration efforts complicates access to remedy. Thus, states are enjoined to ensure strict compliance and punitive actions against businesses that refuse, fail, and neglect to contribute to ecological reintegration and rehabilitation requirements. These obligations must include mandating businesses to set aside some financial tools, such as host community development trust fund,[5] or some form of corporate guarantee before the commencement of the project. The next section discusses practical issues and gaps that must be addressed to guarantee an effective judicial and non-judicial grievance mechanism.

6.3 Effective judicial and non-judicial mechanism

National Human Rights Institutions (NHRIs) have a critical role to play in effectuating judicial and non-judicial mechanisms. Most NHRIs are mandated to investigate complaints arising from corporate-related human rights violations and must be able to address those complaints through a range of approaches – including mediation, conciliation, legal aid, training of relevant stakeholders, and other "culturally appropriate and rights-compatible processes.[6] However, the lack of funds have prevented most NHRIs from accomplishing this task. For example, unlike Nigeria's Human Rights Commission, the South African Human Rights Commission (SAHRC),[7] has been proactively engaging businesses on the importance of the UNGPs. The Commission adopted the BHR concept as its strategic focus area for the 2014–2015 period.[8] The aim was to increase its institutional understanding of the ways businesses impact on the enjoyment of human rights – particularly in respect of the impact on children.[9]

To guarantee effectiveness of the non-judicial grievance mechanism, Principle 31 lists several criteria that should serve as a yardstick for designing and measuring a non-judicial grievance mechanism: legitimacy, accessibility, predictability, equitability, transparency, rights-compatibility, a source of continuous learning, and based on engagement and dialogue. Obstacles to accessibility may include language, illiteracy, costs, and lack of awareness of the availability of grievance mechanisms.[10] Access to justice is the bedrock of sustainable development, and, more importantly, corporations are not excluded from this responsibility. They must provide complaint mechanisms for individuals and communities which are adversely impacted by their activities. Under this Pillar, justice must not only be done, but it must manifestly be seen to be done. Justice must be readily available and effective in meeting complaints from victims of human rights violations. This book construes access to remedies as the availability and effectiveness of formal and non-formal complaint mechanisms – through which victims of corporate-induced human rights violations can seek redress. This avenue enables the public to disagree with projects that are inimical to the sustenance of their environment and community.

The Lake Turkana wind project, oil exploration activities in Niger-Delta/Ogoni, and the Marikana incidents have shown that states lack strong criminal and civil prosecutorial powers to ensure that corporations are brought to justice or that individuals and local communities receive justice. If this is not the case, they are unwilling to exercise those powers. This lack of will on the part of the state presents a legal barrier to litigants. This causes many litigants to seek justice beyond the borders of their countries, despite the jurisdictional challenges posed by the doctrine of *forum non-convenience*, and, relatively recently, the issues surrounding the "presumption against extraterritoriality" rule – which precludes US courts from assuming jurisdiction over cases that do not "touch and concern" the United States with sufficient force. For example, the question before the US Supreme Court in *Kiobel v Royal Dutch Petroleum Co.*,[11] was whether corporations could be sued under international law. This case was a class action suit filed on behalf of Nigerian plaintiffs, who were engaged in peaceful protests in *Ogoniland* against resource exploitation in the Ogoni region of the Niger-Delta. They alleged that Royal Dutch Shell was involved in the suppression of the peaceful protests – by conspiring with and financing the Nigerian military forces to suppress their protests. They further alleged that Shell was complicit in the various human rights violations caused by the Nigerian military. The initial complaint was filed under the Alien Tort Statute (ATS) in 2002.[12] The Supreme Court held that there was a "presumption of extra territoriality against the application of the ATS" to claims brought against companies that had no immediate connection to the United States.[13] Rather than determine whether the ATS forecloses corporate liability, the court avoided the question of corporate liability, and ruled that companies can only be sued under ATS when such cases "touch and concern the territory of the United States . . . with sufficient force to displace the presumption" test.[14] Despite the *Kiobel's* case, the US Supreme Court, again, considered the question of whether corporations can be sued for egregious violations of international law. In *Jesner v Arab Bank*,[15] the plaintiffs alleged that Arab Bank supported international terrorism, financed suicide bombings in Israel and compensated families of suicide bombers.[16] At the lower court,[17] the bank was found liable for violating the US Anti-Terrorism Act. At the Supreme Court, the Court held that foreign corporations may not be defendants in suits brought under the ATS.[18] The Court reasoned that it would be inappropriate for courts to extend ATS liability to foreign corporations absent further action from

Congress.[19] The Court effectively upheld the decision in *Kiobel's* case further affirming that the "presumption against extraterritoriality" applies to the ATS claims,[20] and that even claims that "touch and concern the territory of the United States" must do so with sufficient force to displace that presumption.[21]

African courts should strengthen their ideological orientation in safeguarding people's lives that are at risk at the hands of corporate actors. In *Re: South African Apartheid Litigation*,[22] a group of black South Africans brought claims against the US companies Ford Motors and IBM, for allegedly conducting business that helped perpetuate racial apartheid. The Second US Circuit Court of Appeals held that the parent companies could not be held accountable for the actions of their South African subsidiaries during the time the apartheid regime was in power. On appeal, the US Supreme Court, deferring to the lower court, further limited the contexts in which aliens could hold companies accountable in US courts – for their participation in, or complicity with, human rights abuse abroad.[23]

Lack of access in most African jurisdiction is exacerbated by several factors – including widespread corruption in the justice system, delays in prosecution, unnecessary public holidays, inadequate scientific proof, the inability to secure legal representation, a lack of judicial independence (economic and political pressures), lack of training, and lack of expertise and support for state prosecutors to enable them to investigate individual and corporate-related human rights abuses. An increasing problem is the inability to keep up with new directions and trends in the business and human rights debate. While South Africa is innovative in terms of establishing specialised courts to address emerging issues, Nigeria lumps all manner of claims in the same court – making administration of justice a herculean task. A significant number of judges also need to be re-trained in professional ethics.[24] The principle of a separate legal personality often occasions difficulty, as it becomes difficult to ascribe liability to members of an extensive corporate entity. This was the major factor in excluding Royal Dutch Shell from liability in *Akpan's* case. This is further complicated by the rule of *locus standi*, which determines who has the right or legal standing to sue.[25] Prosecuting cases that fall under business and human rights, is not any easier.[26] These difficulties are compounded by the fact that most litigants, and especially the local communities, are not party to the state-investor contracts, and therefore are oblivious of the contents of such agreements.[27] They therefore lack the requisite knowledge of their rights and responsibilities under the contracts.

There is still no clear evidence that companies have effective grievance mechanisms to settle internal disputes, but the growing challenges demand that companies, and especially extractive companies, should look into the possibility of activating grievance mechanisms that include their host communities. Ruggie points out that most human rights-related grievances between companies and local communities or individuals began as small disputes which the companies largely ignore or dismiss, before they escalate.[28] The failure of companies to have strengthened in-house, early stage conflict-resolution mechanisms led to the Ogoni and Marikana incidents.[29] The underlying basis for access to remedies is that manifest remedial avenues must be unrestricted to the host communities and individuals, which are impacted by development projects. Access to remedies can only be achieved under a transparent and effective judicial system which is capable of delivering justice. However, the challenge seems to be determining what constitutes access to justice. What safeguards are in place to ensure that local communities can access remedies for human rights violations? The next section discusses the essential elements of access to remedies.

6.4 Elements of access to remedies

African states must secure certain elements to safeguard access to justice. Several cases are decided in home states of MNCs due to the worrying situation of judicial remedies in host states. Some of these elements are discussed below.

6.4.1 Effective administration of justice

The twin pillars of natural justice – *audi alterem partem*[30] and *nemo judex in causa sua*[31] – guarantee unhindered access to justice. The effective administration of justice requires the removal of barriers which hinder access to remedies for human rights violations. The rights-based approach prescribes this removal of barriers and legal systems all over the world and supports this. Some of these barriers include long delays, expensive prosecution of cases, prohibitive costs of hiring experienced lawyers, inadequate and/or inexperienced legal representation, expensive legal procedures, bureaucratic bottlenecks, and weak enforcement of laws. As the intended recipients of justice are the poor and marginalised groups in society, access to justice can be made accessible to them through effective traditional justice mechanisms which are devoid of bureaucratic procedures and bottlenecks. To achieve this, stakeholders must be able to bring cases before the complaint's boards, without being confronted with the "standing" issue. The state must ensure that poor and indigent parties are provided with the necessary support to enforce their rights.

There must also be a strong basis for citizenship enforcement of laws. Section 38 of the South African Constitution promotes public interest litigation on the basis of the Bill of Rights. Public-interest litigation not only complements the efforts of public agencies charged with regulating development projects extractive industry, but it is also in conformity with business and human rights norms. Concisely, institution of actions by NGOs or citizens help to shape and set the parameters for public participation in environmental regulation. In *Earthlife Africa (Cape Town) v. Director General of Environmental Affairs and Tourism and another*,[32] the applicant was involved in the campaign against perceived "environmental injustices" in the Cape Town area and to participate in environmental decision-making processes with a view to promoting and lobbying for good governance and informed decision-making. It instituted this action on behalf of the residents of Cape Town who may be exposed to potential risks posed by the construction of a demonstration model 110 MegaWatt class pebble bed modular reactor (PBMR), and in the public interest. On the issue of whether the applicant had first exhausted its internal remedies, the Court held that this case presented an "exceptional circumstances under the Promotion of

Administrative Justice Act 3 of 2000 (PAJA), and that it was in the interests of justice that the applicant be exempted in terms of section 7(2) of PAJA from the obligation of having to exhaust its internal remedies before approaching this court on review. It further held that Earthlife was entitled to an opportunity to make submissions on the final report preceding the Director General's decision. Because no opportunity to do so had been given, the decision was held to be fatally flawed and that part of the process flawed by the irregularity was set aside.

Furthermore, extant statutory legislation empowers South African citizens to enforce environmental and mining-related laws in the interest of the public. For example, section 32 of the National Environmental Management Act (No 107 of 1998) empowers citizens to seek appropriate relief in respect of any breach of their environmental rights, or of any provision contained in any environmental management Act.[33] This provision enables citizens to enforce their rights in court where the protection of the environment is threatened, or the extraction of natural resources is done in an unsustainable way. The ability of citizens to enforce the law extends to situations where a person who is directly affected by corporate-related human rights violations is unable to institute such action.[34] It also encompasses situations of class-action suits, where an action can be brought in the interest of, or on behalf of a group or class of persons whose interests are affected, as well as in the interest of protecting the environment.[35]

In addition, section 33 of the NEM Act, empowers private prosecution of environmental offences. Thus, South African citizens can institute proceedings against extractive companies for environmental offences where public regulatory agencies fail to institute such proceedings against the companies. Without doubt, these statutory provisions effectively displace the doctrine of *locus standi* in South Africa.

6.4.2 Creating a standard legal framework for corporate liability

The UNGPs provide normative principles in the area of access to justice. Seeking justice in the courts at the local, state, and federal levels in Nigeria could be challenging. At the international level, recent cases have shown that seeking justice under the BHR paradigm is a herculean task. For instance, the *Kiobel* case indicates that if the subject matter does not "touch and concern" the United States with sufficient force, the US courts will deny aliens any claim under the ATS. Following this trend, in *Doe v Nestle*[36] the United States Court of Appeals had to deal with the question of whether the defendant corporation assisted and encouraged child slavery, by aiding Ivorian farmers. The case was instituted by former child slaves who were forced to harvest cocoa in Ivory Coast. The defendant corporation had denied liability – claiming that it was not liable for the acts of its subsidiary and argued that if there was any incidence of child slavery, such incidence would relate to the Ivorian farmers and not the company *per se*, because the company never dealt directly with the farmers. Such an argument beggar's belief. If *Kiobel* had not been dealt a death knell on the issue of corporate liability, the company would not have used this line of argument. Rightfully, the court held that there is no definite law of corporate immunity or liability.[37] The court observed that the prohibition against slavery was universal and could be asserted against the corporate defendants in this case. In determining whether a corporation can be held liable, the court believed it must not only look to international law but must apply "customary international law to determine the nature and scope of the norm underlying the plaintiff's claim, and domestic tort law to determine whether the recovery from the corporation is permissible."[38] Interestingly, the court sounded more defiant when the issue of aiding and abetting arose. The court held that the:

> plaintiffs' allegations satisfied the more stringent "purpose" standard by suggesting that a myopic focus on profit over human welfare drove the defendants to act with the purpose of obtaining the cheapest cocoa possible, even if it meant facilitating child slavery.[39]

In this case, Nestlé aided the commission of a crime, and also instigated, planned, and helped with the execution of the crime. To argue that the company was not the party directly responsible for the crime is spurious. The company could not have claimed ignorance of the fact that children were used by Ivorian farmers on the Ivorian farms; it was more concerned about profits. Under the BHR debate, knowledge and foreseeability of risks can trigger liability. Initially, the Supreme Court rejected Nestlé's bid to dismiss the suit – affirming the lower court's reasoning.[40] Recently, the Supreme Court conclusively held that the respondents improperly seek extraterritorial application of the ATS.[41] The Court found all the conduct alleged – forced labour, providing training, equipment, and financial incentives to farmers – occurred in Ivory Coast. Applying the test in *Kiobel*, the Court ruled that the plaintiffs must establish that the conduct must have occurred in the United States, even if other conduct occurred abroad.[42] The consequence of this decision is that the ATS will continue to apply domestically, and an extraterritorial application will be impermissible.

African states must provide adequate mechanisms for citizens to seek redress domestically. There should be a legal milieu, where citizens can activate a complaint mechanism when their existence is threatened by the activities of MNCs. The question of expensive domestic litigation and spurious adjournment wears out plaintiffs who are seeking environmental justice. The exhaustion of local remedies, for instance, has proven not to work effectively in weak zones.[43] In the first place, litigation in local communities is haphazard due to the constant tension in such communities.[44] Complaint bodies at the international level should therefore understand that local remedies may not be effective or sufficient. Hence, home state or international legal jurisdiction should not operate to deprive litigants of the opportunity to seek legal redress in weak zones.

6.4.3 Access to appropriate forums

In *SERAC & Anor v Nigeria*,[45] two NGOs – Social and Economic Rights Action Committee (SERAC) and the Center for Economic and Social Rights (CESR) – on behalf of the Ogoni people in 1996, claimed that the Nigerian state was in violation of articles 2 (right to non-discrimination), 4 (right to life), 14 (right to property), 16 (right to health), 18 (right to family), 21 (right of peoples to freely dispose of their resources), and 24 (right to environment) of the African Charter on Human and Peoples' Rights. The Nigerian military government had been involved in oil exploration through the state enterprise Nigerian National Petroleum Corporation (NNPC). The NNPC operates a joint-venture programme with various oil companies, at the ratio of 60:40. The NNPC is the majority shareholder, while Shell is the largest oil company in this consortium. The relationship between Shell and the NNPC has led to environmental degradation and health problems for the Ogoni people.

The complaint seriously indicted the oil companies for their harmful activities – such as disposing toxic wastes into the environment in violation of international environmental standards, so causing contaminated air, water, and soil with serious short- and long-term effects. The complaint further alleged that the Nigerian government had condoned the activities of Shell, by placing the legal and military powers of the state at the disposal of the oil companies. One such incident led to the series of events that culminated in the execution of the leader of the Ogoni people, Ken Saro Wiwa, and also several other residents. In their judgment, the African Commission on Human and Peoples' Rights found that the Nigerian government had violated articles 2, 4, 14, 16, 18(1), 21 and 24 of the African Charter, and directed the government to ensure the protection of the environment, health and livelihood of the people of Ogoniland.[46] It also enjoined the government to conduct an investigation into the human rights violations described above, and to prosecute officials of the security forces, the NNPC, and any relevant agencies involved in the human rights violations.[47] The government was directed to pay adequate compensation to victims of the human rights violations and to undertake a comprehensive clean-up of lands and rivers damaged by oil operations.[48] The government was also tasked to provide information on health and environmental risks – and to provide meaningful access to regulatory and decision-making bodies for communities likely to be affected by oil operations.[49] Curiously, the decision of the Commission was against the Nigerian state, but the main perpetrator of the various criminal acts, the NNPC, was never indicted or sanctioned, neither was the company joined as a party. To date, Nigeria has not enforced this judgment.

The question of access has also created a vacuum in seeking justice in local courts. Consequently, cases are decided in home states of the MNCs despite the significance of African courts as appropriate forums. Most of these cases have been allowed on the basis of jurisdictional convenience.

In *Okpabi v Royal Dutch Shell Plc*,[50] a set of claimants who lived in Nigeria's Niger Delta brought claims against Shell Nigeria, alleging that Shell's persistent oil leaks from the pipelines caused serious water and ground contamination. This case was initiated in England against the parent company and the Nigerian based subsidiary, apparently on the premise that adequate justice may not be obtainable in Nigeria. They alleged that Shell Nigeria failed to prevent the oil spills or to remediate the impact of their activities and were in "breach of a duty of care owed to them not only by the subsidiary but also by the parent company, the latter on the basis that it exercised a high degree of control, direction and oversight in respect of the subsidiary's pollution and environmental compliance and the operation of its oil infrastructure."[51] The defendants challenged the English court's jurisdiction arguing that there was no duty of care on the part of the parent company to the claimants.[52] Consequently, there was no "connection between England and the claims against the subsidiary on which to found the court's jurisdiction over the subsidiary."[53] The trial judge agreed that there was no arguable case that the parent company owed the claimants a duty of care. On appeal, the Court of Appeal ruled that the trial judge erred in his approach to the evidence presented. However, the Court of Appeal, despite new evidence bothering on internal corporate documents, also concurred that there was no arguable case that the parent company owed the claimants a duty of care. On final appeal, the Supreme Court held that where a jurisdictional challenge on a claim against the parent company raises a triable issue, the defendants are not obliged to "dispute the facts alleged through evidence of its own, save where the allegations of fact were demonstrably untrue or unsupportable".[54] The Court consequently ruled that important issues of consideration for the courts are: particulars of claim; the cause of action asserted had a real prospect of success; disclosure might materially add to or alter the evidence relevant to whether the claim had a real prospect of success; the claimants pleaded case, which had not been shown to be demonstrably untrue or unsupportable, together with the two internal documents and the real prospect of further relevant documentation emerging on disclosure, established that there were real issues to be tried.

The Court allowed the action to proceed on the condition that the parent company can successfully challenge the English court's jurisdiction om the grounds it had raised. In granting jurisdiction over the case, the court noted that the question is not one of control but the degree of management responsibility over the subsidiary in the relevant activity, and the "extent to which the parent did take over or share with the subsidiary the management of the relevant activity, which may or may not be demonstrated by the parent controlling the subsidiary."[55] As considered in *Akpan's case*, the English court further noted that there is no unique principle in tort law of legal responsibility on the part of the parent company with respect to the activities of the subsidiary and those affected by those activities. Certain principles that guarantee access to remedies can be gleaned from this case. First, corporate practice of issuing policies and standards will not necessarily give rise to a duty, except the following applies: the company establishes manifest control over the subsidiary in a substantial manner; the policies were defective or inadequate; there was lack of active training, and parent company claims to exercise supervision and control but fails to do so.[56] Second, companies are obliged to produce evidence of enforcement of standards before such manner of control can be determined. In *AAA and others v Unilever PLC and Tea Kenya Limited*,[57] the English Court of Appeal held that UK domiciled parent company does not generally owe a duty of care to third parties who may have been affected by the operations of its foreign subsidiary. Rather, the parent company must produce evidence that it actively enforced the advice provided, and there was no consideration of whether crisis management policies were defective. The Court of Appeal held that the parent company does not have sufficient proximity to the Claimants, to the extent that no "anchor defendant" exists to establish jurisdiction against the subsidiary. Here, the parent company was not involved in the management of the subsidiary, neither did the subsidiary receive any advice from the parent on how to manage its domestic political risk, or risk management policy.[58]

In *Vedanta Resources PLC & another v Lungowe and others (Respondents)*,[59] the claimants are a group of Zambian citizens who reside in four rural communities within the Chingola District of Zambia. They are poor, peasant farmers who rely on watercourse which provide their only source of water for drinking, for their livestock and as irrigation for their crops. They claim that defendant's Nchanga Copper Mine has caused toxic emissions, affecting their health and farming activities, which have been damaged by the repeated discharges of toxic matter from the Mine into the watercourses.[60] The first defendant in this case is Vedanta Resources plc ("Vedanta"), a company incorporated and domiciled in the United Kingdom. It has substantial interests in Konkola Copper Mines plc (KCM), the second defendant and a public company incorporated in Zambia. KCM is not a wholly owned subsidiary of Vedanta, since the Zambian government has a significant minority stake, but internal documents from Vedanta claims that "its ultimate control of KCM is not thereby to be regarded as any less than it would be if wholly owned."[61] The claimants action based on the common law negligence and breach of statutory duty is on the premise that Vedanta has "very high level of control and direction that the first defendant exercised at all material times over the mining operations of the second defendant and its compliance with applicable health, safety and environmental standards."[62] The defendants challenged the jurisdiction of the England and Wales court to determine these claims against both defendants. The Supreme Court held that a parent company domiciled in England could be liable for the harms caused to community members impacted by the activities of its subsidiary in Zambia.

The Court noted that the critical question is whether Vedanta sufficiently intervened in the management of the KCM, to have incurred, "itself a common law duty of care to the claimants or, a fault-based liability under the Zambian environmental, mining, and public health legislation in connection with the escapes of toxic materials from the Mine alleged to have caused the relevant harm."[63] While Zambia appeared to the appropriate forum to adjudicate the claim, the Court noted that substantial justice may not be available to claimants in Zambia, hence consideration will be given to the extent to which and the manner in which the parent company took over, "intervene in, control, supervise or advise the management of the relevant operations (including land use) of the subsidiary."[64] The court found that Vedanta produced materials where it asserted its own responsibility for "maintenance of proper standards of environmental control over the activities of its subsidiaries."[65] It also committed to proper implementation of these standards through training and monitoring. Although the court noted that the claimants had real prospects of success, it did not apportion liability to either Vedanta or KCM. However, it held that the claimants could proceed with their claim in England.[66]

There are instances where businesses operating in conflict zones and challenging environments seek protection from State security agencies, and these agencies commit serious human rights violations. When this happens, the UK courts have been reluctant to assume jurisdiction or find business entity liable. In *Kadie Kalma & Ors v African Minerals Ltd & Ors*,[67] Sierra Leonean police were involved in brutal clampdown on civil unrest at the defendants mine. The claimants sought to hold the defendant, AML, liable for the police's actions. The Court of Appeal dismissed the claimants' appeal as "unsustainable" and found that AML's activity could be seen as supporting the police to "to restore and keep the peace," by providing financial and operational assistance to the police.[68] The provision of these logistics "cannot give rise to the inferred intent required for the new case on common design."[69]

Affordability is key in terms of gaining access to the judicial system. One may be given access to a court but may not be able to afford initiating or prosecuting the case to the end. Certain administrative costs usually demanded in local courts, should be dropped when it comes to business and human rights cases before the courts. The ineptitude and corruption of court officials frustrates the diligent prosecution of cases. To obtain certified copies of court decisions is sometimes problematic. To gain access to justice – there must be manifest efforts to ensure that indigent litigants are allowed access to the courts. Some of these plaintiffs are peasant farmers who do not have the financial means to pursue private litigation. Even when they have the resources or where the NGOs can pursue private litigation on their behalf, there is no assurance that these parties can financially enforce the judgment in the face of immeasurable financial resources from MNCs who can oppose litigation and the enforcement of judgments.

The UNGPs constitute a normative platform for preventing and addressing corporate-related human rights abuses. They have prescribed minimum standards of behaviour for companies and bring to the fore the less talked about separation of human rights from corporate objectives. The remedial differentiated responsibility status for both states and businesses under the UNGPs will facilitate a robust and holistic development of rights protection. For example, the judicial remedy is state-based, adversarial, and comes after the violation, while the non-judicial remedy prevents any potential violation and recourse to litigation – and starts the moment a relationship is created between the community and the company. Therefore, a non-judicial remedy and preventative measures should be utilised by businesses. To this extent, the UNGPs have been able to form an "integrated, logically coherent, and comprehensive platform for action."[70] Thus, corporations must align their profitable opportunities with their social personalities – closely safeguarding corporate responsibility.[71]

A major challenge to corporate liability stems from the parent-subsidiary theory.[72] Until recently, parent companies are rarely held responsible for the damages inflicted by their subsidiaries, irrespective of the level of control and management of the parent company over the subsidiary. The *Vedanta* and *Okpabi* cases have created an avenue for impoverished host communities, especially in Africa, to hold extractive companies accountable for oil spills and environmental degradation. As evidenced in the *Vedanta* and *Okpabi* cases, the determining factor should be whether there is a duty of care between the parent and subsidiary company. The

Nigerian Companies Act provides for fiduciary duties of directors towards the company.[73] This could extend to not only the best interest of the company but to ensuring the success of the company in the areas of environmental responsibility, participatory democracy of the local community, and respect for the local community.

Principle 2 obligates states to set out clear expectations that companies domiciled in their territories/jurisdictions respect human rights through their operations. One of the ways of setting out this clear expectation, is to adopt an approach that requires parent companies to "report on the global operations of the entire enterprise."[74] When applied, parent companies will find it difficult to avoid liability when their subsidiary companies are found to have violated the human rights of local communities. It would be unusual if Royal Dutch Shell did not have any relationship or derive any financial benefit from its Nigerian subsidiary, to prevent the application of these principles. In fact, companies in developed nations set up subsidiaries in developing nations to either overcome high trade barriers or to take advantage of cheap labour in those weak zones.[75] Unfortunately, the drive for FDI dictates liberalisation of markets, deregulation of products, and privatisation – which allows developing countries to turn a blind eye to enforcement of laws in order for MNCs to operate.

The use of the word "responsibility" instead of "duty" to denote corporate respect for human rights should not be construed to mean that corporations do not have any legal duties under national laws. After all, social responsibility needs are paramount in areas where governance structures are porous.

6.5 Conclusion

This chapter considered judicial and operational level grievance mechanisms. In understanding the importance of effective judicial remedies, this chapter outlined essential elements of remedies. It is imperative that companies must continue to engage in dialogue with community stakeholders. This enhances transparency and corporate legitimacy. Dialogue and empowerment are effective tools which forestall corporate human rights violations. Some of the identified cases show that victims of human rights abuses may find it difficult to seek remedies in the home states of MNCs. Therefore, the host state should be able to enforce and ensure adequate protection of its citizens, when negotiating state-investor contracts.[76] Additionally, public interest litigation should be used to invoke human rights protection across Africa. This intervention should take an expansive view of rights – so as to include all human rights relating to the impact of the extractive industry – including the right to health, clean drinking water, legal aid, a speedy trial, and a healthy environment. For example, Civil Society Organizations are more well-informed of developments in law and policy than local communities. In effect, these organizations can systematically organize to challenge any development project that violates human rights or affects the environment. They can also advance the inclusion of citizenship education that integrates business and human rights with other civic issues in the school curriculum up to university level. In this way, the youth of communities that host extractive industries are informed and empowered in ways that ultimately advance development for their communities. Furthermore, implementation of these human rights norms will give companies an avenue to project their human rights policies and programmes – and at the same time provide citizens with a platform from which to exercise and secure their rights. Moreover, public-interest litigation not only complements the efforts of public agencies, but it is also in conformity with the UNGPs.

Indeed, firms have sufficient legal personality to bear legal rights and duties. This is more evident if companies show commitment to due diligence and incorporate internal remedial complaint mechanisms for the company and the public. This will ensure that complaints are immediately addressed before there is breakdown in relationship between the company and society.

Notes

1 Principle 23.
2 Principle 27.
3 ICMM, "Integrated Mine Closure" (2019) <www.icmm.com/website/publications/pdfs/environmental-stewardship/2019/guidance_integrated-mine-closure.pdf> accessed 24 August 2021.
4 See section 121 of the Nigerian Minerals and Mining Act (NMMA), 2007, which establishes an Environmental Protection and Rehabilitation Fund (EPRF) to be funded by contributions by mineral title holders on a yearly basis for the "purpose of guaranteeing the environmental obligations of Holders of Minerals title."
5 See section 234 of the Petroleum Industry Act, 2021 (Nigeria).
6 Commentary to Principle 27.
7 See the South African Human Rights Commission Act, 2013. The Act establishes the Human Rights Commission to address human rights violations and seek effective redress for such violations, it also engages in monitoring, investigating, and reporting on human rights. See also section 184 of the Constitution. The South African Constitution has robust mechanisms for indirect implementation of the UNGPs. It has defined competent authorities, which can investigate alleged violations of human rights in the extractive resource industry. These include the SAHRC; the Public Protector (the Public Protector Act of 23, 1994 enables a Public Protector to investigate and redress improper and prejudicial conduct, maladministration, and abuse of power in government); the Commission on Gender Equality (the Commission protects human rights by advancing gender equality in all spheres of society); the Commission for Conciliation, Mediation and Arbitration (a dispute resolution body established under the Labour Relations Act, 66 of 1995). These bodies can attribute harm to the perpetrator at any point in time.
8 SAHRC, "Annual Report 2015/16" <www.sahrc.org.za/home/21/files/SAHRC%20Annual%20Report%202016%20full%20report%20low%20res%20for%20web.pdf> accessed 24 June 2021.
9 Ibid.
10 Commentary to Principle 31.
11 (2013) S. Ct. 133 S. Ct. 1659, section 3 (paragraph 16). See also *Republic of Ecuador v. Chevron Corp*., 638 F.3d 384 (2d Cir. 2011). [The court noted that a notice of arbitration and ongoing litigation can coexist without undermining a courts dismissal of *forum non-convenience*].
12 28 U.S.C. S 1350 (ATS).
13 For arguments on Kiobel, see Ralph G. Steinhardt, "Kiobel and the Weakening of Precedent: A Long Walk for a Short Drink" (2013) 107 *Am. J. Int'l L.* 841. [Arguing that

what is law in *Kiobel* isn't clear and what is clear in *Kiobel* isn't law, but a continuing, seemingly visceral resistance to treating modern international law in both treaty and customary form as law of the United States].

14 *Kiobel* (n 11) 1669.

15 548 U.S. (2018).

16 Ibid.

17 *See Jesner v. Arab Bank* 16–499, 2d Cir. (2017).

18 Ibid.

19 Ibid.

20 Ibid.

21 Ibid.

22 No. 14–4104.

23 See also See *Ntsebeza v. Ford Motor Co.*, 15–1020 (February 12, 2016).

24 Issues of impartiality, integrity, and ability to accord due process are still challenges.

25 See J.G. Ruggie, *Just Business: Multinational Corporations and Human Rights* (2013) 103.

26 See "The Corporate Crimes Principles: Advancing Investigations and Prosecutions in Human Rights Cases" (October 2016) <www.commercecrimehumanrights.org/wp-content/uploads/2016/10/CCHR-0929-Final.pdf> accessed 9 June 2021.

27 To ensure transparency, there must be a determination as to what is an appropriate level of contract disclosure? How may state-investor transparency requirements be balanced? How can the public be more engaged in monitoring of the extractive projects?

28 Ruggie, above (n 25) 118.

29 See Linus Gitahi, "Involve Communities to Reduce Conflicts" *Daily Nation* (1 July 2016).

30 Hear the other side.

31 No person shall be a judge in his own court.

32 Case No. 7653/03 [2005] ZAWCHC 7.

33 Section 32 (1) of the National Environmental Management Act, 107 of 1998 (South Africa).

34 Ibid.

35 Ibid.

36 No. 10–56739. D.C. No. 2:05-CV-05133- SVW-JTL.

37 Ibid.

38 Ibid.

39 Ibid.

40 See *Nestle Inc v. John Doe*, US Supreme Court, No. 15–349.

41 *Nestle USA, Inc. v. Doe et all.*, 593 U. S. No. 19–416.

42 Ibid.

43 This is procedure whereby international courts will only attend to a claim if it can affirm that all available domestic remedies have been invoked and exhausted.

44 A notorious militant once threatened a judge who was handling his case, see Ise-Oluwa Ige, "Nigeria: Dokubo Threatens to Kill Judge" *AllAfrica* (6 February 2007) <https://allafrica.com/stories/200702060052.html> accessed 8 May 2021.

45 (2001) AHRLR 60.

46 Ibid. at 9.

47 Ibid.

48 Ibid.

49 Ibid.

50 [2021] UKSC 3. [This case bothers on negligence and duty of care owed by a parent company to a subsidiary].

51 Ibid.

52 Ibid.

53 Ibid.

54 Ibid.

55 Ibid.
56 Ibid. para 53.
57 [2018] EWCA Civ 1532.
58 Ibid.
59 [2019] UKSC 20. On appeal from: [2017] EWCA Civ 1528.
60 Ibid.
61 Ibid. 2.
62 Ibid.
63 Ibid. para 44.
64 Ibid. para 49.
65 Ibid. para 61.
66 Ibid. para 85.
67 [2020] EWCA Civ 144. Case No: B3/2019/0682.
68 Ibid. para 105.
69 Ibid.
70 Ruggie (n 25) 125.
71 See Madhumita Chatterji, *Corporate Social Responsibility* (2011) 6.
72 See Daria Davitti, "Refining the Protect, Respect and Remedy Framework for Business and Human Rights and Its Guiding Principles" (2016) *Human Rights Law Review* 57 [noting that home state jurisdiction implies the relationship between the state and company and therefore, a *de facto* power of authority over the company].
73 Section 279 of the Companies and Allied Matters Act, 1990.
74 Commentary to GP 2.
75 Scott Jerbi, "Business and Human Rights at the UN: What Might Happen Next?" (2009) *Human Rights Quarterly* 299.
76 Most extractive contracts, hiding under confidentiality clauses are shrouded in secrecy. Sometimes, the government invokes these clauses to control information without a legitimate reason for doing so. The public opinion is however drifting towards lifting confidentiality clauses so that the citizens can have a basis for demanding for responsible governance where it is lacking.

Part III

Implementing the protect, respect, remedy framework in Africa's energy and extractive sectors

7 Policy and legal framework in Nigeria

7.1 Introduction

This chapter examines the adequacy of domestic laws in Nigeria, considering that the responsibility to implement business and human rights principles is placed primarily on the states. Principle 1 provides that "States must protect against human rights abuse . . . by business enterprises . . . through effective policies, legislation, regulations, and adjudication." The UNGPs effectively places positive responsibility on states to protect citizens from corporate abuse through a mix of approaches. Accordingly, the UNGPs effectively fulfil human rights by obliging states to prevent corporate abuse, identifies rights-holders (states' citizens) and strengthens the capacity of rights-holders to make their claims through various mandatory and voluntary approaches. This chapter examines whether Nigeria has failed to take appropriate steps to prevent corporate abuses and whether those approaches (legislation, regulations, policies, and adjudication) have passed the litmus test represented by Principle 1. The breach of relevant environmental, corporate, and labour laws by corporate bodies will also be examined.

Nigeria has a plethora of laws that regulate the energy and extractive sectors.[1] In principle, these laws should constitute a "smart mix" of methods to advance corporate respect for human rights. However, the challenge is not the adequacy of laws but the ability to enforce existing laws that directly or indirectly regulate business respect for human rights. This chapter therefore assesses existing laws and determines their compliance with human rights standards as well as level or extent of integrating business and human rights principles.

7.2 Constitution (1999)

Constitutional provisions safeguard citizens' right to challenge government and corporate abuse.[2] Hence, the inclusion of Bill of Rights in most country's constitution. The Nigerian constitution does not mandate business respect for human rights.[3] Rather, it places the responsibility for the protection of environmental human rights among the federal and state governments.[4] Under the Second Schedule, Part I (Exclusive Legislative List) of the Nigerian Constitution, Items 29, 36, 39, 60, and 64 lists the exclusive jurisdictions of the federal government in terms

DOI: 10.4324/9781003290124-11

of legislation.[5] These areas comprise mines and minerals – including oil fields. Part II of the Second Schedule (Concurrent Legislative List) specifies the capacities of both the federal and state governments to legislate on. Furthermore, section 20 of the Constitution vests on the state, the obligation to "protect and improve the environment, and preserve the water, air and land of Nigeria."

There has been scores of literature on the non-justiciability of Chapter of the Constitution.[6] This book argues that; indeed, Chapter II of the 1999 Constitution is realisable. The basis for this is extensively justified subsequently. However, it can be noted here that section 17 (2) (b) and (d) recognise the sanctity of a human person, in order to guarantee social order. In furtherance of this objective, "exploitation of human or natural resources in any form whatsoever for reasons, other than the good of the community, shall be prevented."[7] The non-justiciability of this provision is not in doubt; it falls under Chapter II which covers "Fundamental Objectives and Directive Principles of State Policy." They merely serve as recommendations to the state to pursue and are therefore non-justiciable by virtue of section 6(6)(c) of the Constitution. Despite the non-justiciability of this provisions, they can be realised through the fundamental human rights provisions contained in Chapter IV – as a pathway to guarantee salient human rights, including environmental rights under the Constitution. Moreover, section 12 provides that any treaty the state enters into must be domesticated, through an enactment by the National Assembly, before having the force of law. The UNGPs have not become a treaty yet; however, victims of human rights violations can pursue their environmental rights through the African Charter on Human and Peoples Right (Ratification and Enforcement) Act.[8] In *Fawehinmi v Abacha*,[9] the court held that the African Court on Human and Peoples' Rights exists to provide justice to victims of human rights violations, where such victims cannot claim their rights in local courts. Likewise, in *Social and Economic Rights Action Centre (SERAC) v Nigeria*,[10] the court laid down the principle that the African Charter on Human and Peoples' Rights can be enforced in Nigerian courts, even though some of the provisions of the Charter conflict with the non-justiciable provisions in Nigeria's Constitution. The Court found that Nigeria had violated the rights to environment under article 24, life under article 4, and health under article 16 of the African Charter on Human and Peoples' Rights.[11]

Principle 1 is to the effect that the states are not directly responsible for human rights violations by third parties, including business enterprises, but can shape those enterprises' behaviour through laws and regulations.[12] The Constitution is the *grundnorm* of all laws,[13] and is therefore an avenue for protecting human rights. All other laws find their legitimacy in the Constitution, to the extent that where other energy and environmental laws provide for human rights compliance, such provision could, "to the extent it is inconsistent with the Constitution," be deemed to be null and void.[14]

Principle 3 encourages states to implement laws that requires businesses to respect human rights. As earlier indicated, Nigeria's Constitution does not mandate business respect for human rights. Furthermore, section 44 (3) of the Constitution vests the control of all extractive resources on land or upon waters on the Nigerian government. The provision that would have allowed for the implementation (section 17) is non-justiciable. The UNGPs are voluntary, and two persuasive documents cannot be used for claiming rights before the courts. Nigeria's Constitution is therefore not conducive for enforcing business respect for human rights.

The right to life guaranteed under section 33(1) of the Constitution could be threatened where the deleterious activities are left unchecked – especially where such activities are sanctioned by the state. Environmental rights which can be linked to the right to life should therefore be enforceable under the Constitution. In any case, environmental rights and socio-economic rights can still be enforceable in proactive jurisdictions, by courts who cherish the ideals of freedom and the "right to dignity of the human person."[15]

It is imperative that the Constitution safeguards the International Bill of Rights, and its applicability to all persons, including non-state actors. MNCs do not violate the Constitutions or domestic legislation of their home states. They must comply with home state regulations and laws. Since corporations are bound by the provisions of Chapter IV of the Constitution, enforcement of Chapter II (such as environmental rights) can be achieved through the actualization of the right to life under Chapter IV. This is logical when one considers that civil and political rights under Chapter IV is applicable to persons and corporations. Therefore, corporate accountability can easily be achieved if claims are brought under Chapter IV of the Constitution. Hence, environmental rights (socio-economic rights) will indirectly have an effect under the Constitution. As the Constitution presently is, the civil and political rights under Chapter IV are applicable to the state, individuals, and corporations.[16] This effectively creates a "vertical and horizontal" application of the rights.[17]

The issue of non-justiciability of Chapter II of the Nigerian Constitution has erroneously gained traction in the literature. Section 6(6)(c) of the Constitution excludes the exercise of judicial powers over Chapter II of the Constitution. The phrase "except as otherwise provided by this Constitution" lends itself to different interpretations which can be found in the same Constitution. Hence, where other provisions in the same Constitution allow, Chapter II will be justiciable. Firstly, section 13 of the Constitution mandates all organs of government, including the judiciary, to comply with the provisions of Chapter II. This is evident in the use of the word's "duty" and "responsibility" in that section. Under the Second Schedule, Part I (Exclusive Legislative List), Item 60 (a) obliges the federal government to promote and enforce the observance of Chapter II. In effect, Chapter II seems to run through the entire Constitution. In *FRN v Anache*,[18] the court held that since the justiciability of Chapter II is qualified by the phrase "save as otherwise provided by the Constitution," this gives room for the justiciability of Chapter II. The implication of the foregoing is that if the Constitution references Chapter II in another part which makes the said Chapter II justiciable – the courts will be inclined to give legal teeth to the enforcement of Chapter II. In *Olafisoye v Federal Republic of Nigeria*,[19] the Supreme Court held that section 6 (6) (c) of the Constitution is not absolute or sacrosanct. Since the said provision defers to other parts of the Constitution by using the words "except as otherwise provided by this Constitution," it therefore provides an opportunity for Chapter II to be justiciable.

In *Okogie and Others v The Attorney-General of Lagos State*,[20] the Lagos State government abolished private schools – thereby preventing the proprietors of such schools from providing access to education under section 18 of the Constitution. The Court of Appeal held that the government had no power to abolish private schools under the state laws. Hence, government's act "violated the right to freedom of expression" under the Constitution.[21] In effect, the court used a provision in Chapter IV to actualise Chapter II provisions.[22] On appeal, the Supreme Court laid down the principle that Chapter II can be enforceable when a law has been made to give force to the provisions of Chapter II. Hence, in granting the applicant's relief, the court held that sections 16 (1) (c) and 18 of the Constitution safeguard the Applicants right to contribute to Nigerian economy. Furthermore, in *Attorney-General of Ondo State v Attorney-General of the Federation*,[23] the Supreme Court justified the enactment of the Corrupt Practices and Other Related Offences Act (which established the Independent Corrupt Practices and Other Related Offences Commission) – based on the "Fundamental Objectives and Directive Principles of State Policy." The Court further held that the provisions of Chapter II fall under the jurisdiction of the executive (contained in the Exclusive Legislative List).[24] Thus, the state and parliament must work together to make legislation that will give teeth to the provisions of Chapter II, as the occasion demands. The Supreme Court also held in *Attorney-General of Lagos State v Attorney-General of Federation*,[25] that the Nigerian legislature was exercising its functions under the fundamental objectives when it enacted the Federal Environmental Protection Agency Act (1988) – in order to protect the environment. These cases affirm that a rejection of the justiciability of Chapter II has not been handed down. Much depends on the legislature enacting laws based on Chapter II, and litigants exploring all the provisions of the Constitution that support Chapter II. Rather than limit their argument based on a dogmatic and strict interpretation of section 6 (6) (c), public interest litigators should be innovative when seeking the enforcement of socio-economic rights.

7.3 The Petroleum Industry Act (2021)

On 16 August 2021, the Petroleum Industry Act, 2021 (PIA) was signed into law by the Nigerian President, Muhammadu Buhari. The comprehensive and holistic Act regulates the financial, administrative, and operational activities of the petroleum industry. The Act seeks to "create efficient and effective governing institutions";[26] facilitate transparency and accountability, good governance, and sustainable administration of the petroleum industry.[27] It is not immediately clear whether the Act adequately supports the upstream sector considering the low rate of development and investment in the sector, the difficulties in energy transition and ramifications for green energy. The Act effectively repeals the Associated Gas Reinjection Act, 1979,[28] while some laws will continue to apply until the expiration of any license and oil mining leases granted under the laws.[29] The relevant laws are the Petroleum Act, and the Oil Pipelines Act, Petroleum Profit Tax Act.[30] Subject to certain exemptions, these laws will continue to apply as if they had been issued by the Commission or Authority under the PIA, unless they are revoked or replaced by an amendment to this Act.[31] An examination of the PIA and its relevance to business and human rights debate follows.

7.3.1 Regulatory and institutional reforms

The Act establishes the Nigerian Upstream Petroleum Regulatory Commission,[32] to regulate technical, operational, and commercial activities in the upstream sector.[33] The Commission's responsibility is also to facilitate sustainable and effective conduct of the upstream petroleum operations in an "environmentally acceptable and sustainable manner,"[34] and ensure that environmental policies, laws, and regulations are strictly enforced.[35] The Commission oversees the granting of new licenses and license interests under the Act. The Commission transitions the existing state-owned enterprise, Nigerian National Petroleum Corporation (NNPC) to a limited liability company within six months of the commencement of the Act.[36] The most innovative and significant arrangement is the unbundling of the NNPC. The NNPC has continued to be a powerhouse of corruption and also a bureaucratic bottleneck. For about a decade, the NNPC did not audit its account once[37] – this while it was used as a conduit for money laundering.[38] The Limited liability company will operate on a commercial basis, without government control and funding, publish annual reports, and oversee all Production Sharing Contract (PSC), Profit Sharing and Risk Service Contracts.[39] However, government owns all shares, and selects the management of the company.[40] Section 29 establishes the Nigerian Midstream and Downstream Petroleum Regulatory Authority with the objective of regulating the midstream and downstream petroleum operations in a safe, effective and sustainable manner.[41]

While the Minister retains supervisory capacity over operations of the petroleum industry,[42] Ministerial powers with respect to granting petroleum prospecting licenses and petroleum mining licenses are subject to the recommendations of The Commission.[43] The Act effectively curtails the hitherto unchecked powers of the Minister to ensure transparency and accountability.[44] Furthermore, the current rate of petroleum profits tax under the Petroleum Profits Tax Act, 1959,[45] should be reviewed in order for the tax to promote meaningful impacts on the indigenous community. The current tax rate is 50% for operations in the deep offshore and the inland basin – while 85% is for operations onshore and in shallow waters.[46] Despite this huge amount of money, however, the local community does not feel the impact of the Nigerian state in terms of using the tax proceeds for the development of its citizens.

7.3.2 Establishment of a host community development trust

Section 234 of the Act provides for the socio-economic benefits from petroleum activities to host communities.[47] The Act also heightens a robust peaceful and harmonious relationship between operators and host communities. An operational level grievance mechanism is established to settle disputes between project proponents and host communities. Furthermore, section 235 creates a Host Communities Development Trust (The Trust) for the benefit of host communities. The Trust Fund is designed to finance infrastructural developments, accelerate economic opportunities, and promote the sustainable development of the host communities.[48] Each project proponent must make an annual contribution of 3% of its annual operating expenditure of the preceding financial year to the Trust Fund.[49] Project operators have 12 months to establish this Trust. This contribution is to be applied to the "development of the economic and social infrastructure" of the host communities. This is intended to safeguard the interests of the host communities and to encourage transparency and accountability in the operations of the industry.

There are concerns whether the 3% operating expense allocated to host communities is adequate or more than the 30% profit share as part of the fund for the frontier basin exploration development.[50] Comparatively, the 30% profit share for oil exploration in the "frontier basins" is about $400 million per annum,[51] while the 3% allocated to host community will cost $500 million annually.[52] However, some Niger Delta communities have protested that allocation to frontier basins should be the responsibility of investors and not the state.

7.3.3 Environment management plan

Licensee or lessee operating in the upstream and midstream petroleum sector must submit an environmental management plan of the projects which require environmental impact assessment to the Commission within one year or six months after the grant of the license or lease.[53] This plan is expected to contain the licensee's written environmental policy, objectives and targets, and commitments to comply with the relevant laws, regulations and guidelines. The plan should also investigate, assess, and evaluate the impact of the licensee's proposed activities on the environment. Furthermore, the licensee will also develop an environmental awareness plan which details the manner in which it intends to inform its employees of any risks which may result from their operations, and the ways the risks may be curtailed so as to avoid pollution or environmental degradation.

It is also the responsibility of the licensee or lessee to rehabilitate and manage negative impacts of the project on the environment. Furthermore, as a pre-condition for the granting of a license or lease, the project proponent must pay a prescribed amount to an environmental remediation fund established by the Commission or Authority.[54] This fund will be utilised for the rehabilitation of negative environmental impacts of the project. The amount to be contributed by the project proponent will be determined by the size of the project and the potential level of the environmental risk that may exist.[55]

7.3.4 Gas flaring

In repealing the Associated Gas and Re-Injection Act, the PIA permits the flare of gas to a limited extent.[56] Aside from the exemptions, flaring of gas is prohibited and will constitute a criminal offence and such offender will be liable to a fine under the Flare Gas (Prevention of Waste and Pollution) Regulations.[57] Proceeds of the fine will be applied to environmental remediation of the host communities where the gas is flared.[58] Prior to commencement of petroleum production, each licensee is expected to install metering equipment,[59] and submit a "natural gas flare elimination and monetisation plan" to the Commission.[60]

Nigeria loses around N900 million daily to gas flaring.[61] Extractive and energy companies currently flare about 700 million standard cubic feet of gas per day.[62] Gas flaring should be made unattractive to oil producers, by placing penalty on every cubic foot of gas flared.[63] The negative effects of gas flaring cannot be quantified. It has potentially harmful effects on the health and livelihood of the host communities, as they release a variety of poisonous chemicals.[64] The social and environmental costs of gas flaring are extensive. They include destruction of wildlife and biodiversity, pollution of air and drinking water, degradation of farmland, and damage to aquatic ecosystems.[65] Rather than depend on kerosene or firewood, further depleting the forest, natural gas could serve as a veritable source of sustainable energy. In fact, it could generate megawatts of electricity that is in dire need for Nigerians.

Nigeria will greatly benefit from the development of its conventional and unconventional sources of gas.[66] Partnering with development agencies, Nigeria can utilise its gas deposits for socio-economic development of the country. The utilisation of natural resources in Nigeria should not be to the detriment of host communities, even where domestic laws are silent on punitive measures to polluters of the environment. Indeed, it can be argued that failure to completely prohibit gas flaring is a human rights violation, particularly of the host communities where gas continues to be flared.[67] Gas flaring has led to acid rain and have destroyed the resources that once sustained millions of Delta region inhabitants who farmed and fished in the now bleak environment.[68]

Gas flaring and pipeline leakages have certainly damaged the resources that previously sustained the Niger-Delta communities who farmed and fished in the now unproductive environment. This is compounded by the fact that MNCs rarely complete clean-up of the numerous and often massive oil spills, nor do they compensate affected communities. Resistance by communities against these practices have been met with a callous clampdown through military force. Other than utilising the flared gas for domestic use, there is no basis for continuous flaring of gas in the manner the PIA prescribes.

Gas flaring in Nigeria is not only wasteful, but also releases large amounts of methane, which has very high global warming potential. While flaring in developed countries has decreased, in Nigeria it has grown proportionately with oil production. For instance, Nigeria loses "about 1.2 trillion standard cubic feet of gas annually"– a quantity that could "generate over 12,000 megawatts of electricity."[69]

7.3.5 Access to information

The Commission is obliged to share information and data on the upstream petroleum operations with other government entities,[70] and publish any information regarding royalties, fees, profit oil shares, and other payment to government on its website for public consumption.[71] Extractive agreements will no longer be confidential and must also be published on the Commission's website.[72] These are commendable provisions that will safeguard sustainable development of the petroleum sector and guarantee mutual trust between community and companies.[73]

In the extractive sector, investor-state contracts are the bastion of non-disclosure. Extractive companies should do much more than the PIA demands. They should periodically make available project information – such as parties involved, the names of companies and the Board of Directors, non-judicial grievance mechanisms to address complaints in relation to the project and the impact on the immediate environment, the cost involved, the number of local employees, and the benefit of extractive projects to the immediate community. This information does not in any way compromise or threaten national security, and instead provides a basis for the grant of a social licence. This information must be readily available through the life of the project – as there may be changes in the contract sum and transfer of an oil concession, for instance. Furthermore, government must establish an Extractive Sector Information Management Centre (ESIMC) where information concerning oil concessions and other extractive projects is made readily available. The information must be provided in the languages spoken in the project area and must be easily accessible by local communities. The ESIMC must be managed by an effective communicator. Periodic town-hall meetings, the use of town criers and assembly forum should be a matter of necessity – not only for the dissemination of information, but for making available documents that are crucial to the projects undertaken. There can be no exception to transparency; it is a fundamental part of extractive resource governance. TV and radio programmes must be utilised by the government as an avenue to put information before the public. The trust of local communities is gained when the necessary information is made public, without first demanding it. This gives key stakeholders confidence and trust in the MNCs. Information about any project must be detailed and given in the language understood by the community. Considering the low literacy levels in most local communities, extractive industries must provide information in the language spoken by the community where they operate.[74] If it means using language interpreters, that should and must be done. This will ensure that the message gets to the intended beneficiaries. The era of stating that the plaintiffs, who are mostly poor indigenous people, should bring scientific proof that companies are engaged in environmental pollution should end. Increasingly, companies are inundated with calls to be more transparent and open in their daily operations and access to information is one of the ways to demonstrate this.[75] Extractive companies have a duty to the public and the local community to periodically provide appropriate information about their activities, in a language which is understood by their host communities. For example, the $700 Million Assa North and Ohaji South [ANOH] Gas Development Project in Imo State, Nigeria, is a key infrastructural development project aimed at reducing Nigeria's energy poverty.[76] The project was designed to supplement Nigeria's objective of achieving the generation of 15 gigawatts (GW) of electricity by 2020. The project failed to achieve any form of meaningful consultation or ensure that local communities understand the complexities of development projects. Furthermore, the project distorted local and leadership structures by creating divisions between established traditional modes of community engagement. Divide and rule tactics by energy and extractive companies only serve to reduce community ties and heighten tensions. Hence, where communities attend meetings convened by companies, they may not understand details of the project without expert guidance and local knowledge and language adaptation to these projects.[77]

Government cannot just state that there are exemptions to disclosure – they must clearly state the reasons for these exceptions. Other than national interest, it is difficult to justify other grounds for restricting information provision. The purpose of positive extractive resource governance is defeated if litigants go through a long and arduous process of requesting information from the public service.[78] At any point in time, the denial of information requests from citizens must be based on the genuine reason that such denial will be more beneficial than releasing such information. Public officials must show cause why releasing such information would lead to the violation of an existing law. For instance, releasing information on the following elements should not ordinarily constitute a threat to national security: extractive projects, bidding processes, parties involved, any conflict of interest, operational cost of the project, human rights and environmental impact assessment, and community participation. This burden of proof lies squarely with the government.

7.3.6 Transparency and accountability

In addition to the objectives of the Act which is anchored on transparency, efficiency, sustainable development, good governance accountability, section 83 broadly provides for the full discourse of information on contracts, licenses and leases with NNPC. Such contractual information must be provided to the Commission and published on the Commission's website within one year of granting the license or lease.[79]

To safeguard accountability, the Nigerian Minerals and Mines Act 2007 provides for a binding agreement with the host community before the commencement of any development project.[80] The aim of the agreement is to ensure that there is a framework for the transfer of social and economic benefit to the community.[81] This is a condition precedent to the commencement of any developmental project. This is a novel provision which is absent from previous mining Acts and is especially absent from the PIA. Community Development Agreements can be used by extractive companies as instruments for consulting with local communities.

7.3.7 Abandonment, decommissioning, and disposal

Decommission and abandonment or petroleum wells, installations, structures, utilities, plants, and pipelines requires the prior approval of the Commission before decommissioning or abandonment can take place.[82] The process of decommission and abandonment must not only confirm with international best practices, licenses must first inform the Commission of its intention to decommission indicating the estimated cost, details of the shutdown procedure, clear descriptions of the methods to be employed, and assessment of the environmental and social impact of the decommissioning and abandonment measures.[83] The permit holder must endeavour to restore the land to its original state. Furthermore, the lessee and licensee must establish and maintain a decommission and abandonment fund with an independent financial institution in the form of an escrow account accessible by the Commission.[84] This Fund will be exclusively utilised for decommissioning and abandonment costs.

7.4 Transitional provisions

The Petroleum Industry Act (PIA) preserves certain laws, subsidiary legislation or regulation repealed by the PIA in so far as they are not inconsistent with the PIA. These laws, regulations, and directions will continue to operate as if they were issued by the Commission or Authority until revoked or amended by the PIA.[85] This section discusses these transitional provisions – laws and regulations that could be reviewed in conformity with human rights standards.

7.4.1 Petroleum Act (1969)

The current Petroleum Act as it currently stands vests ownership of all petroleum resources, and the revenue obtained therefrom, in the federal government.[86] Granting the state exclusive ownership over natural resources could however hamper the state-corporate-community relationship, as the debate rages on concerning who owns natural resources. Despite this provision, the state can use its unhindered authority to facilitate the implementation of Principle 4. This is because states are objects – "duty bearers under international law" and are therefore the "trustees" of the UNGPs.[87]

Section 2 of the Act which regulates the granting of oil licences and mining leases should be amended to provide for local community participation in the granting of an oil licence. Any licensed company must be required to incorporate and provide for due diligence requirements and a human rights impact assessment which incorporates the Free, Prior, Informed Consent (FPIC) of the host community. Furthermore, the Petroleum (Drilling and Production) Regulations, 1969, which were made incidental to the Petroleum Act should include human rights content which makes local community participation and consultation imperative – before any oil prospecting or mining activity starts. Section 1(2) (h) of the Regulation which provides for the employment quota of Nigerians in the oil and gas industry, must be amended to further favour the local community of the extractive activity. Additionally, Section 17 of the Regulation limits the entry of a licensee into sacred lands – which are usually used for spiritual purposes. However, the question of which land is sacred is determined by the state authority, whose decisions are final. This provision however makes a mockery of the rights-based approach to development projects. In the face of foreign direct investment and state complicity with MNCs, asking the state to determine which land is sacred is spurious and alarming. Niger-Delta communities hold their land in reverence for spiritual and agricultural purposes. The state government is not the right body to determine the designation of land as sacred – without the input of the local community. Furthermore, if the Act can prohibit pipeline construction near a building, it should prohibit such construction on sacred sites.[88]

The condition of the determination of sacred land by a state authority should be removed. The Regulation should be amended to allow for a representative body in such a community, or in the case of the Niger-Delta community, a body comprising different ethnic groups and clans, to negotiate collective interests with the government in determining any land as sacred land. Every group represented in this body should partake in the election of their representatives and where such a representative goes beyond the wishes of a clan or tribe, the community should be able to impeach such a representative. This process must be free and fair. Elderly and vulnerable members of society can provide social and historical contexts on issues when needed. Participation in determining which land is sacred should be done without coercion and with the central input of the local community. Under no circumstance should there be the granting of operational licences or leases without consulting community members.

The 1969 Regulations oblige licensees or lessees to take adequate precautions to "prevent the pollution of inland waters, rivers, and territorial waters of Nigeria, by oil or other fluids or substances which might contaminate the water, banks of rivers or the Nigerian shoreline."[89] They further mandate the corporate actor to control and remedy any such pollution or harm.[90] Crafting regulations around this preserves the states' own reputation, and also ensures predictability for business enterprises.[91] Furthermore, Principle recommends state support for departmental agencies to be conscious of and to observe the states' human rights obligations when carrying out their mandates.

The Department of Petroleum Resources (DPR) is the regulatory agency for the enforcement of petroleum regulations in Nigeria. Some of the key functions of the Department are to: supervise all petroleum-related operations carried out by businesses;[92] to monitor the petroleum industry to ensure it is in line with national goals and aspirations; and ensure that health, safety, and environment policies adapt to global and domestic best practices.[93] The Department does not have any programme or activity on business and human rights – and does not indicate whether the state has provided adequate mechanisms for information, training, and support for key staff who shape business practices. The Nigerian government should therefore ensure that the DPR is aware of government's human rights obligations (if any exist) – by providing the Department with sufficient information and training on human rights standards. Furthermore, section 9(1) (b) (iii) of the Act empowers the DPR to make regulations for the enforcement of safety and environmental guidelines. Pursuant to this, the DPR issues guidelines which cover the control of pollution from various aspects like petroleum and processing operations. These guidelines are set in the Environmental Guidelines and Standards for the Petroleum Industry in Nigeria (EGASPIN).

A. *The Environmental Guidelines and Standards for the Petroleum Industry in Nigeria (EGASPIN)*[94]

EGASPIN controls pollution from various aspects of petroleum operations. It sets out to regulate the environmental management practices relating to the accidental discharge of oil from oil and gas installations. It also establishes monitoring requirements for oil and gas production.[95] It specifically limits the extent of gas flaring and controls the number of emissions in flares.[96] The Guidelines are enforceable against the MNCs in the areas of oil pollution. The Guidelines thus aim to establish standards for environmental quality control of the petroleum industry.

7.4.2 Oil Pipelines Act (1956)

The Oil Pipelines Act (OPA)[97] provides for a licence to be "granted for the establishment and maintenance of pipelines constructed for use in oil mining and oil fields."[98] One of the main causes of oil spillage in Nigeria is sabotage by the local community – causing pipeline bursting or rupturing. Some of these pipelines predated Nigeria's independence and are not being maintained periodically. While sabotage could be a potent reason, businesses do not adequately maintain the pipelines. For instance, the Act provides permit holders must take all reasonable steps to avoid preventable damage to any land, buildings, crops, or profitable trees and must pay compensation when any damage occurs.[99]

Section 25 allows holders of permit to violate the rights of people by depriving them of the right to property. This arises when such permit holders enter a particular land area and give the occupant only 14 days of advance notice.[100] Any attempt to deny the permit holder entry will be punishable under the law – with "three months' imprisonment or the option of a fine."[101] These provisions complicate application of human rights principles. Not only have these particular occupants been on the land for years, but they are also now possibly subject to imprisonment if there is resistance. Nobody would allow their land to be taken at will – even under the law – where such persons have a spiritual attachment to and derive other benefits from the land. In the *Endorois* case,[102] the Kenyan government evicted the Endorois people from their indigenous land for the building of a national reserve and tourist facilities. Only minimal compensation was paid to the Endorois people. The African Commission on Human and Peoples' Rights held that the Kenyan government infringed on the rights of the Endorois people by evicting them from their land. These violations included the right to property, health, culture, religion, and natural resources. It therefore ordered Kenya to reinstate the Endorois people to their land and also to compensate them. Under the OPA, the compensation regime does not identify how much is to be paid where a license holder causes injury to the land in question.[103] It is only where there is a dispute on the amount to be paid as compensation that recourse can be made to a court.[104]

Section 9 should be reviewed to protect the human rights of landowners. Where land has been affected by the granting of a licence, not only should adequate compensation be paid, but alternative housing or landed property should be provided for residents or victims. The granting of licences under Part III of the Act should be modified to include consultation and local community participation in decision-making – leading to the granting of such licenses.

Like the Petroleum (Drilling and Production) Regulations discussed above, the OPA also prevents the usurpation of sacred land. However, it does not place the burden of determining which land is sacred on the state. Section 15 (1) (a) prohibits a licensee from entering or taking possession of any land held to be "sacred or the object of veneration" unless express permission has been given by the owner. However, the determination of which land is sacred or who owns or occupies such lands is left to the court to determine. FPIC would ensure that project proponents consult with the local community – to avoid any usurpation of sacred land. In this regard, the views and historical account of the elderly and aged in the community will go a long way in determining which land is sacred.[105] After all, the court will still rely on evidence brought by the elderly and chiefs in the community, to determine issues of customary law or sacred land. Extractive and energy companies can avoid tortuous litigation processes by consulting with affected stakeholders, as encapsulated in Principle 18.

It is recommended that the OPA should indicate how such assent, under section 15(1), is obtained – and the processes and procedures involved in obtaining the assent, such as consultation, language (or the use of interpreters), gender representation, and the participatory framework. Furthermore, host communities must be involved in oil pipeline construction. The involvement can take various forms, and this could include employment by the MNCs, using an orderly and recognised representative platform to question the motives of an investor in terms of complying with environmental laws and standards, prevent access to spiritual and communal lands, and receive guarantees that investors will comply with any pre-project arrangement.

To ensure local community-corporate trust, section 21 of OPA provides that the court may consider, where the local community's interests have been seriously injured by the acts of the MNCs, that compensation be paid to the ruler, headman or member of the community concerned (on behalf of the community). However, why should the court have to wait until the community is seriously injured? Local communities have sentimental attachments to their land, which range from spiritual to commercial issues, and any deprivation may cause them injury. This provision – with noble intentions in terms of compensation – creates an easy regime for MNCs to violate local community human rights. Furthermore, the amount of compensation is insufficient reason for a victim to officially or orally object to the destruction of the occupant's land.[106] The incongruity in determining the amount of compensation speaks volumes on the approach of the state to human rights violations relating to the local community. Presently, the Ogoni land has been devastated by years of exploitation and no extractive company currently operates there. Stipulating and measuring adequate compensation will send a clear message to companies: there are serious complications and large fines to be paid when best practices are not ensured. The determination of compensation is discretionary. The court assesses the land or interests on the land, in determining the loss in value.[107]

Thus, if the court is not inclined to the BHR agenda – the progressive realization of the UNGPs through an instructive Act like OPA could be very challenging.

Sequel to sections 33 and 34 of the Act, the DPR published Guidelines for the Operation and Maintenance of Oil and Gas Pipelines.[108] The Guidelines require a prospective applicant for the construction of an oil pipeline to submit to the DPR a preliminary environmental impact assessment.[109] The Guidelines also oblige an applicant to establish an emergency plan – should there be system failures, accidents, and other emergencies.[110] This emergency plan shall include plans for prompt and pragmatic remedial action for the protection of the property, environment, and pipeline.[111] These provisions conform to GP 3(c), which recommends to states that they provide operational direction to companies on "how to respect human rights throughout their operations."

7.5 Environmental Impact Assessment Act (1992)

Within the last decade, the Environmental Impact Assessment (EIA) process has evolved to a wider consideration of the socio-cultural and health consequences of such projects. This evolution, now referred to as Environmental and Social Impact Assessment (ESIA), envisages an evaluation of the effect of a developmental project on a people's culture, community, health, and well-being.[112] This evolution combines health, socio-economic, environmental, cultural, and psychological well-being and an ell encompassing assessment of inter-relationships between human beings and the natural environment.[113]

The EIA Act was promulgated as Decree No 86 of 1992. Under the Act, it is compulsory for any extractive project to establish whether such activity may likely, or to some extent, affect the environment or have any environmental effect.[114] Before deciding to approve the proposed activity, government authorities at all levels, corporate bodies, and any person – must take such environmental effect into account before either granting or applying for a grant.[115] The EIA Act therefore forbids the undertaking of or embarking on projects which may significantly affect the environment, without prior consideration of their environmental effects.[116] This process must include sharing information and consultation between the project developer and local community members which are host to the extractive project.[117]

The Act provides a mandatory list of the development projects that must be preceded by an EIA.[118] Thus, any extractive resource projects must be subjected to an impact assessment process. Section 12 provides that where an extractive project is identified, the government or any of its agencies shall not permit such projects to be done in any form, shape, or manner – unless such an agency has, in accordance with its statutory powers, assessed that such projects should proceed with or without any conditions. Despite this, where a project will affect the environment – even though it is not contained in the mandatory list, the Act provides that appropriate environmental issues should be identified and studied before such a project or activity commences.[119] An impact assessment must contain information on how the proposed activity affects the environment, and whether there are alternative means for carrying out the project and ways to mitigate adverse environmental impacts of the project – including human rights violations.[120] Principle 18 provides that, in order to measure human rights risks, companies should "identify any actual or potential adverse human rights impacts" that may arise in the course of their activities; this makes impact assessment imperative. Likewise, Principle 19 provides that companies "should integrate the findings from their human rights impact assessment" into their business activities. Consequently, under the UNGPs, human rights impact assessments must be incorporated into other processes like environmental and social impact assessments.[121] Businesses are capable of potentially impacting practically on any internationally recognised human rights. Thus, the EIA Act must be expanded to accommodate human rights impact assessment, as part of its impact assessment processes. Furthermore, efforts to avoid or lessen unfavourable human rights impacts must be geared to integrating the outcomes of EIA within corporate human rights policy commitments. This will facilitate a regime of corporate culture in terms of preparing for any potential human rights impact of corporate behaviours.

The EIA ensures that the local community is aware of potential developmental projects. This is possible through public participation in public hearings – and the proceedings of such hearings, including public comments, shall be detailed in a panel's report.[122] Through this process, opportunity is given to government, the public, and specialists to make comments on the EIA of a proposed project.[123] The extent to which the local community is to be involved is however, unclear. That said, the Act specifically mentions "public," and it therefore seems that project developers and government officials may only allow the public to attend public hearings and voice their concerns, but after that their concerns may not necessarily be included in a "panel's report"– since the report is not subjected to any referendum. Besides, the mere fact that an EIA is only useful in a pre-development stage, makes the enforcement of an EIA questionable. An impact assessment must follow the life cycle of any project. The EIA does not mention any human rights impact assessment; thus, it is possible that while carrying out the environmental impacts of a project, certain rights of local communities may be violated, such as the right to property – which is different from environmental impacts (oil pollution, gas flaring). However, under the Act, human rights violations are not included. Any violation of the provisions of the Act carries a term of imprisonment or the offender is liable to fines.[124] Like other extant environmental laws, the financial penalty for a corporate body carries a fine of N1 million ($3,275). These paltry penalties will, however, not ensure serious compliance with the Act.

The EIA Act must be amended to cater for preliminary assessment of extractive projects. Preliminary assessment goes beyond mere screening and scoping stages. This assessment must integrate the host communities, consider the viability of the project in terms of human rights implications, health consequences of such projects and costs of relocation of community members. Currently, the Act does not require human rights considerations in conducting preliminary assessments.

Before development projects are conducted, there must be detailed description and analysis of the objectives and impact of such projects on the community at the first instance, and on the country at large. Issues here would include relocation of members of the community, the siting of the project (in relation to spiritual affinity to the land), closeness to natural habitats or monument sites, post-completion operations such as decommissioning and the closing of mines, and the effect of such activity on the immediate environment. Thus, an EIA remains crucial for identifying these issues. However, while the current law prescribes that an EIA is to be done before the project, it is submitted that an EIA should be done before, during, and after the completion of the project. This will be in form of a monitoring plan that assesses the effect of a developmental project on the host community's culture, community, health, and well-being. This would enable various stakeholders to determine whether the intended objectives have been met, and if not, whether reparations are possible.[125]

The Environment Impact Assessment Act (Amendment) Bill (2010) has been before the Nigerian legislature since 2010.[126] The Bill seeks to amend the Environment Impact Assessment Act and make it more responsive to the aspirations of the people. It seeks to ensure that project developers, approving authority, and persons whose livelihood will be affected by the proposed project are involved in the decision making to safeguard the environment and ensure adequate re-mediation of the environment. The passage of this Bill will lend credence to the recommendations highlighted in this book that seeks to ensure that preliminary assessment is done before, during and after the project as well as involving the host communities in decision making. For instance, paragraph 9 of the proposed amendment provides that project proponents shall submit a security bond, the value of which the Assessment Agency shall stipulate for the remediation of any adverse environmental impact after completion of the project. This guarantees that where the host communities have been impacted, appropriate compensation and remediation will be done. An Impact Assessment done during and after the completion of the project can only give effect to this proposed amendment.

The Nigerian regime on impact assessment should designate a competent authority, devoid of government patronage or control, which will administer impact assessment. Currently, the Department of Petroleum Resources is saddled with this responsibility. A government agency solely in control of such a responsibility cannot truthfully and objectively work against the interests of MNCs, for obvious reasons.[127] Furthermore, impact assessment in Nigeria does not encourage the participation of local communities which will be impacted by the environmental work.[128] The importance of this assessment is key in determining the liability of such a project and its potential to acquire the social licence to operate. For instance, this report will indicate if there will be environmental effects of gas flaring, acid rain, oil pollution – and how the company intends to mitigate or reduce this. The report will also address the social, economic, cultural, and environmental impacts of the project, and what percentage of the host community will be employed. The information yielded by this assessment will determine how many homes will be lost, how many locals will be displaced, the possibility of land expropriation, and whether there is an alternative site for the project. It is only at the planning stage that these issues can be identified – and if such issues cannot be resolved, extractive projects should not proceed. These issues are more pertinent when the oil wells and activities are onshore. The extent of contamination and corporate-induced human rights violations are more visible onshore compared to when oil activities are undertaken offshore.

7.6 The Land Use Act (1978)

Every individual has the immutable right to own immovable property in any place where such individual is lawfully permitted to reside.[129] Although section 44 (1) of the Constitution provides that "any right over, or interest in," immoveable property shall not be taken possession of or acquired compulsorily, except where a law provides for such compulsory acquisition, section 44 (3) effectively grants the entire property and control of natural resources "in, under or upon any land, territorial waters and the Exclusive Economic Zone" to the Federal Government of Nigeria. The management of such resources is, however, to be prescribed by parliament.

Extractive resource projects have the potential to deprive individuals of land rights. More compelling is that in many cases of compulsory acquisition, compensation is not paid by the state. Article 17 of the Universal Declaration of Human Rights protects the right of individuals to ownership and use of property. The United Nations Declaration on the Rights of Indigenous Peoples provides that states shall, *inter alia*, "provide effective mechanisms for the prevention of, and redress for, any action – which has the aim or effect of dispossessing indigenous peoples of their lands, territories or resources."[130] Article 14 of the African Charter on Human and People's Rights guarantees the right to property,[131] though this right can be infringed in the interests of the public, community, and must be done within the purview of appropriate laws.[132] The Land Use Act (LUA) entrusts all the land in the "urban area of a state in the governor of that state"– who "holds the land in trust for the people and manages it for them."[133] The rights to land in non-urban areas are vested in local governments.[134] The rights of the state or the local government to hold these lands in trust does not apply to lands owned by the federal government[135] – which includes lands on which extractive resource projects are built.

The commentary to Principle 3 directs states to review whether their laws and policies provide a conducive environment for corporate respect for human rights. Principle 3 particularly recommends that states clarify the area of law pertaining to "access to land, including entitlements and ownership of land necessary to protect rights-holders" and corporate entities.[136] The LUA unnecessarily strips Nigerians of ownership over their land and natural resources. Section 66 explicitly states that the exclusive right of landowners (subject to a 99-year of right of occupancy) is restricted against the governor of a state, and any land where there is prospecting for natural resources.[137] Thus, local communities do not have access to and ownership over the properties where extractive projects are undertaken. Where they are already in possession of the land, the governor can withdraw a "right of occupancy" over the land where there is a prospect of an oil pipeline or mining. To avoid this right deprivation, most indigenes keep quiet if they discover natural resources on their land – so preventing the government from accessing the resources.

The LUA does not consider the rights to property or potential violation of local community human rights, when communities are relocated or dispossessed of their land.[138] Adequate compensation is not paid to victims of land grabs by the state and companies, while victims are not resettled very well. The weak human rights regime does not facilitate the sustainable development of extractive resources. This could have serious implications for the implementation of the UNGPs. The government must provide a guarantee "that project sites and lands have not been indiscriminately acquired – and where procedurally acquired, adequate compensation must have been paid to those whose lands have been affected. This policy would prompt the government to take the human rights agenda seriously."[139]

The right to own immoveable property is subject to the overriding states' authority to utilise that land in the interest of the public. Such state authority must be exercised prudently in the interests of the host communities, not the MNCs.[140] Occasionally, lands are appropriated for political reasons – exclusive of reparation. Indigenous communities have deep ancestral ties to their land, if for any reason, these communities are to be relocated, adequate compensation must be paid. Since the idea of compensation is based on public interest,[141] it is therefore morally and ethically sensible to pay adequate compensation. Perhaps, host communities should be included in the contractual negotiations between state and MNCs before any land is expropriated. Under this arrangement, extractive and energy projects on land taken from communities will not be stifled by those communities.

7.7 Companies and Allied Matters Act (CAMA) 2020

CAMA is the only statutory document that regulates corporate entities in Nigeria.[142] However, it does not provide for human rights protection in any of its sections. Nonetheless, under section 300 the court may grant injunctions against company actions that contradict or are *ultra vires* the company's Articles of Incorporation or are in breach of shareholder rights. Due to the lack of human rights provisions in CAMA, it is difficult to know whether the actions of directors or the company in human rights compliance, will amount to a breach of the fiduciary duties of the directors. The provision enabling the company to sue in order to remedy any wrong is contained in the "Protection of Minorities from Illegal and Oppressive Conduct" section of the Act.[143] CAMA must be revised to adapt to changing dynamics of globalisation in the context of business and human rights. It must contain the human rights interests of key stakeholders in the resource sector – host communities to extractive resource projects.

The CAMA requires Directors to have duty of care towards their stockholders.[144] Furthermore the Act compels Directors to act in "utmost good faith towards the company."[145] Thus, at the Management level, rational decisions should be taken, that will not lead to human rights violations of stakeholders. Executives of the company should consider human rights obligations to be in the best interests of the company. Can it therefore be said that a director may have authorised human rights infringements which the company actively took part in? This book submits that the company's "best interest" does not only end in satisfying the shareholders, but also extends to complying with human rights duties available under domestic corporate and environmental laws. For instance, Principle 3 (b) provides that, states must "ensure that their laws and policies in the area of corporate law do not constrain but enable business respect for human rights." To achieve this, CAMA must require companies to commit to respecting human rights in their activities. Human rights commitments must be incorporated into their Memorandum and Articles of Association. Any company dealing with the extractive industry must include in its Article of Incorporation how it commits to socially responsible custom – which must include the responsibility to respect human rights. Furthermore, for any such companies listed on Nigeria's stock exchange, there must be a requirement that companies commit to their human rights responsibilities through their CSR, ethical dealings, and social commitments. South Africa has been able to achieve this listing requirement under the King Code of Corporate Governance.

CAMA must be reviewed to accommodate human rights provisions in the corporate set-up. The 2020 amendment did not incorporate or consider human rights provisions. At the point of company registration, the Principles can be included in the incorporation documents to be submitted by the companies, who must commit to human rights principles.[146] Nigeria can take a cue from India in this regard. In 2013, India directed all its registered companies earning above a particular threshold – to "spend at least 2% of their average net profits over three years in pursuance of" CSR within India."[147] After all, some of Nigeria's environmental laws – as discussed above – recognise human rights, and corporate law can do more than that.

The courts have been divided on whether corporations have human rights obligations. In *Ategie v Mck Nigeria Ltd*,[148] the court declined jurisdiction over an enforcement of fundamental rights claimed on the basis that the case could not be brought against a company – even though there was an allegation of a breach of fundamental rights. In *Abdulhamid v. Akar*,[149] the Supreme Court held that where the violation of human rights is committed by non-state actors, the victim would have a right to proceed against the perpetrator. In *Uzoukwu v Ezeonu II*,[150] the Court of Appeal held that infringements of civil and political rights under the 1979 Constitution were enforceable against the state, non-state actors and individuals.[151] In *Peterside v IMB*,[152] the Court rejected the notion that fundamental rights guaranteed under Chapter IX of the Constitution can only be enforced against government but cannot be enforced by one individual against another, including corporate actors.[153]

It seems the courts are more inclined to entertain public interest litigations in human rights brought under the Fundamental Rights (Enforcement Procedure) Rules, 2009.[154] The Rules prevent the striking out of a case for want of *locus standi*.[155] Instructively, section 3 (b) advances applications which may be brought under the UNGPs. It provides that the Court "shall respect municipal, regional and international bill of rights" brought to its attention, whether these bills form instruments themselves or they constitute parts of a larger documents like constitutions.[156] Under the Rules, the Courts are enjoined to proactively ensure fairness for all classes of petitioners: "poor, illiterate, uninformed, vulnerable, incarcerated, and the unrepresented."[157] The Rules oblige Courts to ensure the speedy and effective enforcement and realisation of human rights.[158] This can be done by advancing good governance, human rights and culture through positive deference to human rights enforcement. Provision of human rights obligations under CAMA would be the only solution to states' duty to protect human rights under Principle 1. How can human rights be integrated under CAMA? The next section discusses this.

7.7.1 Human Rights Due Diligence (HRDD)

The requirement for corporate HRDD will require companies to identify real and possible impacts of their projects on the human rights of their host communities, and how they intend to avoid or mitigate such impacts. This would include integrating and acting upon the findings. The lack of HRDD has led to corporate disasters such as the deleterious effects of gas flaring and acid rain. Regrettably, this same gas that can be converted to domestic use, is lost through indiscriminate flaring.

Due diligence must include a community-based human rights impact assessment (HRIA), which advances the aim of due diligence by "knowing and showing" how companies respect human rights. HRIA complements EIA and due diligence processes, and hence are an integral part of the UNGPs. Through the HRIA, companies will be obliged to demonstrate the extent to which their activities have been subjected to HRIA. HRIA would also help identify if there is potential for the displacement of people from their homes, the loss of fishing and farming by local communities, and potential for oil spillage.

HRDD should also commence at the initial stage and run through the life cycle of the project. This should be mandated by the state as a pre-condition for granting oil exploration rights. This gives companies guidance on how to avoid or mitigate human rights violations. The UNGPs support the continuous conduct of HRDD. When a project ends, due diligence will determine whether the project had negatively affected the host community. For example, the failure of Shell to do HRDD after its operations, when it decided not to secure a wellhead it was no longer using, caused the company to pay huge fines in the *Akpan v Shell* case.[159]

The concept of incentivising is key to achieving corporate HRDD. For instance, the Indian government launched National Corporate Social Responsibility (CSR) awards to recognise companies that contribute to social welfare and that have made an impact on society through their sustainable CSR initiatives.[160] This forms part of the government's efforts to incentivise companies that contribute to social welfare. Under India's Companies Act 2013, a class of companies that meet a designated profit threshold is required to spend 2% of its average annual net profit on CSR. Incentivized companies are expected to have focused on the following areas: human development, economic development, welfare, the environment, and sustainable development. Nigeria can also incorporate similar provisions in its corporate law. The use of national awards and TV shows will encourage MNCs to do more in terms of integrating human rights into their practices. Furthermore, mandating MNCs in Nigeria to adopt environmental impact assessment and human rights due diligence aligns with the UNGPs.

7.8 The National Oil Spill Detection and Response Agency (NOSDRA)

The Law establishing the Agency is known as the National Oil Spill Detection and Response (Establishment) Act No. 15 of 2006. This Act empowers the Agency to regulate oil and gas industries with regard to oil spillages,[161] and to detect and respond to oil spills in Nigeria.[162] The core functions of the Agency are to: ensure compliance with environmental legislation concerning oil spills;[163] coordinate oil-spill response activities throughout Nigeria;[164] co-ordinate the implementation of the National Oil Spill Contingency Plan (NOSCP) for the elimination of dangerous substances, as may be published by the government from time to time;[165] assist with arbitrating between host communities and the environment degrader; measure any harm triggered by an oil discharge; and supervise the clean-up operations, in order to guarantee full restoration of the affected areas.[166]

The procedure for NOSDRA when an oil spill occurs, includes:

1. Receive report of incident with the location and date of the oil spill, as well as the name of the facility from which the leak occurred.
2. Participate in a Joint Investigation Visit (JIV) to determine the cause and extent of the pollution. Members of the JIV include representatives of NOSDRA, DPR, the Rivers State Ministry of Environment, the spiller (the oil company), and the community.
3. Geo-reference all oil-spill sites, by recording the coordinates of the site using a Global Positioning System (GPS).
4. Enter details of the oil spill in the Agency's online data bank.
5. Receive a clean-up/remediation plan from oil companies.
6. The Agency will monitor the clean-up or remediation work.
7. Certify and close-out the oil-spill incident. This is done by visiting the site after the clean-up/remediation work is completed, to collect soil or water samples for laboratory analysis to determine if the level of harmful substances like Total Petroleum Hydrocarbon (TPH), Benzene, Toluene, and Xylene in the contaminated site or medium, are within allowable regulatory limits.[167]

In some instances, NOSDRA does not certify and close-out the oil-spill incident – even when it is obvious that remediation has been concluded. When an oil spillage occurs, payment for compensation is based on the law.[168] First, the operator of the facility where the oil has spilled shall pay compensation to an oil-spill victim for damages caused.[169] Second, compensation is not paid when the cause of the spill is due to sabotage.[170] Third, the operator shall internalize the cost of compensation – as part of the polluter-pays-principle.

The Agency – being a regulatory body in nature – does not respond to oil spillages directly, but rather the owner of a facility where spills occurred (MNCs) is expected by law to report and inform the Agency about the spillage within 24 hours. Furthermore, the Agency does not carry out clean-up operations; it monitors clean-up activities carried out by the spiller, to ensure that the clean-up is done in line with the regulations. Practically, the Agency seeks advice from the community in carrying out joint investigations to determine the cause of a spill incident and oil-spill-related activities, and, as such, they are part of those that contribute to decision-making in the field during investigation and assessment.

7.9 Niger-Delta Development Commission (NDDC)

To protect the Niger-Delta environment, the National Assembly enacted the Niger-Delta Development Commission Act, 2000 – which established the NDDC. The Commission was set up to facilitate the "sustainable development of the Niger-Delta" region. The core functions of the NDDC are to: prevent environmental problems that arise from the extraction of natural resources; and to advise the state on the avoidance and control of oil spillages and environmental contamination. The terms of this Act are in consonance with Principle 1, which provides for the state's duty to protect against human rights through effective legislation

7.10 National Environmental Standards and Regulations Enforcement Agency (Establishment) Act 2007 (NESREA Act)

The NESREA Act repealed the Federal Environmental Protection Act and established the National Environmental Standards and Regulations Enforcement Agency (the Agency). The Agency is generally responsible for the "protection and development of the environment, biodiversity conservation and sustainable development of Nigeria's natural resources",[171] as well as the enforcement of environmental standards regulations, rules, laws, policies and guidelines.[172] The Agency is specifically saddled with the responsibility of enforcing compliance with the provisions of international agreements, protocols, conventions, and treaties on the environment including conventions on climate change, ozone depletion, amongst others. Unfortunately, the Agency is excluded from regulation of air pollution in the oil and gas sector.[173]

In furtherance of its mandate to protect the environment, the Agency has released several regulations to protect the environment. An important Regulation which is instructive for this book is the National Environmental (Pollution Abatement in Mining and Processing of Coal, Ores, and Industrial Minerals) Regulations (2009).[174] This Regulation basically to minimize pollution from mining and processing of coal ores and industrial minerals. Extractive industries are obliged to apply up to date, efficient and cleaner production technologies, and also pollution prevention measures that will bring environmental and economic benefits.[175] They further provide that extractive companies must ensure compliance with prescribed guidelines for safe levels of air pollutants tolerable to human, plants and animals.[176]

7.11 Nigerian National Human Rights Commission Act (1995)

The Nigerian National Human Rights Commission of Nigeria (the Commission) was established by the National Human Rights Commission Act, 1995, as amended by the NHRC Act, 2010.[177] The Commission functions as an extra-judicial mechanism which safeguards the human rights of the Nigerian population, provides and enabling environment for promotion, protection, and enforcement of human rights.[178] It monitors human rights in Nigeria, assists victims of human rights violations, and helps in the formulation of the Nigerian Government's policies on human rights.[179] The Commission has been instrumental to the development of a National Action Plan on Business and Human Rights. It has led collaborative efforts with CSOs to facilitate stakeholder consultations on BHR between 2012 and 2017. In February 2017, the joint efforts led to the drafting of a Consultative Draft of Nigeria's NAP.[180]

7.12 Corporate criminal jurisdiction

The Malabo Protocol which allows for corporate criminal liability in African courts, has not been ratified by African states.[181] Although Nigeria has adopted corporate criminality into its corporate law, it is not yet clear how the concept can be adopted and applied. That said, it remains a useful tool for ensuring that corporations are held liable for their human rights violations and an extension of the state's duty with regard to Principles 1 and 2. The discussion here is concerned with the criminal liability of the corporation itself, and not of officers or individuals who commit crimes while being employed by the company.

Nigeria provides for corporate criminal liability under its environmental and corporate laws. In the environmental sector, The Harmful Waste (Special Criminal Provisions) Act,[182] criminalises the conduct of a corporate body – where such conduct was done with the consent or in connivance with the Director or other officers of the company.[183] The corporate body and any such officers shall be guilty of the crime and punished accordingly. Furthermore, section 6 of the Oil in Navigable Waters Act[184] provides that "a person shall be guilty of an offence under sections 1, 3, and 5, and liable to a fine." The "persons" referred to in the mentioned sections are the "owner or master" of the ship or vessels. Thus, where a corporate body owns a ship, such a body will be held liable and convicted for the offence. Section 27 (2) of the NESREA Act, 2007, bans the release of harmful and hazardous substances on the land and waters of Nigeria, except where such a discharge is allowed under Nigerian law. Any corporate body that violates this provision commits an offence and is liable, upon conviction, to a fine of not more than N1 million ($2,800) and an added fine of N50,000 ($140) for each day the offence exists.[185] Furthermore, this Act defers to the Harmful Waste (Special Criminal

Provisions) Act in respect of any hazardous substance constituting harmful waste under section 37 of the Harmful Waste Act. Section 60 of the EIA Act stipulates that a firm shall be guilty of an offence where such a firm fails to comply with the provisions of the Act, and, upon conviction, is liable to pay a fine of not less than N50,000 ($140) and not more than N100,000 ($280).

In the corporate sector, sections 65–67 of CAMA regulate liability for the acts of the company. The sections provide for criminal and civil liability of the company. This liability accrues to the company in much the same way, as if it were a natural person. However, it imputes the acts of Directors and other offices of the company as being that of the company – if such acts took place during the ordinary course of the company's business. Nevertheless, there is an exception. The company will not incur civil liability for any person's act, if such a person had actual knowledge that the company had no power to act in such a manner or that he or she was acting in an irregular manner.[186] Furthermore, where an activity is carried out by the company, it is not the defence of the company to say that such an activity did not take place during the ordinary course of business of the company, or authorised by its memorandum and therefore it cannot be held criminally liable.[187] The company will still be liable, though the activity did not take place in the course of the business of the company.

Prosecution of companies for egregious conduct strengthens good governance, rule of law, and encourages accountability.[188] It is often the case that the personal liability or mental state of employees is inputted on the company. Sometimes, the veil of the corporation is lifted to discover which individuals are responsible for the corporate crime. This book takes the position that it is quite possible to impose criminal liability on the corporation based on the shared knowledge of the company employees.[189] Companies do not want to be associated with crime, however, they engage in illegal conduct, thereby betraying the public trust. The mere fact that they have become monstrous and outgrow the financial capacity of most developing states means that they should be held responsible for their criminal conduct, separate from individuals who work for the company. Occasionally, corporate practice and beliefs may affect the behaviour of officers of the company. Thus, creating a separate criminal liability system puts a check on an illegal corporate culture. Therefore, the CAMA must be amended to authorise corporate criminal liability separate from the criminal liability of its employees or agents. After all, if companies can be legal persons for the purpose of juristic personality, companies can be legal persons when sued for torture, murder, and other egregious crimes.

7.13 Conclusion

The inadequacy of human rights protection in local laws is a challenge to the implementation of business and human rights principles. Adequate legal and institutional frameworks that safeguards human rights standards creates a robust regime of sustainable development of country's infrastructure and resources. Consequently, human rights language must be easily identified in relevant domestic laws. States, as duty bearers, are obliged to protect rights holders from human rights violations. Introducing legally binding obligations to protect human rights in their activities provide a legal basis for local communities to demand for accountability. Without a legal framework that outlines corporate respect for human rights, business and human rights challenges such as discrimination, social exclusion, lack of participation endures. Domestic laws must adequately capture business' responsibility to prevent and mitigate environmental damage in their activities.

Notes

1 This book does not advocate for the creation of new laws but to integrate human rights dynamics into existing laws.
2 Charles Fombad, "Strengthening Constitutional Order and Upholding the Rule of Law in Central Africa: Reversing the Descent towards Symbolic Constitutionalism" (2014) 14 *African Human Rights L J* 414.
3 Constitution of the Federal Republic of Nigeria (1999). [CFRN].
4 O. Abe, "Utilisation of Natural Resources in Nigeria: Human Rights Considerations" (2014) *India Quarterly: A Journal of International Affairs* 3.
5 CFRN (n 3).
6 See F.O. Oleghe, "Nigeria's Ratification of International Human Rights Instruments and the Question of the Non-Justiciability of Chapter II of Its 1999 Constitution" (2020) 1(1) *Carnelian J.L. & Pol.* 5–19; O.F. Olayinka, "Implementing the Socio-Economic and Cultural Rights in Nigeria and South Africa: Justiciability of Economic Rights" (2019) 27(4) *African Journal of International and Comparative Law* 564–587.
7 Section 17 (2) (b) (d) of CFRN.
8 Cap A9, Laws of the Federation, 1999.
9 (1996) 9 NWLR (Pt. 475) 990.
10 Communication No. 155/96, 2001.
11 Abe (n 4) 3.
12 Commentary to Principle 1.
13 Section 1(1) of the Nigerian Constitution.
14 Section 1(3) of Nigerian Constitution.
15 See *Aturu v Minister of Petroleum Resources & Ors*, FHC/ABJ/CS/591/2009. [Holding that governments decision not to control the national economy in a way that would guarantee social justice and happiness of its citizens is in clear violation of Chapter II of the Constitution.] Though the law in Nigeria today is that socio-economic rights are not justiciable, see further *Okogie v. The Attorney-General of Lagos State* (1981) 2 NCLR 350.
16 See Emeka Polycarp Amechi, "Millennium Development Goals (MDGs) and Policy Reform: Realising the Right to Environment in Africa" (Saarbrucken: Verlag Dr. Müller (VDM), August 2010) 83; see also *Agbai & Ors v. Okogbue* (1991) 10 S.C.N.J. 49, 87.
17 Ibid. ICT Access to Justice: Human Rights Abuses Involving Corporations – Federal Republic of Nigeria (2012) 5.
18 2004 14 WRN 1.
19 (2004) 4 NWLR {Pt. 864} 580.
20 (1981) 1 NCLR 281.
21 Ibid. at 220.
22 See also *Adewole v Jakande* (1981) 1 NCLR 262, 279.
23 (2002) FWLR (Part 111) 1972 at 2144.
24 Ibid.
25 (2003) 15 NWLR (Pt. 842) 113, 175.
26 Section 2.

27 Ibid.
28 Section 310.
29 See further section 311 (9).
30 The Act includes any subsidiary regulation made under it and the Act will remain in operation until it is repealed or revoked and be considered enacted under the PIA.
31 See Section 311 (1).
32 [The Commission].
33 Section 6 of the Act.
34 Section 6(c) of the Act.
35 See sections 6 and 7 of the Act.
36 Section 53 (1).
37 Anjli Raval, & Maggie Fick, "Nigeria Unveils First Accounts in Decade" *Financial Times* (15 February 2016) <www.ft.com/content/b5a5f5f0-cf20-11e5-92a1-c5e23ef99c77> accessed 5 May 2021.
38 "Nigeria's NNPC 'Failed to Pay' $16bn in Oil Revenues" *BBC News* (15 March 2016) <www.bbc.com/news/world-africa-35810599> accessed 5 May 2021.
39 Section 64.
40 Section 53(1).
41 See sections 30–31.
42 Section 3(1) (b).
43 Section 3 (1) (g-h).
44 See Principle 21.
45 The law continues to apply as if enacted as part of the PIA.
46 Section 21 and 22 of the Petroleum Profits Tax Act, Cap P13, LFN, 2004.
47 The Nigerian Constitution provides for the payment of 13% of the revenue from the Federation Account be paid to oil producing States.
48 Section 239.
49 Section 240.
50 See section 9 where at least 30% of the profit to be generated by the proposed Nigerian National Petroleum Company Limited will go to oil exploration in the "frontier basins." Kayode Oyero, "3% to Host Communities More Than 30% Profit Share for Oil Exploration in Sokoto, Others: Kyari" *Punch* (24 August 2021) <https://punchng.com/3-to-host-communities-more-than-30-profit-share-for-oil-exploration-in-sokoto-others-kyari/?utm_medium=Social&utm_source=Facebook&fbclid=IwAR3bOh-dY0Cgf4N-HckSCcgRxLIfWT3zx8gV8F3Jv6VUc-IcoMJBXiE5oJ3M#Echobox=1629822277> accessed 26 August 2021.
51 Frontier Basis are the Chad Basin, Gongola Basin, Sokoto Basin, Dahomey Basin, Bida Basin, Benue Trough, Anambra Basin, amongst others.
52 Ibid.
53 Section 102.
54 Section 103.
55 Ibid.
56 The exemption applies in cases of emergency, where the Commission allows the flare, for instance, as required for facility start up or strategic operational reasons, including testing, and as an acceptable safety practice established under regulations. See further sections 104 and 107.
57 Sections 104–105.
58 Ibid.
59 Section 106.
60 Section 108.
61 Micheal Eboh, "Nigeria Losing N868m Daily to Gas Flaring" *Vanguard News* (6 March 2018) <www.vanguardngr.com/2018/03/nigeria-losing-n868m-daily-gas-flaring-nnpc/> accessed 11 May 2021.
62 Ibid.

63 David M. Doya, & Antony Sguazzin, "Gas Flaring Law Error Cost Nigeria Billions of Dollars" *Bloomberg* (29 January 2018) <www.bloomberg.com/news/articles/2018-01-29/gas-flaring-law-error-cost-nigeria-billions-of-dollars> accessed 11 May 2021. [The federal government imposed a penalty of $3.50 per thousand standard cubic feet (SCF) of flared gas on defaulting company].
64 C. Nwaoha, & D. Wood, "A Review of the Utilization and Monetization of Nigeria's Natural Gas Resources: Current Realities" (2014) 18 *Journal of Natural Gas Science and Engineering* 424. [Noting different gas utilization options, export potential, and government's policies that are stimulating gas investments in Nigeria].
65 Eman A. Emam, "Environmental Pollution and Measurement of Gas Flaring" (2016) *International Journal of Scientific Research in Science, Engineering and Technology* 252. [noting that gas flaring is a major contributor to air pollution and acid rain].
66 Ibid.
67 See further Uwem Udok, & E.B. Akpan, "Gas Flaring in Nigeria: Problems and Prospects" (2017) 5(1) *Global Journal of Politics and Law Research* 16.
68 See further *Jonah Gbemre v SPDC* Unreported suit No: FHC/B/CS/53/05.
69 E. Ojijiagwo, C. Oduoza, & N Emekwuru, "Economics of Gas to Wire Technology Applied in Gas Flare Management" (2016) *Engineering Science and Technology* 2109.
70 Section 7 (aa).
71 Section 83.
72 Section 83 (3).
73 For example, the Freedom of Information Act (2011) is currently only applicable to public institutions. Among other things, the Act seeks to make "public records and information more freely available, protect public records and information and protect serving public officers from adverse consequences of disclosing certain kinds of information." The Act should be amended in line with the PIA and Constitution (section 39) to ease the process and to reduce the burden of requesting and accessing information.
74 In Nigeria, the Freedom of Information Act has been translated to the three main Nigerian languages: Hausa, Igbo, and Yoruba, see Leadership, "Nigeria: NOA Unveils Information Act in Three Nigerian Languages" *AllAfrica* (19 April 2013) <https://allafrica.com/stories/201304200142.html> accessed 7 June 2021.
75 States should inform, train, and support government departments and agencies on how it fulfills its human rights obligations. See further Principles 8 and 21.
76 Victoria Ibezim-Ohaeri, et al., "Natural Resource and Benefit-Sharing Negotiations between Host Communities and Extractive Companies: A Case Study of Assa North & Ohaji South [ANOH] Gas Development Project" <https://spacesforchange.org/wp-content/uploads/2021/10/S4C-ANOH-EXECUTIVE-SUMMARY.pdf>.
77 Ibid.
78 see further the Report of the Special Rapporteur, Promotion and Protection of the Right to Freedom of Opinion and Expression, I UN Doc. E/CN.4/2000/63, 18 January 2000.
79 See generally section 83.
80 Section 116 of the Nigerian Minerals and Mining Act, 2007.
81 Section 117.
82 Section 232.
83 Ibid.
84 Section 233.
85 Section 311.
86 Ibid.
87 See the commentary to Principle 4.
88 See section 17 (1) (a) of the Petroleum Act.
89 Section 25 of the Petroleum (Drilling and Production) Regulation, 1969.
90 Ibid.
91 See commentary to Principle 2.

92 See Department of Petroleum Resources, "What We Do" <www.dpr.gov.ng/functions-of-dpr/> accessed 2 May 2021.
93 Ibid.
94 Department of Petroleum Resources, "Environmental Guidelines and Standards for the Petroleum Industry in Nigeria" (2002) ['Guidelines'].
95 Ibid.
96 Ibid. at paras 3.8.8.1 (iii)-(ix); para 5.6.2.2.
97 Cap O4, Laws of the Federation of Nigeria, 2004. ['OPA'].
98 See Preamble to the Act.
99 Section 6(3) of OPA.
100 Ibid.
101 Ibid.
102 See 276/03, *Center for Minority Rights Development (Kenya) and Minority Rights Group (on behalf of Endorois Welfare Council)/Kenya*; see also Derek Hawkins, "Activists and Police Trade Blame after Dakota Access Protester Severely Injured" *The Washington Post* (22 November 2016) <www.washingtonpost.com/news/morning-mix/wp/2016/11/22/activists-and-police-trade-blame-after-dakota-access-protester-severely-injured/?utm_term=.83f18b473638> accessed 4 May 2021.
103 Section 6 (3).
104 See Part IV of OPA.
105 See further Deanna Kemp, & John Owen, "Corporate Readiness and the Human Rights Risks of Applying FPIC in the Global Mining" (2017) *Business and Human Rights Journal* 164. [FPIC must be adapted to local context and corporate ability to support the principle].
106 Section 9(2) of OPA.
107 See generally section 20 of OPA.
108 See Department of Petroleum Resources, "Guidelines and Procedure for the Construction, Operation and Maintenance of Oil and Gas Pipeline Systems in Nigeria" (2007), DPR P-1P.
109 Ibid. at sections 1.2.3.7 and 1.2.3.8.
110 Section 2.4.1.
111 Ibid.
112 See further T.C. Nzeadibe, et al., "Integrating Community Perceptions and Cultural Diversity in Social Impact Assessment in Nigeria" (2015) 55, *Environmental Impact Assessment Review* 74; Z.A. Elum, K. Mopipi, & A. Henri-Ukoha, "Oil Exploitation and Its Socioeconomic Effects on the Niger Delta Region of Nigeria" (2016) 23 *Environmental Science and Pollution Research* 12880.
113 Nzedibe, et al. (n 102).
114 Section 1(a) of the EIA Act.
115 Ibid.
116 Section 2(1) (2)(3) of the EIA Act.
117 Sections 4 and 9(1) provides the minimum contents of an EIA; human rights impact is not included.
118 See Section 12, Schedule to EIA Act.
119 Section 3(1) of EIA Act.
120 Sections 4, 17(1) (2) of the EIA Act.
121 See Commentary to Principle 18.
122 Section 27 of the EIA Act.
123 See sections 6–11 of the EIA Act.
124 Section 62.
125 See further Aoife McCullough, "Environmental Impact Assessments in Developing Countries: We Need to Talk about Politics" (2017) 4(3) *The Extractive Industries and Society* 448. [Finding that the implementation of EIA in developing countries has been

found to be relatively ineffective]; Allan Ingelson, & Chilenye Nwapi, "Environmental Impact Assessment Process for Oil, Gas and Mining Projects in Nigeria: A Critical Analysis" (2014) 10(1) *Law, Environment and Development Journal* 37. [Arguing that although EIAs have become a standard legal requirement for all oil, gas, and mining projects in Nigeria, not much is achieved in terms of managing the impacts of these projects].

126 See National Assembly, Nigeria, "Environmental Impact Assessment Bill, 2019 (HB. 85)" <www.nass.gov.ng/documents/bill/10438> accessed 24 June 2021.

127 Where an impact assessment does not meet the minimum standards, the DPR can decide to look the other way to enable them to receive foreign direct investment from the MNCs.

128 See section 7, EIA Act (Nigeria).

129 Sections 43 and 44 of the Nigerian constitution (Nigeria); sections 25, 26 of South African Constitution (1996).

130 Article 8 (2) (b) of the United Nations Declaration on the Rights of Indigenous Peoples.

131 See Article 14.

132 Ibid.

133 Ibid.

134 Sections 1 and 2 of the LUA.

135 Section 49 of the LUA.

136 See Commentary to Principle 3.

137 Section 28 of the LUA.

138 In *SERAC v Nigeria* (2001) AHRLR 60 (ACHPR 2001), the African Commission held that the forceful possession of Ogoni land, without compensation, violated article 14 of the African Charter on Human and Peoples Rights. In South Africa, customary land rights have a tortuous history because of the land policy under the apartheid government. For instance, the Communal Land Rights Act, 2004 (No. 11, 2004), transfers communal lands to communities and regulates the democratic administration of communal lands by communities; the Restitution of Land Rights Act (No. 22 of 1994-the Act sets up a process of giving redress to persons and communities that lost land during the apartheid government.

139 Oyeniyi Abe, "The Feasibility of Implementing the United Nations Guiding Principles on Business and Human Rights in the Extractive Industry in Nigeria" (2016) *Journal of Sustainable Development Law and Policy* 155.

140 Ibid.

141 Section 28 of the LUA.

142 Cap C20, LFN, 2004.

143 See Part X of CAMA.

144 Section 279 of CAMA.

145 Ibid.

146 See Alexor Limited, Integrated Report 2014 (2014) at 17. Companies do need to understand the importance of negotiating with local communities in provision of essential services, such as health care, housing, water and education. Integrity, business ethics, and compliance with domestic law are *sine qua non*-to protecting the safety and health of the host local communities.

147 See section 135 of India's Companies Act 2013. It further requires companies to disclose their CSR programmes in their financial reports and on the company's website. Reasons for failure to spend the required amount must also be indicated in the report. See Companies (Corporate Social Responsibility Policy) Rules, 2014.

148 Suit No. M/454/92. See generally, ICT Access, above (n 42) 21.

149 (2006) 5 S.C., 44. See in particular, *Ale v. Obasanjo* (1996) 6 NWLR (Pt. 458) 394; *Aderinto v. Omojola* (1998) 1 FHCLR 101.

150 (1991) 6 NWLR [Pt. 200] 708.
151 Ibid.
152 (1993) 2 NWLR (Pt. 278) 377.
153 See further *Onwo v. Oko* (1996) 6 NWLR (Pt. 456) 584 at 603; *Okoi v. Inah* (1998) 1 FHCLR 677; *Anigboro v. Sea Trucks Ltd* (1995) 6 NWLR (Pt. 399) 35.
154 Section 3 (e) of the Fundamental Rights (Enforcement Procedure) Rules, 2009. ["FREP"].
155 Ibid. section 3(e); see further: *Adesanya v The President of Nigeria* (1981) 2 NCLR 258; Tunde I. Ogowewo, "Wrecking the Law: How Article III of the Constitution of the United States Led to the Discovery of a Law of Standing to Sue in Nigeria" (2017) 26 *Brooklyn Journal of International Law* 527 [tracing the problem with standing to sue in Nigeria to the construction placed by the courts on section 6(6) (b) of the Nigerian Constitution].
156 Ibid. section 3 (b).
157 Ibid. section 3 (d).
158 Ibid. section 3 (f).
159 Case Number: C/09/337050, HA ZA 09–1580.
160 News, "Government Launches Awards for CSR Nominations Open Till June 18" *The Economic Times* (15 May 2017) <https://economictimes.indiatimes.com/news/economy/policy/govt-launches-awards-for-csr-nominations-open-till-jun-18/articleshow/58685469.cms> accessed 7 June 2021.
161 NOSDRA Act No. 15 of 2006, see also Statutory Instrument No.25 Oil Spill Recovery, Clean-up, Remediation and Damage Assessment Regulations, 2011.
162 See Preamble to the NOSDRA Act.
163 See section 5 of NOSDRA Act; see also Statutory Instrument No.25 Oil Spill Recovery, Clean-up, Remediation and Damage Assessment Regulations, 2011.
164 Ibid.
165 Ibid.
166 Ibid.
167 Ibid.
168 Part III, section 26, statutory Instrument No.25 Oil Spill Recovery, Clean-up, Remediation and Damage Assessment Regulations, 2011.
169 Ibid. section 26(1).
170 Section 26(2).
171 Sections 2, 18 of the NESREA Act.
172 Ibid.
173 See section 7 (c), (d), (h) of the NESREA Act.
174 National Environmental (Pollution Abatement in Mining and Processing of Coal, Ores and Industrial Minerals) Regulations (2009).
175 Ibid. articles 1–3.
176 Ibid. article 30.
177 See the National Human Rights Commission (Amendment) Act 2010.
178 Ibid.
179 May Agbamuche-Mbu, "Nigeria and Its Human Rights Commission" *This Day* (21 October 2014) <https://web.archive.org/web/20150402095128/http:/www.thisdaylive.com/articles/nigeria-and-its-human-rights-commission/191769/> accessed 11 May 2021.
180 NHRC, "National Action on Business and Human Rights in Nigeria to Support the Implementation of the United Nations Guiding Principles on Business and Human Rights" <https://globalnaps.org/wp-content/uploads/2017/11/nhr-national-action-plan.pdf> accessed 20 August 2021.
181 Protocol on Amendments to the Protocol on the Statute of the African Court of Justice and Human Rights, A.U.Doc. No. STC/Legal/Min. 7(1) Rev. 1 (May 14, 2014. The

African Heads of State adopted the Malabo Protocol on June 30, 2014, at its Twenty-Third Ordinary Session. [Malabo Protocol].

182 Cap H1, Laws of the Federation of Nigeria, 2004.

183 Section 7 of the Act.

184 Cape 06, LFN, 2004.

185 Section 27 (3) (4) of the NESREA Act.

186 Section 65 (a) of CAMA.

187 Section 65 (b) of CAMA.

188 David Uhlmann, "The Pendulum Swings: Reconsidering Corporate Criminal Prosecution" (2016) 49 *UC Davis L. Review* 1235.

189 See further David Uhlman, "Erosion of Corporate Criminal Liability" (2013) 72 *Maryland L. Review* 1301.

8 Policy and legal framework in South Africa

8.1 Introduction

This chapter examines the adequacy of domestic laws in South Africa, considering that the responsibility to implement business and human rights principles is placed primarily on the states. South Africa has provided a robust legal regime through which business and human rights standards can be met. However, serious concerns exist on the implementation of these laws and their potential to address human rights challenges. As indicated in Chapter 6, the question is not of adequacy of laws, rather, the ability of these laws to guarantee social inclusion and sustainable development of development projects.

8.2 Constitution of the Republic of South Africa (1996)

South Africa mandates business respect for human rights. Under Chapter 2 (Bill of Rights), Article 8(2) provides that the Bill of Rights binds "natural or a juristic person." Thus, victims of corporate induced human rights violations can seek justice before South African courts. The horizontal application of this provision lends credence to the fact that it imposes positive obligations on the corporations – instead of the "*do no harm*" obligations of the UNGPs which scholars have cited as the basis for the passive nature of the UNGPs.

This constitutional horizontal application has created a fundamental pathway for human rights victims to seek justice against corporate actors. In *Glenister v. President of the Republic of South Africa,*[1] the Constitutional Court laid down the principle that the "*do no harm*" responsibility goes beyond the "mere negative obligation not to act in a manner that would infringe a right."[2] It also includes "positive duties on the state to take deliberate, reasonable measures to give effect to all of the fundamental rights contained in the Bill of Rights."[3] Thus South Africa appears to have taken the intentions of the UNGPs even further. This is facilitated by the proactive nature of the judiciary in terms of the radical realization of socio-economic, cultural, and human rights. In *University of Stellenbosch Legal Aid Clinic and others v Minister of Justice and Correctional Services and others,*[4] the issues surrounding debt collection procedures employed by the micro-lending industry which raises significant irregularities were considered. The First

DOI: 10.4324/9781003290124-12

Applicant on behalf of the other Applicants encountered large scale abuse of emoluments attachment orders (EAO) by credit providers and allegations of fraud in the process of issuance of the EAOs. Unfortunately, the fact that the debtor is a low-income earner is immaterial. There is "no statutory limit for deductions, neither is there a limit on the number of EAOs which may be made against a judgment debtor. The employer must deduct from employees" salaries the amount stated in the EAO and pay to the creditor."[5] The Applicants argued that the grant of EAOs by the courts clerk is inconsistent with the constitution and invalid as they fail to provide for the judicial oversight over the issuance of the EAO.[6] The Western Cape Division of the High Court of South Africa considered a litany of international human rights instruments including the International Labour Organisations' Protection of Wages Convention; ILO's recommendation concerning the Protection of Wages; the UNGPs; and the Human Rights Council resolution 26/22 of 15 July 2014. With particular reference to the UNGPS, the court noted that the UNGPs "place a duty upon the state to take measures to prevent the abuse of human rights in their territory by business enterprises. States are obliged to reduce legal and practical barriers that may deny individuals a remedy."[7] Consequently, the court held that the South African EAO system fails to comply with human rights principles as encapsulated in various instruments. In declaring the issued EAOs to be unlawful, invalid and of no force and effect, the court found that EAOs may be issued by the clerk without an oversight by a judicial officer; employees were not given an opportunity to make representations before an EAO is issued; the ineffective remedy when an excessive portion of a debtor's earnings is attached.[8]

On appeal, the Constitutional Court did not confirm the order of constitutional invalidity made by the High Court.[9] However, it considered some changes to the wordings of the legislation relied on by the High Court to align with the intent and purposes of the Constitution. While the Court did not rely on the UNGPs, it did confirm the Courts obligation to consider factors before EAOs are issued to avoid a punitive effect on the debtors and ensure that those orders apply to excess earnings after the costs for the debtor's maintenance must have been considered.

Due to the nature of mining activities, safeguarding property rights have remained challenging, especially for the vulnerable members of the society. The South African Constitution guarantees the right to property ownership without any form of deprivation,[10] although this right is subject to grounds under which lands may be expropriated.[11] Court decisions have exemplified post-apartheid property rights and supremacy of the constitution. In *Alexkor Ltd and Another v Richterveld Community*,[12] there was a dispute between the Richtersveld community and a diamond miner concerning the return of ancestral land to the indigenous community. The court held that allowing the miner to continue possession of the land will amount to grave injustice considering the fact that the community had been disposed of their land rights by the government. The court subsequently ordered the return of the land in dispute, with its mineral resources, to the community. Furthermore, section 26 of South Africa's Constitution created a fundamental right to housing. In *Government of the Republic of South Africa v Grootboom*,[13] the land in question, occupied by the claimant, was being repossessed for redevelopment.

The Constitutional Court held that section 26 created a justiciable right to housing in South Africa. Although the Court realized the practical difficulties in achieving socio-economic rights, it nonetheless granted temporary housing for the claimant. In *Port Elizabeth Municipality v Various Occupiers*,[14] some members of a community had been illegally residing on a vacant, private land. The municipality of Port Elizabeth sough to evict this group of people. The Constitutional Court declined the municipality's request, holding that the eviction could not proceed. This decision represents a "new task"[15] of the court which was to manage "the counter positioning of conventional rights of ownership against the new, equally relevant, right not to be arbitrarily deprived of a home, without creating hierarchies of privilege."[16]

8.3 Companies Act (2008)

The Companies Act enjoins compliance with the Bill of Rights as guaranteed under the Constitution.[17] Section 15(a) provides that a company's "Memorandum of Incorporation must be consistent with the Companies Act." By necessary implication, the Memorandum of a company must integrate human rights standards.

South African companies must consider human rights violations and take appropriate measures to avoid them. The failure to consider these human rights norms led to the various silicosis cases,[18] Marikana incident, and the mine – community distrust. Thus, there is the duty on the part of corporate actors to go beyond the do no net harm requirement in respecting human rights when operating in weak zones. The question is how may officers of the company ensure that their company does not engage in egregious conduct? The Act gives some guidance. The Board makes decisions for the company. Such decisions must be in the interest of the company and to the satisfaction of the shareholders. Furthermore, the fiduciary duties of a director, under Section 76 (3), provides that a director, in the course of his employment, must exercise his functions in good faith, in the best interest of the company, and with a reasonable degree of care, skill and diligence. The exercise of these fiduciary duties is discretionary. However, in the "best interest" of the company would amount to taking appropriate measures not to infringe the rights of the company's host community. These are non-derogable provisions which should be implemented strictly, especially against corporate actors.

The discretionary nature of the exercise of fiduciary duties of directors impedes the ability to say, with certainty, that companies act in accordance with human rights obligations. However, since section 15 requires that the Articles of Incorporation is consistent with the Companies Act, this book submits that the Companies Act should expressly stipulate that operational document of the company must include human rights obligations. This would give support to the promotion of compliance with the Bill of Rights as contained under section 7 of the Act.

To promote transparency and accountability, the Institute of Directors, South Africa (IoDSA) published the King Report on Corporate Governance in South Africa.[19] The Report obliges companies to document their social responsibility projects and commit to human rights standards.[20] Although a voluntary document, companies seeking to trade on the Johannesburg Stock Exchange (JSE) must comply with the requirements of the Code. Furthermore, like the MPRDA discussed below, the Companies Act requires companies to report on their social impact and environmental duties.

8.4 Mineral and Petroleum Resources Development Act 28 of 2002 (amended in 2008) (MPRDA)

Human rights and mining are not usually coterminous in the South African extractive industry. The inequality which inevitably follows the beneficent extraction of minerals is invidious. Host communities to mining projects have been despoiled and degraded due to activities of state and corporate actors. This situation presents some form of inconsistency with the purpose and intent of the Constitution and corporate law. For example, mining activities have exacerbated social exclusion, forced labour, discrimination on the basis of gender, deprivation of cultural lifestyle due to land relocation for development projects, community displacement,[21] and exposed local communities to high levels of radiation.[22]

The MPRDA is the overarching legislation for the extractive industry in South Africa.[23] It seeks to ensure that all South Africans have "equitable access to the nation's mineral and petroleum resources,"[24] and mining companies contribute "to the socio-economic development of their host communities."[25] The Act ensures that the custody of "mineral and petroleum resources is the common heritage of all South Africans";[26] the state is, however, the custodian of the resources.

Under the Act, the Minister is obliged to provide assistance to any historically disadvantaged person in conducting mining operations.[27] This is aimed at achieving equitable access to the nation's mineral resources.[28] Furthermore, the holder of an Environmental Impact Assessment (EIA) must conduct an EIA and communicate the impact of that EIA.[29] Where the impact has caused damage to the land, the holder of the mining right must manage such environmental impact by rehabilitating the environment affected by the damage.[30]

The MPRDA promotes equity in mining through granting access to "historically disadvantaged persons" provided for under the Act. In 2007, Luxembourg and Italian investors brought a claim against South Africa at the International Centre for Settlement of Investment Disputes (ICSID) – arguing that the MPRDA expropriated their mineral rights.[31] The investors argued that these expropriations were unlawful because they did not follow due process and were not adequately compensated. Not only was the MPRDA in line with the South African Constitution, but it served as the "custodian" of the country's mineral resources for the benefit of the people. The MPRDA was also an extension of the Broad-Based Black Economic Empowerment Policy. Both parties settled the case in 2010. However, shortly after the settlement, South Africa initiated a review of its Bilateral Investment Treaties (BIT), and terminated several of its BIT, claiming that such BIT "pose risks and limitations on the ability of the government to pursue its constitutional-based transformation agenda." On 23 June 2013, South Africa "served a notice of termination of its BIT with Spain."[32] The implication of South Africa's move is that investors must consider South Africa's racial history and modern attempt to empower economically disadvantaged people through the instruments of the law.[33] These BIT create economic advantages for states, and thus the redistributive tendencies under the MPRDA could be contrary to the "fair and equitable treatment provisions" under most BIT. Additionally, BIT protect investors against any arbitrary treatment by the host government and should ordinarily protect the citizens against any high handedness on the part of investors. In a bid to attract FDI, host governments enter onerous contractual agreements with MNCs. The terms of those agreements protect foreign investors against arbitrary conduct by host governments. Sometimes, however, these agreements can prevent the application of existing domestic laws when certain acts beyond the contemplation of the parties arise. Government is thus locked-in for the entire duration of the project, and may not be able to apply, for instance, a new environmental law. Where government enacts a new environmental law as a result of emerging environmental challenges, investors could seek to challenge such new laws – especially where they will violate the terms of existing BIT. When this happens, the BIT becomes the only point of reference.

It appears African states lack bargaining power when negotiating these BIT. Very protective and extreme provisions are agreed to with investors – making it clear that the primary interests are not those of the community. For instance, while the Nigerian Investment Promotion Commission Act No 16 of 1995 makes no mention of human rights. The South African government remedied this defect when it enacted the Black Economic Empowerment programme – which sought to empower the black majority by giving them an opportunity to partake in governance. Despite criticism of the programme, it did in fact create a more balanced approach and tightened investment agreements.

To integrate the black majority into the economic development of South Africa and to correct the racial disparities of the apartheid regime, the Broad-Based Black Economic Empowerment (BBBEE) Act (Act 53 of 2003) was enacted as a form of affirmative action. Under this programme, wealth was distributed across a cross-section of historically disadvantaged South Africans. In furtherance of the Act, the Codes of Good Practice, 2007, were designed to fulfil the ideals of the programme. Among other things, the Act measures ownership, management control and employment – to ensure that equitable transfer of the above indices is met. Some key themes that identify a sustainable approach to extractive activities can be gleaned from the Act. The next section briefly discusses these themes.

8.4.1 Social and labour plan

Mining companies must present a Social and Labour Plan (SLP) in consultation with local communities.[34] The Plan must indicate how the company will ensure fair and equal treatment of the company's own workers, and also infrastructure development within the community.[35] The plan must be published in English and one other dominant official language generally used in the mine community, within

30 days of approval, on the company's website or websites, local newspaper or newspapers, and other platforms that can be easily accessible by the public.

The MPRDA obliges the Minister to grant mining rights only when mining will not result in environmental pollution or degradation,[36] and when the applicant has provided for a SLP.[37] The SLP requirement does not end at the application stage, it runs throughout the duration of the project. In renewing the mining licence, the Minister can only grant the renewal if the applicant has consistently shown commitment to the SLP.[38] The holder of a mining right must also "submit to the Director-General an annual report detailing the holder's compliance with the SLP."[39] The foundation for a mining right in South Africa is therefore hinged on the mandatory design, commitment to, and execution of a SLP.[40] These provisions are in line with Principles 3, 8, and 28 – which oblige states to gauge their human rights impacts and produce programmes and policies, which will ensure that deleterious activities of businesses are curtailed.

8.4.2 Closure and abandonment

Section 43 of MPRDA places the responsibility for remedial activities on the permit holder. The holder is liable for any environmental and ecological degradation, and pollution. Within 180 days of the closure of mining activities, abandonment or completion of a project, the permit holder must complete and submit a prescribed closing plan including an environmental risk report to the Regional Manager of the area the land in question is situated.[41] The closure plan must include closure objectives such as: elimination of any immediate harm to human health and safety, fitness of the groundwater for current and future domestic and other uses consistent with the agreed current and future land use, surface water must be fit for current and future basic human needs and aquatic ecosystems requirements.[42] Furthermore, the EIA Regulations also mandates a mine to prepare a closure plan and objectives, including measures to rehabilitate the environment affected by the project.[43]

8.4.3 Mineral rights ownership

The question of mineral right ownership has created some tension between communities and the mines. The case of Royal Bafokeng community and Anglo-American Platinum conveys how mining companies undermine traditional governance mechanisms in local communities. Mines must engage with local communities in the most productive way through understanding of the local customary laws. Anglo American Platinum (Amplats) decided to mine in Mapela, Limpopo Province. The mining later resulted in community discord and violence – because the company failed to understand the power dynamics and local governance in a community. Amplats set aside R175 million for settlement claims with the community.[44] The community leader, Kgoshi Langa, was the head of the trust where the money was paid, and he had significant control over other trustees. Chief Langa started living a profligate life: acquiring properties and disposing of country land in favour of the mining operations.[45] Unfortunately, Amplats did not negotiate with the right people – which exacerbated the whole scenario and led to more violent clashes and tensions. The Mapela community was outraged because Amplats refused to negotiate with them directly, and instead negotiated with compromised community leaders, and detail about the settlement was withheld from them.[46] The violence escalated when the community heard that the leader, Kgoshi Langa, had signed the settlement agreement which the whole community had kicked against. A clash of community ideals ensued. Amplats agreed with the traditional leader's position that he was only obliged to consult with his traditional council and not the entire community. Amplats failed to cross the transparency and accountability rubicon.

In another development, Amplats set up a Royal Bafokeng Development Trust to cater for development projects and an educational system.[47] Despite, this, the mining benefitted a few elites and not the entire community. However, it is the community members – workers and miners – which are greatly impacted by the activities of the mines. In October 2015, mineworkers sought permission from the South Gauteng High Court to bring a class action against mining companies in respect of mine workers who have silicosis and tuberculosis due to hazardous work environments.[48] The mineworkers claimed that the management of the mines failed to protect them from excessive levels of dust and the risks of silicosis and tuberculosis.[49] Despite the fact that as early as 1912 South Africa had introduced compensation for silicosis as an occupational disease – getting the mines to implement this directive has proved abortive. The state simply seems to have turned a blind eye to the mine companies' culture of impunity. The mining industry has been immune to liability for injuries sustained by mineworkers due to exposure to silica dust.[50]

8.5 The National Environmental Management Act 107 of 1998 (NEMA)

NEMA regulates South Africa's environmental governance architecture with particular emphasis on environmental decision-making. In line with the polluter pays principle under international environmental law, section 28 enhances the duty of care and remediation efforts by mandating a polluter to prevent and mitigate any pollution from continuing or recurring.[51]

Some regulations have also mandated project proponents to ensure the sustainable development of their projects. The National Environmental Management Act: Regulations Pertaining to the Financial Provision for Prospecting, Exploration, Mining or Production Operations (2015),[52] require project proponents to provide financial costs for remediation and management of environmental impacts of the project. Section 4 of the Proposed Regulation Pertaining to Financial Provisioning for the Rehabilitation and Remediation of Environmental Damage Caused by Reconnaissance, Prospecting, Exploration, Mining or Production Operations (17 May 2019),[53] mandates the permit holder to manage and implement post completion project plans that addresses human rights impact of such projects, with particular reference to the mine closure plan and environmental risk assessment.

8.6 Environmental impact assessment

Environmental Impact Assessment (EIA) process in South Africa typically involves desktop research, a scoping phase, preparation of an EIA report,[54] public participation, and the formulation of an Environmental Management Plan (EMP).[55] The EMP must include information on mitigation measures to be taken to address the environmental impact, identification of persons responsible for the implementation of the mitigation measures, and measures to rehabilitate the environment affected by any environmental impact – among others.[56] The burden of proving environmental mitigation is on the "holder of a prospecting or mining right,"[57] and thus where there has been any form of environmental damage, pollution, or ecological degradation which can be traced to the activities of the mining company – that company will be solely responsible.[58] Remarkably, the MPDRA mandates prospective companies to conduct the impact of their mining activities on cultural resources, as part of the EMP.[59] Furthermore, an approved Environmental Management Programme (EMPr) or EMP is the foundation for prospecting or mining.[60]

The EIA provides for an Environmental Assessment Practitioner (EAP).[61] The Practitioner is obliged to give notice to affected parties of the application for environmental authorisation by a MNCs.[62] This gives room for the local community to discuss the proprietary of allowing such project proponent to work on its land. It is the responsibility of the Practitioner to ensure that the information is made available to interested and affected persons and that participation is done in a way that gives room for stakeholders to comment on the application.[63]

The Practitioner must be an independent practitioner with expertise in conducting impact assessments.[64] Such a Practitioner must be versed in the relevant laws, objectives, and must disclose material information that may influence any decision to be taken.[65] An EIA with strong participation from an affected affluent community in Mossel Bay, South Africa, reveals the impact of community input. An EIA for the Mossel Bay community was suspended because there was an allegation that the EIA was non-compliant with South Africa's environmental regulations, and, most importantly, the EAP was not fully independent.[66] Likewise, after some years of bickering, the national government approved the shale gas development in the Karoo region. There has, however, been fierce criticism and petitioning for the project not to commence.[67] In *Silvermine Valley Coalition v Sybrand Van Der Spuy Boerderye and Others*,[68] the court held that an EIA was designed to ensure that official authorisation is given before any land is put to specific use – with particular reference to extractive activities.

8.7 South African Human Rights Commission (SAHRC)

Section 184 of the Constitution establishes the South African Human Rights Commission (SAHRC) with the mandate to promote respect for human rights and a culture of human rights; promote the protection, development, and attainment of human rights; and monitor and assess the observance of human rights in the Republic. The SAHRC has been proactively engaging businesses on the importance of the UNGPs. The Commission adopted the BHR concept as its strategic focus area for the 2014–2015 period.[69] The aim was to increase its institutional understanding of the ways businesses impact on the enjoyment of human rights – particularly in respect of the impact on children.[70]

On 27 June 2013, the Commission held a conference on "Business and Transparency" which aligns with the Commissions broader mandate in relation to corporate accountability for human rights, as articulated in the UNGPs. Participants noted that the role and responsibility of financial and business institutions in the financial crisis highlighted the need for compliance with human rights obligations such as transparency and accountability. Other critical reflections included the South Africa's arms deal which raises the question of how easily global arms corporations could re-orient the country's priorities. Furthermore, Marikana has not only focused attention on police brutality and on the labour and social conditions of employees, but also opened the critical debate of how the mining industry can break with its past to uphold human rights.

In March 2015, the Danish Institute for Human Rights (DIHR) and SAHRC produced a Business Country Guide which provides country-specific guidance to help companies respect human rights and contribute to development.[71] The Country Guide refers to the several cases the Commission is involved with and further makes recommendations to government and other stakeholders on issues including business, such as setting a minimum wage in sectors such as agriculture; improving monitoring of employment contracts; enforcing environmental obligations.[72] In April 2016, the SAHRC organised a discussion on BHRs with a thematic focus on "access to justice: creating access to effective remedies for victims of business-related human rights violations".[73] The discussion noted the importance of the right of access to justice, especially for the poor. In March 2018, the Commission in collaboration with DIHR released a Business and Human Rights Dialogue Report which builds on the earlier activities of the Commission.[74] The Dialogue focused on key human rights challenges in South African business sectors and sought to enhance public understanding and awareness of the roles and responsibilities of stakeholders in upholding and protecting human rights.[75] The objective of the Dialogue is to create a platform for further engagement and identification of the role of busines in equality and development, corporate accountability and SOEs as well as community engagement and employment equity. These capacity development programmes are geared towards positioning the Commission to fulfil its mandate of protecting human rights and investigate corporate abuses.

A "Shadow" National Baseline Assessment of Current Implementation of Business and Human Rights Frameworks was launched by the Centre for Human Rights, University of Pretoria, in conjunction with the International Corporate Accountability Roundtable (ICAR).[76] The Baseline Assessment found lack of access to judicial remedies for victims of human rights abuse. Other findings include land reform as a controversial issue due to South Africa's historically discriminatory and turbulent dispensation of land, lack of human rights due diligence requirements and impact assessments in business conducts.[77] The South African government has not committed to developing a NAP.

8.8 Conclusion

The legal and institutional provisions discussed in this chapter addresses the negative consequences of ineffective and inadequate requirements for extractive activities at the same time focuses on environmental management through the introduction of stricter requirements and sound principles for the extractive industry. The regulatory environment in which businesses operate must be constantly monitored and supervised to ensure compliance with human rights standards.

Corporate disregard for human rights standards and states' reluctance to enforce its laws leads to social tension, poverty, and corruption. Therefore, States must establish an autonomous and independent monitoring department – with the authority to ascertain and implement best corporate practices in the extractive industry. Where there is failure on the part of any company to respect human rights, appropriate sanctions should apply. An inability to present institutional checks or audit accounts of state-owned enterprises leads to rent-seeking conduct. Beyond good policies at national and industry levels, making extractive resources work for development will also require building constructive partnerships between MNCs and host communities based on trust, mutual interests, and a common understanding of the challenges and opportunities. Harnessing the dividends of extractive resources within an accountable, human rights-friendly regulatory framework, will contribute significantly to local community development.

Notes

1 (2011) 3 SA 347.
2 Ibid.
3 Ibid.
4 Case No. 16703/14 (8 July 2015) <https://cisp.cachefly.net/assets/articles/attachments/55805_university_of_stellenbosch_99.pdf> accessed 25 August 2021. The case went on appeal to the Constitutional Court where the highest Court did not refer to the UNGPs. See *University of Stellenbosch Legal Aid Clinic and Others v Minister of Justice and Correctional Services and Others* [2016] ZACC 32.
5 Ibid.
6 Ibid.
7 Para 71.
8 Para 75.
9 See *University of Stellenbosch Legal Aid Clinic and Others v Minister of Justice and Correctional Services and Others* [2016] ZACC 32.
10 Section 25 of the Constitution.
11 Section 36 of the Constitution.
12 [2003] ZACC 18.
13 [2000] ZACC 19.
14 [2004] ZACC 7.
15 Ibid. para 23.
16 H. Mostert, & A. Pope (eds.), *The Principles of the Law of Property in South Africa* (2010) 15–16.
17 Section 7 (a).
18 *Bongani Nkala & 68 ors v. Harmony Gold Mining Company & 31 ors*, Consolidated Case Number: 48226/12.

19 See IOD, South Africa, "King Report on Corporate Governance in SA" <www.iodsa.co.za/page/kingIII> accessed 23 June 2021.

20 Ibid.

21 Some South African mine companies have, however, incorporated human rights standards in their spheres of operations. For example, Gold Fields has a human rights policy anchored on the UNGPs, and it has adopted several international human rights instruments such as the International Council on Mining and Metals, The Global Compact, and EITI. See further Gold Fields, "Human Rights" <www.goldfields.com/human-rights.php> accessed 18 June 2021. Sibanye-Stillwater has also adopted human rights standards and norms contained in the UNGPs, Global Compact, UDHR, and Voluntary Principles on Security and Human Rights. See further Sibanye-Stillwater, "Human Rights Policy" <https://thevault.exchange/?get_group_doc=245/1623770079-ssw-human-rights-policy-june-2021.pdf> accessed 18 June 2021.

22 See further Tracy-Lynn Humby, "Environmental Justice and Human Rights on the Mining Wastelands of the Witwatersrand Gold Fields" (2013) 43 *Revue Générale de droit* 67–112.

23 Some of the relevant laws that have human rights implications for extractive governance include: The Basic Conditions of Employment Act (right to fair labor practices as provided for in Section 23(1) of the Constitution, it also regulates basic working conditions such as hours of work, leave, remuneration, termination of employment); The Employment Equity Act (prohibits unfair discrimination, embodies South Africa's affirmative action policy); The Labour Relations Act (gives effect to Section 27 of the South Africa Constitution, it regulates trade union activities and guarantees freedom of association, right to strike and ADR; and collective bargaining); The Occupational Health and Safety Act (provides for the health and safety of persons at work); National Environmental Management Act, 1998 (regulates EIA); The Communal Land Rights Act (transfers communal lands to communities and regulates the democratic administration of communal lands by communities); The Expropriation Act (expropriation of land and other property for public use).

24 Section 2 (e) of MPRDA. See also section 24 of the Constitution.

25 Section 2 (i) of MPRDA.

26 Section 3 (1) of MPRDA.

27 Section 12(1) of MPRDA.

28 Section 13(3)(a) of MPRDA.

29 Section 38, 39 (1) of MPRDA.

30 Ibid.

31 N. Peacock, & H. Ambrose, "South Africa Terminates Its Bilateral Investment Treaty with Spain: Second BIT Terminated as Part of South Africa's Planned Review of Its Investment Treaties" *Lexology* (21 August 2013) <www.lexology.com/library/detail.aspx?g=daf93855-71f9-425e-92d3-5368d104f8ff> accessed 5 May 2021. See further South Africa, "Bilateral Investment Treaty Policy Framework Review" (June 2009) 5 <www.gov.za/sites/default/files/gcis_document/201409/32386961.pdf> accessed 5 May 2021.

32 Ibid.

33 See also section 4 of the Protection of Investment Act, No. 22 (2015) which affirms the Bill of Rights as applicable in the South African Constitution.

34 See section 25 of the MPRDA.

35 Ibid.

36 Section 23 (1) (d) of the MPRDA.

37 Section 23 (1) (e) of the Act.

38 Sections 24 (3) (c), 25 (2) (f), 85 of the Act.

39 Section 28 (2) (c).

40 section 84 (1) (g); Item 5 (2) (f).

41 Section 43 (4) of MPRDA.
42 Ibid.
43 See Appendix 5. South Africa, "NEMA: Environmental Impact Assessment Regulations" (2014) <www.environment.gov.za/sites/default/files/legislations/nema_eia-2014regulations_g38282_0.pdf> accessed 23 July 2021.
44 Tamara Jewett, "Mining, Land and Community in Communal Areas III: Community Governance" (11 August 2016) <https://hsf.org.za/publications/hsf-briefs/mining-land-and-community-in-communal-areas-iii-community-governance> accessed 11 May 2021.
45 Lucky Biyase, "Anger Mounts against Bafokeng King" *Business Day* (16 June 2013) <www.businesslive.co.za/bd/companies/land-and-agriculture/2013-06-16-anger-mounts-against-bafokeng-king/> accessed 11 May 2021.
46 Ibid.
47 Sobantu Mzwakali, "Rural Community's Attempt for Redress Sidelined by Leadership" (13 May 2016) <www.larc.uct.ac.za/news/rural-community's-attempt-redress-side-lined-leadership> accessed 23 July 2021.
48 See the *Bongani Nkala & 68 ors*' case. See further, Alide Dasnois, "The Long Battle to Get the Mines to Cough Up" (3 September 2015) <www.groundup.org.za/media/features/silicosis/silicosis_0022.html> accessed 22 July 2021.
49 Ibid.
50 Ibid.
51 See also *Hichange Investments (Pty) Ltd v. Cape Produce Co (Pty) Ltd t/a Pelts Products* [2004] 2 SA 393 (E), where the court found that there had been a significant pollution of the environment as contemplated by NEMA. Consequently, the polluter (first respondent) who had failed to minimise the significant pollution it was causing or to prevent such pollution from occurring, continuing, or recurring, was in clear breach of NEMA.
52 South Africa, "NEMA: Regulations Pertaining to the Financial Provision for Prospecting, Exploration, Mining or Production Operations" (2015) <www.gov.za/sites/default/files/gcis_document/201511/39425rg10526gon1147.pdf> accessed 22 May 2021.
53 South Africa, "NEMA: Proposed Regulation Pertaining to Financial Provisioning for the Rehabilitation and Remediation of Environmental Damage Caused by Reconnaissance, Prospecting, Exploration, Mining or Production Operations" (17 May 2019) <www.environment.gov.za/sites/default/files/gazetted_notices/nema107of1998_proposedregulations_financialprovision.pdf> accessed 22 May 2021.
54 An assessment report must contain a detailed description of the proposed activity and the environment that may be impacted by the activity, the need for and importance of the activity, a description and comparative analysis of identified possible alternatives to the activity, and a statement on how an environmental impact is defined. See generally Regulations 19–21, 23 of EIAR (2014). In Nigeria, the EIA process requires companies to undergo an environmental assessment of their activities before commencement, and this does not include a detailed procedure. However, a process for mitigation must be indicated in the report. See sections 3(1), 16 and 17 of the Nigerian EIA Act.
55 Section 39 of MPRDA. An EMP allows the mines to show how they intend to prevent or mitigate the adverse effects of their activities on the environment. See further Environmental Impact Assessment Regulations (2014) [EIAR]; Section 39 of the MPRDA. See also SADC Environmental Legislation Handbook (2012) 331.
56 Regulation 19.
57 See section 38(1)(e) of the MPRDA.
58 Ibid. see further section 38(2) [stipulating culpability of directors of the company]; 21 (1)(b) [noting report on compliance with the approved EMP].
59 Regulations 1, 2 (h) (iv).
60 Regulation 19.

61 Regulations 1, 7 of EIAR. ["The Practitioner"]. See also sections 1 and 24H of the National Environmental Management Act (1998).
62 Ibid. This can be done through placing advertisements in newspapers, an official gazette, or a notice at a conspicuous place.
63 See generally Regulations 39–44.
64 Regulation 13.
65 Ibid.
66 See Southcapenet, "EIA for Proposed Mossel Bay LNG Terminal Suspended after Objections" (26 November 2013) <http://thegremlin.co.za/mossel-bay-news/wordpress/2013/11/26/eia-for-proposed-mossel-bay-lng-terminal-suspended-after-objections/> accessed 5 May 2021.
67 Jenna Etheridge, "Government Gives Green Light for Shale Gas Fracking in Karoo" *News24* (30 March 2017) <www.news24.com/news24/SouthAfrica/News/govt-gives-green-light-for-shale-gas-fracking-in-karoo-20170330> accessed 5 May 2021.
68 2002 (1) SA 478 (C).
69 SAHRC, "Annual Report 2015/16" <www.sahrc.org.za/home/21/files/SAHRC%20Annual%20Report%202016%20full%20report%20low%20res%20for%20web.pdf>.
70 Ibid.
71 SAHRC, "Human Rights and Business Country Guide" <Human Rights and Business Country Guide South Africa>.
72 Ibid.
73 SAHRC, "Business and Human Rights: Access to Fairplay for Those Affected by Business-Related Human Rights Violations Is Possible Via SA's Constitution." <www.sahrc.org.za/index.php/sahrc-media/opinion-pieces/item/372-business-and-human-rights-access-to-fairplay-for-those-affected-by-business-related-human-rights-violations-is-possible-via-sa-s-constitution>.
74 SAHRC, "Business and Human Rights Dialogue Report" <www.sahrc.org.za/home/21/files/Business%20and%20Human%20Rights%20Dialogue%20Report.pdf>.
75 Ibid.
76 "Shadow National Baseline Assessment of Current Implementation of Business and Human Rights Frameworks" (April 2016) <www.chr.up.ac.za/images/centrenews/2016/files/Shadow-SA-NBA-Final.pdf>.
77 Ibid.

9 Policy and legal framework in Kenya

9.1 Introduction

Kenya's mineral deposits makes it an attractive destination country for foreign direct investment.[1] However, human rights concerns associated with resource exploitation have been widespread.[2] On the one hand, the history of the social and ecological structures currently contributes to a thriving environment for the exploitation of natural resources and the chance for economic development,[3] while, on the other, human rights abuse has led to the impoverishment and marginalization of rural communities,[4] an ineffective environmental preservation strategies,[5] systemic gender discrimination,[6] labour fairness concerns,[7] and degradation of the environment.[8] This chapter examines the legal and institutional framework regulating business and human rights regime in Kenya's energy and extractive sector. It also discusses Kenya's approach to developing a National Action Plan on Business and Human Rights. In doing so, it considers whether Kenya's legal framework has a strong normative foundation establishing both vertical and horizontal human rights obligations, and a clear legal mechanism for redress in the event of violation of those rights. In offering a paradigm shift in the discourse of the dynamics of business, law, and human rights from a regional perspective, this chapter focusses on the regulatory capacity, institutional efficacy, and democratic legitimacy of governance institutions that shape development projects in Kenya.

9.2 Constitution of Kenya (2010)

Kenya's Constitution offers a paradigm shift from the traditional vertical application of the Constitution to the horizontal application of the Bill of Rights to juristic persons. It mandates business respect for human rights.[9] Thus, victims of corporate induced human rights violations can constitutionally challenge corporate activities that encroach on their fundamental rights. In *Ngugi v Nairobi Hospital and 2 ors*,[10] the Court held that "person" includes a corporate entity and business entities must comply with the Constitution, including observing human rights standards. In *Mambo and 2 Others v Limuru Country Club and ors*,[11] the court stated that: "it cannot be safe, in a progressive democratic society, to arrive at a finding that allows

DOI: 10.4324/9781003290124-13

private entities to hide behind the cloak of "privacy" to escape constitutional accountability."[12]

A serious human rights concern in Kenya's extractive activities has been access to property and land. The constitution protects the right, either individually or in association with others, to acquire and own property of any description and in any part of Kenya.[13] According to Pilon, "the right to property is the foundation of every right including the right to be free."[14] By recognizing the right to property, the Constitution provides a framework for the recognition and protection of community property and other human rights.[15] Although this is not an absolute right,[16] adequate compensation must be paid for and land displacement, relocation or deprivation of land. Additionally, the Land Act emphasizes inclusivity of communities where decision making relating land is concerned.[17] The Constitution also guarantees every person the right to a clean and healthy environment which includes the right to have the environment protected for the benefit of present and future generations through legislative and other measures.[18]

Article 2(5) of the Constitution recognizes that general rules of international law form part of the laws of Kenya. Although the UNGPs are normative instruments of international law, Kenyan courts have held that normative instruments, such as UNGPs, Resolutions, UN Guidelines, Declarations, are intended or designed to further bolster socio-economic and fundamental human rights as provided under the Constitution and the International Bill of Rights.[19]

9.3 Companies Act (2015)

While the Constitution mandates business respect for human rights, the Companies Act does not make any reference to the Constitution or obliges businesses to comply with human rights in their spheres of operations.

The Act introduces the concept of enlightened shareholder value approach which implies the prospect that the directors can consider the interests of a wider spectrum of stakeholders in their decision-making. In section 655 of the Act, directors are required to prepare a business review report which is a balanced and comprehensive analysis of the development and performance of the business of the company during the company's financial year; and the position of the company at the end of that year, consistent with size and complexity of the business.[20] For quoted companies, the review must include information about environmental matters (including the impact of the business of the company on the environment), the employees of the company, and social and community issues, including information on any policies of the company in relation to those matters and the effectiveness of those policies.[21] Though the enlightened shareholder model encourages the inclusion of other stakeholders, the requirement is largely voluntary and the text uninspiringly passive without clear guidelines even to the corporations that may be disposed to apply them.

A business review report enables a company to track its performance especially in measures that ensure they respect human rights. It shows that directors have complied with their obligations which require them to make decisions on behalf of the company.[22] Failure to prepare reports may lead to the director's disqualification, under a derivation action by a member of the company.[23]

9.4 The Petroleum Act (2019)

The Act governs the negotiation and conclusion of petroleum agreements and the exploitation production and transportation of petroleum. The Act guarantees the sustainable development of petroleum in several ways. First, petroleum agreements must be subject to public participation in the ratification process before approval. This ensures that Kenyans can actively determine whether such agreements will contribute the social-economic development of the country.[24] Second, the Act mandates local content requirements.[25] Not only must qualified and skilled Kenyans be employed at all levels of the value chain in the upstream petroleum sector, but priority must also be given to services provided and goods manufactured in Kenya. Project proponents must submit local content plans to the Energy and Petroleum Regulatory Authority (EPRA) before commencing any petroleum operations. However, the Act does not provide monitoring and implementation mechanisms to ensure project proponents are actively complying with local content requirements. Third, the Act guarantees transparency and accountability in project design, planning, and implementation.[26] The Cabinet Secretary must develop a framework for reporting, transparency, and accountability in the upstream petroleum sector. Such reporting must include the publication of all "petroleum agreements, records, annual accounts and reports of revenues, fees, taxes, royalties and any other relevant data and information."[27] The public access to these critical information safeguards a rights base approach to extractive governance. Local community tensions are triggered when access to information is restricted by the state or project proponents.

9.5 Mining Act (2016)

The Act applies to construction and industrial minerals, precious stones, precious, semi-precious, base, and rare metal groups, fuel mineral, and gaseous minerals.[28] The mineral resources belong to the people but held in trust by the state.[29] In applying for mineral rights, the project proponent must demonstrate that it meets the prerequisite technical capacity, expertise, experience, and financial capacity.[30] However, the same threshold is not required of artisanal miners.[31]

The Director of Mines is mandated to ensure access to information by the public, subject to any confidentiality restrictions.[32] Additionally, the Act establishes a Mineral Rights Board which requires mineral rights applicants to seek the approval of the appropriate Cabinet Secretary or other authority, where the area in respect of which a mineral right is sought is dedicated or set apart as a place of burial, religious significance, as a public building, or for any other public purpose.[33] Laudably, the Act forbids issuance of prospecting and mining rights with respect to private land without the express consent of the registered owner, which consent must not be unreasonably withheld.[34] Such consent can be deemed to have been issued if the registered owner enters into a legally binding arrangement with the applicant for the prospecting and mining rights or with the Government, which allows for the conduct of prospecting or mining operations; or an agreement with the applicant for the prospecting and mining rights concerning the payment of adequate compensation.[35] On the other hand, for community land, issuance of prospecting or mining rights is forbidden without the prior consent of the authority obligated by the law relating to administration and management of community land to administer community land; or the National Land Commission in the case of unregistered community land.[36] In the event consent in either private or community land is unreasonably withheld, the Cabinet Secretary has been empowered to take steps under the law relating to compulsory acquisition of land or rights or interests in land and vest the land in question in the Government or on behalf of the Government.[37]

Before granting a mineral right, the Mineral Rights Board must satisfy itself that the applicant will protect the environment, develop the community, and ensure the health and safety of persons undertaking the operations.[38] Additionally, as a local content requirement, the holder of a mineral right must give preference in employment to members of the community and citizens of Kenya.[39] As a positive step, the Act requires holders of a reconnaissance licence,[40] to compensate users of land for damage to land and property resulting from reconnaissance operations in the licence area.[41] Furthermore, the Act requires the holder of a mining license to sign a community development agreement (CDA) with the community where the mining operations are to be carried out.[42] CDA facilitates socio-economic development of the country.

9.5.1 *Environmental rehabilitation and restoration plan*

Before the grant of a prospecting licence,[43] applicants must satisfy the Cabinet Secretary that they have submitted an environmental rehabilitation and restoration plan.[44] Project proponents must comply with the environmental rehabilitation and restoration plan.[45] Likewise, the Cabinet Secretary can only grant a retention licence,[46] if the applicant has obtained an environmental and social impact assessment licence and an environmental management plan which relates to the operations to be carried out under the retention licence where required under the Environment Management and Coordination Act.[47] The same is required of an applicant of a mining licence.[48] Failure to comply with these requirements may lead to a revocation of a mineral right.

Mineral agreements must include environmental obligations and liabilities of project proponents, subject to the requirement of the Environment Management and Co-ordination Act and community development plans.[49] Such agreements must be made accessible to the public,[50] and must align with human rights obligations of the Constitution and Mining Act.[51]

9.6 Business and human rights challenges in Kenya

Kenya's development projects have often been met with stiff resistance from the local communities. For example, there were allegations that the Standard Gauge Railway contract (SGR) enabled several improprieties, such as price variations, retendering and several other practices.[52] Despite promising to make the SGR contract publicly available, the Kenyan president failed to do so.[53] Likewise, the Production Sharing Contract (PSC) between Kenyan government and Tullow oil was not released for the public to assess resulting in widespread suspicion and mistrust between the community and the company. This eventually led to interruption of the early oil pilot scheme because of local community protests on security, infrastructure and revenue sharing formula.[54] Eventually the early oil pilot scheme project resumed and limped on until Kenya exported its first oil export to China in 2019.[55]

The Lake Turkana project,[56] has clear potentials to generate economic benefits, including low-cost power, stimulus to local businesses due to rehabilitated road networks, increased tax income, employment opportunities, tourism, and improved communication.[57] The project exacerbated conflicts and caused adverse social and economic impact including job redundancy, lack of FPIC and local community participation.

Despite the challenges of a business approach to integrating human rights standards, the Kenyan courts have been an avenue to progressively realize business respect for human rights. In *Save Lamu & 5 others v National Environmental Management Authority (NEMA) & another*,[58] Save Lamu, a community-based organization representing the Lamu community, challenged the grant of a license for the construction of Lamu Coal-fired Power Plant,[59] as well as the process in obtaining the Environmental Impact Assessment (EIA) license by the energy company contracted by the Kenyan government to develop a coal power generation project. It was the contention of the appellants that the project lacked proper public participation in the preparation of the Economic and Social Impact Assessment (ESIA) report, and a flawed EIA report which was plagued by misrepresentations, inconsistencies, and omissions was drafted. Other contentions were that the project will have adverse effects on the marine environment through the discharge of thermal effluent into the marine environment by using poor and outdated cooling system. The lack of sound mitigation measures also compounded the unviability of the project.[60] The Tribunal subsequently cancelled the license issued to Amu Power by NEMA and ordered Amu Power to conduct a fresh ESIA report before commencement of the project. Additionally, NEMA was required to comply with the relevant regulations by engaging with the lead agencies and the public in determining the report. The Tribunal emphasized on the need for public participation in the preparation as this will create access to information for the community affected, through meaningful and effective participation.[61] The impact of this decision affected funding of the project as some financiers started withdrawing their funding to the project due to its environmental and social risks. Similarly, in *KM & 9 others v Attorney General & 7 others*[62] the petitioners are residents of Owino-Uhuru community. They allege that the seventh Respondent set up a lead acid battery recycling factory in a neighbouring plot which produced toxic waste. The waste seeped into the village and caused petitioners' serious illness and diseases as a direct consequence of lead poisoning.[63] The Court found that the petitioners are entitled to compensation in monetary and non-monetary reliefs and granted them declarative relief to a clean and healthy environment; highest attainable standard of health and right to clean and safe water guaranteed by Article 43 of the Constitution, and a Declaration on the right to life as guaranteed by the provisions of Article 26 of the Constitution. However, the state has appealed the decision, contending that the apportionment of liability to state agencies is contrary to the "polluter pays" principle.[64] The case is yet to be determined. In *Kenneth Gona Karisa v. Top Steel Kenya Limited*,[65] the Petitioner accused the corporate Respondent that its activities have led to serious human rights abuses in violation of the UNGPs.[66]

Extractive investment benefits have not adequately favoured women in particular. Women suffer greater harm, often being employed for poor wages, coerced into signing consent forms that displace them from their land.[67] Gender discrimination can occasionally coincide with cultural gender discrimination. Hence, several women working in Magarini as the salt mines were expanded were forced out of their homes as local customs dictated that women do not own land. Consequently, any benefits or compensation was given to the male members of their household.[68] There are also health risks to the sexual and reproductive health rights of women as the labour associated with salt harvesting with no protective gear has meant that there will be an increase in adverse health conditions.[69] In energy projects, such as the solar power projects in Homa Bay and Kitui, the negative impact on women was evident because the project did not consider gender needs. Consequently, electricity investments will be poorly suited to meet household needs as those needs are often centred around women's participation in household activities and energy usage.[70] Considering that most Kenyan households rely on traditional biomass fuels with the attendant effects of air pollution, environmental degradation, Kenya should aim towards providing modern energy services to households to relieve the strain on women. Furthermore, to be placed in an enviable position, Kenya must develop gender equality policy tools for utilization in the extractive and energy sectors. The objective will be to reduce and ultimately close the gender gap in these sectors.

9.7 National Action Plan (NAP) on business and human rights

To show its commitment to business and human rights, Kenya is one of two countries that have developed a National Action Plan on Business and Human Rights.[71]

In 2016, the Kenyan Attorney General initiated the process of developing a NAP which was officially published on 24 July 2019. In April 2021, the NAP was approved by the Cabinet, to be reviewed after five years. Kenya thus became the first African country to publish a NAP. The NAP is aligned with Kenya's Vision 2030 and government's commitment to achieving the Sustainable Development Goals (SDGs).

The Kenya NAP acts as a guiding tool for all actors in the respect for human rights, rather than creation of new obligations.[72] The strategic objectives of the NAP are to enhance existing policy, legal, regulatory, and administrative framework for ensuring respect of human rights by businesses through legal review and development of specific guidance for business; to enhance understanding of the obligation of business to respect human rights; to enhance access to justice for victims of business-related human rights abuses; and to establish a NAP implementation and monitoring mechanism that will also act as a platform on dialogue on business and human rights issues in the country.[73] The NAP focusses on five thematic areas such as land and natural resources,[74] environmental protection,[75] labour rights,[76] revenue transparency,[77] and access to remedy.[78] It also identifies the following concerns related to business and human rights:

a Sexual harassment is widespread and underreported, with women being the majority of victims. Fear of job loss is a major factor in the reluctance to report. Furthermore, there is low enforcement of the Sexual Offences Act, 2006;
b Lack of access to maternity and paternity leave. While the law provides and protects both maternity and paternity leave, not all workers in the private sector are able to access this benefit for fear of job loss. Once again, enforcement of the law in this respect remains weak;
c Low level of awareness on labour rights among workers (mostly women in low income or low skilled jobs) and employers;
d Lack of effective regulation of recruitment agencies for migrant workers;
e Lack of publicly available statistics disaggregated by sex and other vulnerabilities that could be useful in addressing sex and other forms of discrimination in the workplace; and
f Lack of effective remedies for victims of labour-related grievances resulting in high prevalence of unresolved labour-related grievances. A weak enforcement mechanism, in particular inadequate number of state labour inspectors and the lack of effective operational level grievance mechanisms were cited as contributing factors.

9.8 Conclusion

This chapter has examined the constitutional provisions, legal and institutional framework for developing Kenya's extractive industries in line with human rights standards. A human rights-based approach is fundamental to corporate investments in Kenya. This is evident from its constitutional mandates, strong normative foundation establishing both vertical and horizontal human rights obligations, and a clear legal mechanism for redress in the event of violation of those rights. However, development projects such as the Lake Turkana Wind Power project has been complicated by varied political interest, which has stifled comprehensive and positive approach to development agenda. Accordingly, Kenya needs to proactively implement its laws in a way that assuages the feelings and behaviour of vulnerable members of the public, whether slum dwellers, farmers, indigenous communities, or the general populace, and evident manifestation of reduction in inequality, poverty and marginalization is obvious.

Local communities must be adequately informed of any development projects and FPIC guaranteed as a means to give the community an opportunity to contribute to the management of their land. While Kenyan laws pursue sustainable business practices, it appears there are remarkable lack of enforcement. Without consultation and public participation, local communities will struggle to accept any developmental project that could heighten their socio-economic development benefits and rights. Participation does not end at the point of consent; it is an ongoing process.

Notes

1 Kenya, "Mining and Minerals Policy" (2016) 5 <www.idlo.int/sites/default/files/pdfs/highlights/Kenya%20Mining%20Policy%20Popular%20Version-LowRes.pdf> accessed 15 May 2021.
2 IHRB, "Human Rights in Kenya's Extractive Sector" (December 2016) <www.ihrb.org/uploads/reports/IHRB%2C_Human_Rights_in_Kenyas_Extractive_Sector_-_Exploring_the_Terrain%2C_Dec_2016.pdf> accessed 15 May 2021.
3 Kenya (n 1) 5.
4 MRGI, Kenya, Minorities, Indigenous Peoples and Ethnic Diversity (2005) 15.
5 UNDP, Strategic Environmental Assessment for the Mining Sector in Kenya, Reference No: RFP/UNDPKEN/009/2016, 25–26.
6 The Equal Rights Trust/KHRC, "In the Spirit of Harambee: Addressing Discrimination and Inequality in Kenya" (2012).
7 USDOS, "Kenya 2018 Human Rights Report" 48.
8 UNDP (n 5).
9 See articles 20 and 260 of the Constitution. Article 260 defines a person to include a company, association, or other body of persons whether incorporated or unincorporated.
10 [2013] eKLR.
11 [2014] eKLR.
12 Ibid.
13 Ibid. see article 40(1) of the Constitution.
14 R. Pilon, "Property Rights and the Constitution" in Cato Institute (ed.) *Cato Handbook for Policymakers* (2017) 173.
15 Kanyinke Sena, "Indigenous Peoples and Access to Remedies in the Context of the LAPSSET Corridor, Kenya" in C. Doyle (ed.) *Business and Human Rights: Indigenous Peoples' Experiences with Access to Remedy* (2015) 233.
16 Article 40 of the Constitution.
17 Section 4 of the Land Act (2012).
18 Article 42 of the Constitution.
19 See for example *Mitubel Welfare Society v Kenya Airports Authority & 2 others*, SC Petition No. 3 of 2018, see also *Mitu-Bell Welfare Society v Kenya Airports Authority & 2 others; Initiative for Strategic Litigation in Africa (Amicus Curiae)* [2021] eKLR; *Kepha Omondi Onjuro & Others v. Attorney General & 5 Others Nairobi* HCC Petition No. 239 of 2014; *Satrose Ayuma & 11 Others v. The Registered Trustees of the Kenya Railways Staff Retirement Pension Scheme & 2 Others Nairobi* HC Petition No. 65 of 2010 where the Courts relied on the UN Guidelines on Evictions.
20 Section 655(3).
21 Section 655(4).
22 David Hess, "The Transparency Trap: Non-Financial Disclosure and the Responsibility of Business to Respect Human Rights" (2019) 56(1) *American Business Law Journal* 5–53.
23 Section 238.

24 Section 31 of the Act.
25 Sections 19–24 of the Act. Section 206 of the Energy Act (2019) also obliges the project proponent to prepare and submit an annual and long-term local content plan.
26 See section 119 of the Act.
27 Ibid.
28 See the First Schedule to the Act.
29 Section 6(1) of the Mining Act. In addition to the Mining Act, the mining sector is governed by several regulations, such as the Mining (Licence and Permit) Regulations, the Mining (Use of Assets) Regulations, the Mining Act (Dealings in Minerals) Regulations, the Mining Act (Work Programmes and Exploration Reports) Guidelines, the Mining Act (State Participation) Regulations, the Mining Act (Use of local Goods and Services) Regulations, the Mining Act (Employment and Training) Regulations and the Mining Act (Use of Local Goods and Services) Regulations. In addition, the Guidelines for Work Programmes and Exploration Reports were prepared for additional support to the governance framework. The institutional framework governing mining is robust and includes the Ministry of Mining, Directorate of Mines, Directorate of Mineral Management and Regulations, Directorate of Geological Surveys, Directorate of Mineral Promotion and Value Addition, Directorate of Mine Health, Safety and Environment, Directorate of Resource Surveys and Remote Sensing, Directorate of Corporate Affairs, Geo-data Centre and Minerals Certification Laboratory, National Mining Corporation, Mineral Audit Agency, Mineral Rights Board, Ministry of Energy, County Governments (KCM), Association of Artisanal and Small-Scale Miners (ASSM), National Land Commission and the Kenya Chamber of Mines.
30 See section 11(3).
31 Section 4 defines artisanal mining to include traditional and customary mining operations using traditional or customary ways and means.
32 Section 20.
33 Section 36(2)(c).
34 Section 37(1).
35 Section 37(2).
36 Section 38.
37 Section 40(1).
38 Section 42(1).
39 Section 47(1).
40 Reconnaissance license is given to project proponents who conduct a non-intrusive search for mineral resources by geophysical surveys, geochemical surveys, photo geological surveys or other remote sensing techniques, but excludes drilling and excavations. See further section 4.
41 Section 67(1)(g).
42 Section 109 (i).
43 Section 4.
44 Section 72(3)(c).
45 Section 77(1)(d).
46 Section 85 defines A retention licence is granted where the permit holder discovered mineral deposit of commercial significance, but the minerals cannot be developed immediately due to due to temporary adverse market conditions, economic factors, technical constraints, or other factors. See section 85.
47 Section 86(3)(c).
48 Section 103(c).
49 Section 117(2).
50 Section 119.
51 Section 121.
52 Moses Michira, "How Kenyans May Have Lost Sh29b in SGR Tender" *The Standard* (20 January 2020) <www.standardmedia.co.ke/business/business/article/2001357139/how-kenyans-may-have-lost-sh29b-in-sgr-tender> accessed 17 February 2021.

53 Nahashon Musungu, "Forget It: State House Makes U-Turn in Releasing SGR Contract" *Nairobi News* (29 April 2019) <https://nairobinews.nation.co.ke/news/forget-it-state-house-makes-u-turn-on-releasing-sgr-contract> accessed 5 February 2021.
54 Ibid.
55 Edwin Okoth, "Kenya Sells Its First Oil to China" *Business Daily* (16 August 2019) <www.businessdailyafrica.com/news/China-gains-upper-hand-with-deal/539546-5237392-7c6jrnz/index.html> accessed 18 January 2021.
56 See further chapter 2.3 (c).
57 See "Lake Turkana Wind Power Project, Kenya" (November 2011) <www.eib.org/attachments/registers/53222536.pdf> accessed 29 January 2021.
58 [2019] eKLR.
59 Ibid.
60 Ibid.
61 Ibid.
62 [2020] eKLR, 178.
63 Ibid.
64 Joackim Bwana, "State Appeals Sh1.3b Award for Lead Victims" *The Star* (8 August 2020).
65 Petition No 3 of 2018. (Employment and Labour Relations Court of Mombasa).
66 Ibid. Para 11.
67 GAGGA, "Impacts of Extractives on Land, Environment and Women's Rights in East Africa" (June 2018) 10–11.
68 Ibid.
69 Ibid.
70 T. Winther, et al., "Solar Powered Electricity Access: Implications for Women's Empowerment in Rural Kenya" (2018) 44 *Energy Research and Social Science* 61–74.
71 Uganda published its National Action Plan on Business and Human Rights in August 2021. See further Oyeniyi Abe, "A Study on the State of Business and Human Rights in Africa and Potentials for Adopting the African Union Draft Policy Framework on Business and Human Rights" AU/PAPs-FES Commissioned Study on Business and Human Rights in Africa (Forthcoming 2021).
72 Kenya, "National Action Plan on Business and Human Rights" <http://nap.knchr.org/Portals/0/2019%20FINAL%20BHR%20NAP%20JUNE%20PDF.pdf> accessed 18 August 2021.
73 Ibid.
74 The challenges identified in the NAP relating to land and natural resources rights and business are: lack of a predictable compensation and resettlement framework for the voluntary and compulsory acquisition of land; lack of guidance on community consultation in the context of natural resources governance, resulting in inadequate participation of local communities in decision making; and adjudication has not been undertaken in some areas where businesses are operating or propose to operate, complicating decisions on who are the rightful parties to be consulted and compensated; The Mining Act has not been fully operationalized with regards to the sharing of revenues, effectively denying local communities impacted by the operations of mining companies the rights and protections under the law; Cultural and historical barriers to access to land by women, minorities and marginalized groups such as indigenous persons. These barriers limit these groups' participation in and decision-making power over land-related issues, and Lack of sustainable benefits for host communities from the exploitation of natural resources despite the constitutional imperative for equitable sharing of benefits.
75 The NAP identifies the following two concerns related to the impacts of businesses on the environment: First, environmental pollution by business operations, including through discharge of effluent into waterways, air and noise pollution and poor disposal of solid waste, toxic and hazardous substances. These negative impacts compromise the

rights to; a clean and healthy environment, health, reasonable standards of sanitation, clean and safe water; and second, loss of biodiversity due to destruction and encroachment on the natural environment for commercial purposes which negatively impacts livelihoods, health, and the access to clean and safe water for present and future generations.

76 While the constitution guarantees the right to fair labour practices, including right to fair remuneration, reasonable working conditions and the right to join and participate in the activities of a trade union, the NAP identifies several concerns including sexual harassment, lack of access to maternity and paternity leave, low level of awareness on their workers' rights, ineffective regulation of recruitment agencies for migrant workers, and ineffective remedies for victims of labour-related grievances.[780]

77 Tax revenue is the most important, reliable, and sustainable means of resourcing initiatives that contribute to the realization of human rights such as health and education. However, tax justice and the regulation of financial behaviour of companies can no longer be treated in isolation from the corporate responsibility to respect human rights. Thus, Kenya faces challenges in relation to proper and effective mobilization and utilization of the tax revenues. These challenges include: corruption during collection and management of taxes especially in the business licensing and public procurement processes; non-disclosure of contracts, especially those that have significant economic consequences; lack of transparency in the administration and management of revenues collected from exploited natural resources; and Lack of legal beneficial ownership disclosure aids the veil of secrecy in determining who owns and controls business entities, inhibiting law enforcement ability to "follow the money." See further pages 13 to 14 of the NAP.

78 The NAP identifies the following challenges on access to remedies: lack of specialized courts in remote areas, low prosecution rate for violator of human rights regulations, high cost of litigation, hostility in form of death threats from human rights violators, and limited capacity of the administrative tribunals to offer non-judicial remedies. See further page 3 of the NAP.

10 The future of business and human rights in Africa

10.1 Introduction

A rights-based approach to extractive resource governance provides a just and ethical path towards developing social expectations that corporations ought to make a proactive contribution to solving grave communal problems associated with their activities.[1] Integrating human rights into business as a moral imperative, local community participation, consultation, and awareness – through citizenship education – will contribute to the implementation of human rights standards in Africa. However, certain steps must be implemented. First, irrespective of the nomenclature given a set of norms, their intention and objective are fundamental to their application. Therefore, implementation of the UNGPs is critical to ensure sustainable development of Africa's resources. Second, critically important is determining how to adopt, mainstream and integrate the UNGPs into extant laws and corporate practice – so as not to undermine the social contract that binds society, and in a way that guarantees development and positive governance within the communities.

This book investigated and unpacked the "state duty to protect; corporate responsibility to respect; and access to remedies" under the UNGPs. The strength of the implementation of business and human rights standards lies in the ability and dogmatic determination of the states to strengthen their domestic laws and to adequately regulate corporate activities in a manner consistent with the intents of global human rights standards. When corporations breach host state laws, they breach labour, environmental, criminal, and human rights laws. Those breaches can be latent if domestic laws do not contain human rights provisions to guard against corporate-related abuse.

This chapter discusses the practical implementation of business and human rights standards and the future of business and human rights in Africa. First, it examines the global adaptation of human rights normative principle and what this portends for Africa. Second it identifies the challenges to implementation of business and human rights in Africa. Third, it concludes with opportunities for further engagement.

DOI: 10.4324/9781003290124-14

10.2 Global adaptation of business and human rights principles

Globally, the UNGPs have been incorporated into a number of soft law instruments. These include the revised OECD Guidelines (2011), the revised International Finance Corporation Performance Standards on Environmental and Social Sustainability (2012), the ISO 26000 Social Responsibility Standard, and the UN Global Compact. The UNGPs have also been either adopted or endorsed by the American Bar Association and the European Commission. In some countries, the UNGPs have impacted on domestic legislation such as: the Dodd-Frank Act (US); the Business Supply Chain Transparency on Trafficking and Slavery Act, 2015 (US); the Business Transparency on Trafficking and Slavery Act, H.R. 2759: Global Online Freedom Act, 2013 (US); the California Transparency in Supply Chains Act 2010 (US); and the Modern Slavery Act, 2015 (UK).

Globalization has extended the spread of MNCs into places where gross violations of human rights are endemic. People are speaking of the language of human rights, and the issues have been pushed beyond the traditional confines of human rights. Many initiatives have been helpful in reducing the incidence of human rights abuse – but there has not been sufficient progress in accessing remedies in Africa. For instance, how do we know that the incidences of human rights abuses are declining as a result of various measures taken by the government and companies? To avoid these protracted arguments about the best solution, documentation is needed. As much as there is a call for the tightening of state regulations, states must incentivise companies and support the community without harming business activities. The corporate image is enhanced if the company can show that they actively protect human rights. When human rights have been integrated into domestic law, international human rights norms become naturally applicable – as mandatory and enforceable provisions against the harmful effects of globalisation. After all, MNCs are creations of domestic statutes, and they cannot be seen to avoid compliance with domestic laws.

The state's responsibility stems from its status under international law. In keeping with territorial jurisdiction, states can only protect individuals within their own territories. This makes it extremely difficult for states to discipline erring companies headquartered within their domain, but which operate globally. It is thus a dangerous phenomenon to live in a society where MNCs operate with reckless abandon, unchecked by any known mandatory rule of international human rights law, without avenues for victims of corporate disasters or wrongdoing to seek redress.

10.3 The future of business and human rights

Without a human rights perspective, business enterprises risk exacerbating harm in host communities. National authorities need to develop clear and comprehensive regulatory framework on corporate responsibility to respect human rights.

Most of the existing literature on the UNGPs have focused on the weaknesses inherent in normative instruments, while some question the passive tone of the UNGPs towards the *do no harm* principle directed at corporate entities. The identified human rights concerns of development projects and their impact on the host communities in Africa as well as the adaptation of the business and human rights principles in an African context has not been substantially addressed. The rights-based approach to development projects could help Africa achieve holistic sustainable development of its resources, where the rights of the local community are guaranteed, and fundamental human rights protection is integrated into extant laws.[2]

Although the UNGPs do not provide mechanisms or guidelines on how human rights can be integrated into domestic laws and development projects, this book unpacked the question of how human rights can be integrated into the domestic body of law through legal and institutional frameworks. In doing this, it examined the practical basis for adopting the HRBA as a framework for integrating human rights principles into development projects. Earlier research has not focused on the theoretical and practical applicability of the UNGPs, as a rights-based approach to project execution, hence the continuous and increasing debate over the binding and voluntary nature of the UNGPs.

While concerns about human rights violations in project development, especially in developing countries, are not a novel concept, the consideration of adapting a rights-based approach to local context has not been sufficiently explored in the literature. This book articulates a model for adapting and integrating human rights into extractive projects and domestic legislation. The study explored the imperative of connecting human rights with developmental projects, as well as providing a legal and institutional pathway for sustaining these principles over time. In this regard, the obligations of the state to protect human rights and the UNGPs as a rights-based approach in project execution and implementation were discussed. This is particularly to ensure that resource and developmental projects do not produce adverse human rights consequences, and where they do, that proactive and adequate measures are taken to address and mitigate such violations. The next section recommends institutional mechanism for monitoring and implementing business and human rights standards.

10.3.1 Global Memorandum of Understanding (GMOUs)

The existence of GMOUs between project proponents and local communities has, to some extent, created less tension between these two actors.[3] GMOUs are designed to create a pathway for social legitimacy and promote corporate social responsibility. These agreements constitute important mechanisms for local participation in resource governance.[4] Though voluntary, they are becoming the fastest means of forging corporate-community alliance and trust.[5]

Principle 18 requires project proponents to consult with host communities in assessing human rights risks. GMOUs could be used by companies as mechanisms for consulting with local communities.[6] GMOUs could address issues such as the assessment of actual and potential human rights impacts arising from a project, as well as measures for mitigating such impacts. Where effectively implemented, GMOUs will help companies obtain from their host communities a social license to operate. This social license, through GMOUs or CDAs legitimizes a company's activities within the communities. As it currently stands, GMOUs currently in force are binding in honour only, hence the recurrent tensions and conflicts between host communities and companies.

The ANOH Gas Development Project in Nigeria,[7] institutionalized GMOU for "codifying the negotiations and agreements between the extractive companies and their host communities."[8] However, the project failed the minimum standard in drafting and negotiating meaningful consultations with local communities. The GMOUs were prepared and presented to the local communities to sign without any prior consultation and expert guidance before signing.[9] Thus, despite the existence of GMOU in this instance, the processes leading to the adoption of the GMOU did not satisfy business and human rights standards with particular reference to community participation, consultation, and FPIC. Consequently, development and project proponents must guarantee that GMOUs are genuinely negotiated with local communities in the language they understand in addition to access to legal advice and representation. Project activities must be periodically assessed and reviewed to ensure that compliance with carefully negotiated GMOUs. GMOUs must incorporate modalities on compensation for acquired communal properties, adequate information on remittances to government for concessions and grant of permits, full implementation on the development agreement including periodic review and assessment by a jointly negotiated independent party.

10.3.2 Business and Human Rights Unit (BHRU)

At the continental, regional and domestic level, relevant agencies should consider setting up a BHRU. The BHRU will be responsible for identifying and safeguarding human rights challenges. The Unit will be responsible for coordinating and mandating human rights due diligence, and human rights impact assessment before any development project commences. It will serve as a check on corporation excesses by monitoring their activities, and coordinate settlement of grievances between host communities and corporate actors.

Creating a human rights agency is important due to the continuous extensive human rights violations that have characterized corporate activities in the continent. Undoubtedly there is the linkage between human rights and the environment, trade, and socio-economic factors that face host communities. BHRU would ensure that from design to implementation, development projects do not infringe the human rights of local communities. It would serve as the linkage and rallying point between the local community and corporate actors – as well as other stakeholders. Furthermore, the Unit will ensure that businesses keep to their obligation to respect human rights in their spheres of operation, will be responsible for investigating human rights abuses, and will be authorized to certify a project for having fulfilled human rights obligations. It must make it a matter of policy to ensure that businesses obtain the prior and informed consent of the local community.

This book has identified the local community as important stakeholders in the hierarchy of stakeholders. The community includes its vulnerable members: women, children and the disabled, community leaders, and the youth. In obtaining consent, community representation must be verified to be doubly sure that these are people who share the values and concerns of the entire community. As indicated, consent earlier given can be withdrawn during the pendency of the project. This provides a remedy for consent obtained by dishonest manipulation of corporate actors. The consent must relate to the project, and consent given should not be taken as applying to all projects by the project proponent. Where a project proponent obtains consent for a project and another project comes up, the project proponent must approach the community again for consent for the second project.

BHRU personnel must cut across various disciplines, including environmentalists, labour and human rights experts from various disciplines. They must be trained in quality assessment and monitoring. Human rights education and training should be regularly conducted with corporate entities. To integrate a rights-based approach, implementation, and policy formulators in BHRU must be trained and very well acquainted with the UNGPs, so that monitoring, and implementation is more effective. Periodic assessment and evaluation of staff should be carried out to assess their level of engagement with human rights and business principles. Ongoing staff development through various avenues such as summer school programmes, certificate courses, seminars and conferences would be essential.

The next section identifies and discusses barriers that could impede the implementation of business and human rights principles in Africa and effective mechanism for addressing the barriers.

10.4 Challenges to implementation of business and human rights principles

10.4.1 Gender disparities

The UNGPs recognize the challenges that could be faced by indigenous people, women, and vulnerable members of society.[10]

The focal case studies yielded valuable gendered information with regard to environmental matters. First, lack of education impacts realization of environmental rights. In most African societies, men work mostly in the mines while women are given household responsibilities. In some other societies, women in rural communities are more involved in agriculture, focusing on crop and livestock faming, while the men have an easier access to education and better economic advantage. Second, African societies are still largely patriarchal in nature. This affects the distribution of wealth, which results in an unequal economic advantage of one group over another. The under-representation of women in the decision-making process reflects the socio-economic inequalities between men and women.[11] Activities around mining, such as food vendors and social life, in rural South African communities, for instance, have led to an upsurge in forced prostitution, trafficking of women and girls, and the spread of sexually transmitted diseases. There seems to be a connection between resource extraction and violence against women. Men are also negatively impacted by the presence of extractive industries in communities, however, the impact and level of vulnerability of women is significantly higher. For instance, in South Africa, the added stress and burden on women who must nurse their spouses during illness caused by the environmental conditions of mines cannot be quantified. This is the subject of an ongoing silicosis case in South Africa.[12] Third, social gender roles significantly determine the nature of the impact of development projects – resulting in unequal benefits and risks for men and women. For instance, land allocation and child rearing are based on gender roles. Women principally assume responsibility for the feeding and wellbeing of their family, in addition to their farming roles. The direct impact of acid rain, water contamination, pollution, and land grabbing on these local communities are therefore largely felt by women.

While developmental projects result in land depreciation, the duties of women in terms of attending to the wellbeing of their family do not reduce. In the very few meetings conducting by project proponents, women are not usually allowed to be present. Besides, women are still discriminated against in respect of access to land and property ownership. Furthermore, children work under hazardous or exploitative labour conditions and are involved in illegal oil refining or artisanal mining. Further, the exclusion of women from community meetings and decision-making processes is a challenge to the actualization of the FPIC principle under the participatory framework of the HRBA. Comprehensive consultation involves participation of all genders. Local communities should not impede constructive engagement due to leadership structures that are characterized by power struggles – making it difficult for companies to engage with community leaders.

10.4.2 Developing national action plans

Africa is the richest continent on the planet,[13] although it remains the poorest.[14] Exploitation of the environment has continued to occur at an alarming rate over the last few decades. While humanity has tilled and plundered the earth with reckless abandon, it seems that the earth is running out of resources.[15] Extraction of natural resources is one of those activities which humanity has undertaken, in order to achieve social and economic survival.

Adoption of a NAP on Business and Human Rights should be a policy tool used by government, which sets out priorities that would encourage strategic mechanisms to ensure corporate accountability.[16] It will also serve as a guidance for states to facilitate tougher regulatory enforcement and monitor the implementation of the UNGPs. A NAP which is well structured, adapted to local context, comprehensive, and which follows a transparent process – will expedite the implementation of the GPs. In a continent of 55 countries, it is unacceptable for just two countries to develop NAPs as at today.

10.4.3 Political will

The state's duty to protect human rights builds on the existing legal obligations of states under international law. While the MNCs could frustrate the intentions and enforcement of the laws, local communities could also over-reach their monitoring capacities. When the local community protests, government uses its security apparatus to suppress a legitimate demand for transparent and accountable systems of governance.[17]

Willingness on the part of political leaders and stakeholders is imperative. Political leaders must not block funding avenues to agencies that work towards the development and implementation of human rights standards. At the continental and state level, there must be proactive and speedy development of National Action Plans. The stakeholders must look beyond political affiliation or dis-incentivisation and understand that achieving a holistic governance through a rights-based approach would not only promote social licence to operate, but citizens would develop faith in the capabilities of their elected officials to represent them and to manage their affairs judiciously. It will also prevent resistance to development projects and promote the integrity of human rights regimes in Africa where the rights of those immediately impacted – the local communities – are considered and reflected in government policies and regulations. Government must set clear objectives and framework for transparency and information disclosure, meaningful engagement, and consultation in development projects. These objectives must incorporate environment and social impact assessment of development projects which takes into consideration the concerns of host communities to these projects.

To remedy lack of political will, politicians should be required to divest themselves of any interest in development projects or association with project proponents. It will be unconscionable for political office holders to have vested interests in extractive companies – and still be part of the regulatory mechanism for the companies.

10.4.4 Environmental democratisation

To ensure proper participation in governance, all developmental projects must be presented to the local community in a language understood by that community and should demonstrate a deep knowledge of local customs. The views and concerns of the community captured in any such meeting must be incorporated into the project plan and design. Such a project must adapt the consultation process to the specific customs and concerns of each local community, which is host to the project. This process will give citizens a basis to demand the enforcement of their rights when projects do not go according to the agreed plan.

African communities can adopt popular normative initiatives whereby citizens will promote the adoption of laws or regulations regulating their environment. The local community will take an active role and participate in all the discussions leading to the passing of any such laws. Before any discussions are incorporated into law, a referendum should take place which asks the local communities whether they agree to incorporating such initiatives into any body of law. Here the people, who are direct recipients of the law, would have an opportunity to approve or reject a draft legal order or even revoke one that is in place. However, before this process is activated, there must have been a sensitisation and awareness campaign, followed by an authorisation process such as a collection of signatures or other process. The final draft of the proposed instrument would then be presented to legislature with the caveat that the inputs of the local community to the original version, should be maintained. There must, however, be set criteria for consultation and participation. For instance, there could be a mandatory minimum requirement that stipulates the fraction of the total registered voter population that could be required to cast a vote to validate the community's input into the draft law on the proposed amendment. This would constitute a threshold that confirms that consultations have properly taken place. The lawmakers representing constituencies with extractive activities may be required to demonstrate that this consultation has taken place.

Judicial understanding also forms part of environmental democratization. Judges must be trained on recognizing these normative instruments as critical part of right based approach to development. Adequate training for judges, investigators, and corporate lawyers on business and human rights must be fully supported and encouraged.

10.5 Conclusion

The involvement of the community in negotiations between the state and MNCs for any development project will guarantee the social licence to operate. Furthermore, most development projects are sited in poverty-stricken communities. MNCs must promise that their projects will not further degrade or dehumanise the people and the environment. Environmental impact assessment must clearly set out human rights impact assessment which identify groups at heightened risk of project impact. It is also key that access to information is streamlined to ensure that information on development projects is readily available when requested.

In conducting human rights due diligence, project proponents should work on the identified human rights impact and report to the public how they have been able to overcome pertinent impacts. The public presentation should be in a suitable format such as a workshop or seminar where NGOs, human rights activists, local communities, and other stakeholders are given the opportunity to make presentations. This will remove any one-sided presentation, and company executives will have the opportunity to discuss matters with their stakeholders. Upon presentation to the public, comments and suggestions must be incorporated into the final report presented. Collective efforts will ensure that areas of concern are identified and that solutions are developed to ensure maximum respect for human rights. This process will make the companies socially responsible.

For the sake of humanity's future, we must be conscious of the exploitation of natural resources. A proactive implementation of human rights principles will reduce or prevent the harmful exploitation of natural resources and guarantee sustainable development. Africa is a vast continent with many languages and diverse populations. Its legal mechanisms must be connected to the realities of local people to enhance the possibility of a realistic solution to the legitimate concerns of those impacted by development projects. The rights-based approach adopted in this book provides a pathway for the sustainable development of Africa's extractive and energy resources. Legislation must come from the very people that such legislation aims to protect. As exemplified in South Africa's legal and judicial regime, only credible institutions that appreciate the socio-economic, cultural, and political realities of host communities can legislate properly for them and monitor compliance. Further research is necessary in determining the necessity of a treaty on business and human rights. As it currently stands, the UNGPS present a valuable roadmap for strengthening institutions to ensure that business activities in Africa's development projects are not devoid of pertinent human rights considerations.

Notes

1 Maria Barchiesi, & Andrea Colladon, "Corporate Core Values and Social Responsibility: What Really Matters to Whom" (2021) 170 *Technological Forecasting and Social Change* 120907.
2 See generally, Sam Amadi, "Improving Electricity Access through Policy Reform: A Theoretical Statement on Legal Reform in Nigeria's Power Sector" in Yinka Omoregbe & Ada Ordor (eds.) *Ending Africa's Energy Deficit and the Law: Achieving Sustainable Energy for All in Africa* (2018) 344.
3 GMOUs and Community Development Agreements (CDAs) are largely used interchangeably.
4 See further Austin Shaffer, Skylar Zillox, & Jessica Smith, "Memoranda of Understanding and the Social License to Operate in Colorado's Unconventional Energy Industry: A Study of Citizen Complaints" (2017) *Journal of Energy & Natural Resources Law* 69 at 71. [Arguing that Memoranda of Understanding provides a space for host communities to air their grievances and participate in the governance process as well as integration of local concerns into the planning and regulation of extractive projects].
5 Osamuyimen Egbon, Uwafiokun Idemudia, & Kenneth Amaeshi, "Shell Nigeria's Global Memorandum of Understanding and Corporate-Community Accountability Relations: A Critical Appraisal" (2018) 31(1) *Accounting, Auditing & Accountability Journal* 51. [Exploring the extent to which GMOUs promotes corporate-community accountability necessary for fostering sustainable community development in Nigeria's Niger Delta]; see also Kiikpoye Aaron, "New Corporate Social Responsibility Models for Oil Companies in Nigeria's Delta Region: What Challenges for Sustainability?" (2012) 12(4) *Progress in Development Studies* 259 at 266.
6 See also Principles 17 to 21. By the end of 2011, Shell (Nigeria) had signed and implemented 27 agreements, covering 290 communities in its areas of operation. See further, Shell, "Global Memorandum of Understanding (GMOU)" <www.shell.com.ng/sustainability/communities/gmou.html> accessed 11 May 2021. Section 116 of the Nigerian Minerals and Mining Act, 2007 obliges mining companies to enter into CDAs with host communities prior the commencement of mining project.
7 Victoria Ibezim-Ohaeri, et al., "Natural Resource and Benefit-Sharing Negotiations between Host Communities and Extractive Companies: A Case Study of Assa North & Ohaji South [ANOH] Gas Development Project" <https://spacesforchange.org/wp-content/uploads/2021/10/S4C-ANOH-EXECUTIVE-SUMMARY.pdf>.

8 Ibid.
9 Ibid.
10 See commentary to Principle 3; Principles 7(b) and 18.
11 IHRB, "Human Rights in Tanzania's Extractive Sector: Exploring the Terrain" (2 December 2016) 54 <www.ihrb.org/focus-areas/commodities/human-rights-in-tanzanias-extractive-sector-exploring-the-terrain> accessed 10 March 2021.
12 See the *Bongani Nkala & Ors v. Harmony Gold Mining Company Ltd & Ors* case.
13 See Miriam Mannak, "Africa: Why the Richest Continent Is Also the Poorest" *Climate & Capitalism* (5 September 2008) <https://climateandcapitalism.com/2008/09/05/africa-why-the-richest-continent-is-also-the-poorest/> accessed 29 May 2021.
14 Ibid.
15 Mark Townsend, & Jason Burke, "Earth Will Expire by 2050" *The Guardian* (7 July 2002) <www.theguardian.com/uk/2002/jul/07/research.waste> accessed 29 May 2021.
16 For the essential criteria of a NAP, see UN Working Group on Business and Human Rights, "Guidance on National Action Plans on Business and Human Rights" (November 2016) <www.ohchr.org/Documents/Issues/Business/UNWG_NAPGuidance.pdf> accessed 5 June 2021.
17 Yinka Omoregbe, & Ada Ordor (eds.), *Ending Africa's Energy Deficit and the Law: Achieving Sustainable Energy for All in Africa* (2018).

Index

Page numbers followed by 'n' indicate a note on the corresponding page.

AAA and others v Unilever PLC and Tea Kenya Limited 98–99, 104n57
Aarhus Convention 70, 89n119
abandonment: of mining activities 143; in Nigeria 115–116
Abdulhamid v. Akar 125, 135n149
abuse of human rights: allegations 58, 81; concern for victims of 12; identifying and mitigating adverse 58; International Bill of Rights and 7; platform for preventing and addressing 100; rights-based approach for 64–84; vulnerable to 21
accountability, transparency and: human rights-based approach to development projects 77–81; in Nigeria 115; sine-qua-non for social licence to operate 46
Aderinto v. Omojola 135n149
Adesanya v The President of Nigeria 136n155
Adewole v Jakande 131n22
Adidas 59
administration of justice 93–95
affordability, in gaining access 100
Africa National Congress (ANC) 21
African Charter on Human and Peoples Rights (Ratification and Enforcement) Act 59, 76, 108
African Commission on Human and Peoples' Rights v. Kenya 75–77
African Continental Free Trade Area Agreement (AfCFTA): Agenda 2063 and 28; for conglomeration of territories 27, 33–34n63; expanded Continental Task Force on 28; implementation of Agreement 28, 34n71; importance of human rights and 28; initiatives 27–28; objectives of 28; trade liberalization under 29; transformative agenda of 28
African Development Bank Group (AfDB) 32n41
African Economic Community 27
African Mining Vision (2009) 72, 87n54
African Union: Agenda 2063 65; approach to contextualize business and human rights 26–27; Policy Framework 26–27; role of 26–27, 33n54
Afro-centric (third world) strategic approach 20–22
Agbai & Ors v. Okogbue 131n16
agency theory 41
Agenda 2063; adoption of 65; democratic and sustainable development goals in 28, 29
Akpan v Shell Petroleum Development Company of Nigeria Ltd & Royal Dutch Shell Plc 78–80, 88n96, 93, 98, 136n159
Ale v. Obasanjo 135n149
Alexkor Ltd and Another v Richterveld Community 139, 147n12
Alien Tort Statute (ATS) 92, 102n12
American Bar Association 163
Anigboro v. Sea Trucks Ltd 136n153
appropriate forums, access to 96–101
Assa North and Ohaji South (ANOH) Gas Development Project 114, 165
Associated Gas Reinjection Act (1979) 59, 110, 112, 132n28
Ategie v Mck Nigeria Ltd 125, 135n148
Attorney-General of Lagos State v Attorney-General of Federation 110, 131n25
Attorney-General of Ondo State v Attorney-General of the Federation 110, 131n23
Aturu v Minister of Petroleum Resources & Ors 131n15

audi alterem partem, natural justice 94
Australian Human Rights Commission 85n17
authenticity of commitment 39

Basic Conditions of Employment Act 148n23
Bhopal (1984 – India) disaster 11, 34n84; emergence of participatory mechanisms and 85n32; stakeholder theory and 42
Bilateral Investment Treaties (BIT) 141–142
Bill of Rights: International 7, 17n20, 109; Kenya 151–152; Nigeria 107; Ogoni community 22; public interest litigation on basis of 94; South Africa 138, 140
Black Economic Empowerment programme 142
blood diamonds 8
Board of Directors 45, 114
Bodo Community v. Shell Petroleum Development Company of Nigeria 23, 31n27
Bongani Nkala & 68 ors v. Harmony Gold Mining Company & 31 ors 87n69, 147n18, 149n48, 171n12
Botswana 84n7
Bowoto v. Chevron Texaco Corp. 23, 31n26
Brazil, dam collapse in 52n43
Broad-Based Black Economic Empowerment (BBBEE) Act 69, 141, 142
business and human rights (BHRs): African Union, role of 26–27; Business and Human Rights Unit 165–166; case studies 22–26; challenges, nature and scope of 20–30; contemporary discourse on 20–21; corporate governance, competing theories of 37–44; corporations and local communities 45–47; criticisms and 10; discourse on implementation of 13; environmental democratisation 168–169; firm, board structure of 45–47; future of 163–166; gender disparities 166–167; global adaptation of principles 163; Global Memorandum of Understanding 164–165; in Kenya 154–156; lack of binding 8; Lake Turkana Wind Power Project 24–26; legal context, challenges, and overview 6–10; linkages of 13; Marikana incident 23–24; National Action Plan 156–157, 167; Niger-Delta, Ogoni experience 22–23; political will 168; principles, implementation of 5, 166–169; as public value 47; stakeholder value approach 44–45; sustainable approach to 47–49; theoretical basis for implementing 35–37; third world approach to 20–22; trade regime and human rights implications 27–29
Business and Human Rights Dialogue Report 146
Business and Human Rights Unit (BHRU) 165–166
Business Country Guide 146, 150n71
Business Supply Chain Transparency on Trafficking and Slavery Act (2015) 163
Business Transparency on Trafficking and Slavery Act, H.R. 2759 163

California Transparency in Supply Chains Act 2010 163
Centre for Minority Rights Development & Others v. Kenya 87n73
Centre for Transnational Corporations 8
Choc v Hudbay Minerals Inc 50n14
citizenship education: advancing inclusion of 101; integrating human rights into business by 162
citizenship enforcement of laws 94–95
climate change: globalisation and 41; issues of 48; publishing information regarding 83
closure of mining activities 143
Code of Conduct for Private Security Service Providers (2010) 18n35
Codes of Good Practice (2007) 142
Commission for Conciliation, Mediation and Arbitration 102n7
Commission on Gender Equality 102n7
Communal Land Rights Act 148n23
communities *see* host communities; local communities
Community Development Agreements (CDAs) 154, 170n3
Companies Act 48; of India 126, 135n147; of Kenya 152–153; of Nigerian 101; of South Africa 140–141
Companies and Allied Matters Act (CAMA): 1990 104n73; 2020 124–127, 137n186–187
"comply or explain" approach 48
Constitution: of Kenya 151–152; of Nigeria 107–110; of South Africa 138–140
Constitution and Mining Act 154
Corporate Duty of Vigilance Law, France 19n60

corporate duty to respect human rights: Human Rights Due Diligence 57–60; Human Rights Impact Assessment 60–61
corporate governance: competing theories of 37–44; shareholder value principle 39–42; social change as system of corporate transformation 38–39; stakeholder theory 42–44
corporate liability: challenge to 100–101; standard legal framework for 95–96
corporate reporting: encourage or incentivize 43; in safeguarding accountability and effective communication 82–83; social responsibility and 48
corporate social responsibility (CSR): business and human rights and 35–37, 47–49; corporate governance, competing theories of 37–44; corporations and local communities 45–47; enforcement of initiatives 35; firm, board structure of 45–47; Indian government's 126; innovations in European Union 36; stakeholder value approach 44–45
cost-benefit analysis 47
criminal jurisdiction, corporate 129–130
culture: corporate 38, 51n21; role in life of organisation 49

dam collapse, in Brazil 52n43
Danish Institute for Human Rights (DIHR) 146
decommissioning, in Nigeria 115–116
Department of Petroleum Resources (DPR) 122; for enforcement of petroleum regulations 94, 117, 134n92; Guidelines for Operation and Maintenance of Oil and Gas Pipelines 120
developmental projects: access to information 82–83; expectation of society incoming from 69; human rights-based approach adaptation to 64–84; inclusion of local people in 69–70; non-discrimination and fairness 83–84; participation 68–77; timely and adequate information on 70; transparency and accountability 77–81
diamonds: blood 8; illicit trade in 6, 16n5; tracking sale of 8
Director of Mines 153
Dodd – Frank Wall Street Reform and Consumer Protection Act 18n35, 62n17, 163
Doe v Nestle 50n6, 95–96, 103n36
domestic laws: human rights and 5, 12, 163, 164; in Kenya 151–158; in Nigeria 107–131; in South Africa 138–147; UN Guiding Principles and 9
Dooh v. SPDC 88n96
Draft Norms 9, 18n36
due diligence 57, 58; adoption of 73; impact on host community 59

Earthlife Africa (Cape Town) v. Director General of Environmental Affairs and Tourism and another 94, 103n32
economic efficiency 42
ECOWAS Mining Directive 72, 87n55
emoluments attachment orders (EAO) 139
Employment Equity Act 148n23
Endorois case 75
Energy and Petroleum Regulatory Authority (EPRA) 153
Environmental and Social Impact Assessment (ESIA) 32n43, 33n46, 120; of Lake Turkana Wind Power Project 24
Environmental Assessment Practitioner (EAP) 145
environmental degradation: economic sabotage and 23; extent of 6–7; extractive companies accountable for 100; identifying sources of 60; in Ogoniland 6–7; oil spillage and 47; Shell Petroleum Development Company and 23
environmental democratisation 168–169
Environmental Guidelines and Standards for the Petroleum Industry in Nigeria (EGASPIN) 118
environmental impact assessment 145; environmental management plan and 112; human rights impact assessment and 61; lack of transparent 74; in Nigeria 120; obtaining license 155; in South Africa 141, 145; unmitigated violation of human rights, preventing 47
Environmental Impact Assessment (EIA) Act: of Nigeria 120–123, 134–135nn114–128; of South Africa 141
Environmental Management Plan (EMP) 145, 149n55
environmental pollution: by business operations 160–161n75; costs of remedying 59; issues of 48; liable for damages due to 80; mining and 143; by oil spills 23

Environmental Protection and Rehabilitation Fund (EPRF) 102n4
environmental rehabilitation and restoration plan 154
Environment Management and Coordination Act 154
environment management plan 112
environment restoration fund 91
European Commission 163
European Union (EU): corporate social responsibility and 36; due diligence in 59
Expropriation Act 148n23
Extractive Industries Transparency Initiative (EITI) Act (2007) 8–9, 18n33
Extractive Sector Information Management Centre (ESIMC) 114

fairness, non-discrimination and 83–84
Fawehinmi v Abacha 108, 131n9
firms: board structure of 45–47; as moral agents owing society social service responsibility 47; responsibility and power, validating 46; *see also* multinational companies (MNCs)
Flare Gas (Prevention of Waste and Pollution) Regulations 113
Foreign Direct Investment (FDI) 12
forum non-convenience doctrine 11, 92
Four Nigerian Farmers and Milieudefensie v. Shell 89n109
Framework Principles on Human Rights and the Environment 2018 65
Freedom of Information Act 74, 82, 89n122, 133n73
Freeman, Robert E. 42, 44, 52n37, 53n48
Free, Prior and Informed Consent (FPIC): application of 73; *Endorois* case and 75; occurrence of participation 72–73; United Nations Guiding Principles on Business and Human Rights and 74
Free Trade Agreement (FTA) 29
Friedman, Milton 26, 28, 31, 39–40, 51n25; "Capitalism and Freedom" 39; claim and founders of corporate 41; essence of firm, debate about 40; failure of corporate social responsibility ideas 40
FRN v Anache 109, 131n18

gas flaring: compliance programme and 49; designed to reduce 74; effect of toxic pollutants, and environmental pollution 45; environmental effects of 122; failure to prohibit 113; greenhouse effect due to massive 53n53; human rights due diligence and 126; judgment and ceasing 59; liable for damages due to 80; in local community 58–59; negative effects of 113; in Nigeria 112–113; and pipeline leakages 113; reducing 74; Shell Petroleum Development Company and 59, 74; social and environmental costs of 113
gender disparities 166–167
General Agreement on Tariffs and Trade (GATT) (1947); substitution of single customs territory 33–34n63; trade agreements and 29, 34n79, 81
General Assembly Resolution 18n30
Germany 86n46
Glenister v. President of the Republic of South Africa 138, 147n1
globalisation: and climate change 41; dynamics of 35, 41, 124; and emergence of participatory mechanisms 68; and governance 30; provisions against harmful effects of 163
Global Memorandum of Understanding (GMOUs) 164–165, 170n3
Global North: corporate behaviour and 8; Global South and, inequality between 21; natural resources in 41; sectorial issues in 13
Global Online Freedom Act 163
Global South: factors associated with extractive resource development in 41; and Global North, inequality between 21
Gold Fields, in South Africa 148n21
Government of the Republic of South Africa v Grootboom 139–140, 147n13
gross domestic product (GDP) 6
Guiding Principles 18n39; incorporation and implementation of 13; for multinational organisations 9–10

Hague Court of Appeals 79
Heads of African Regional Economic Communities (RECs) 28
Hichange Investments (Pty) Ltd v. Cape Produce Co (Pty) Ltd t/a Pelts Products 149n51
host communities 46, 58; consent and 73; development projects and 44; development trust, establishment of 111–112; development trust fund 91; duty of care towards 80–81; Free, Prior, Informed Consent of 72, 116;

human rights due diligence and 59, 126; methodical and fundamental injustice 64; mines and 144; multinational companies and 30; responsibilities or duties between corporation and 45–46; right of participation in decision making 68–77
human rights: agency, creating 165; business respect for 38–39; corporate duty to respect 57–61; development and implementation of standards 168; domestic law and 163, 164; duty to protect 163, 168; education and training 166; Human Rights Due Diligence and 57–60; Human Rights Impact Assessment and 60–61; implications, trade regime and 27–29; integrating into business 162; *see also* abuse of human rights; business and human rights (BHRs); violations of human rights
human rights-based approach (HRBA): access to information 82–83; adaptation to development projects 64–84; factors, necessary for 64–65; for integrating human rights principles into development projects 164; non-discrimination and fairness 83–84; participation 68–77; Swedish government using 66; transparency and accountability 77–81; United Nations Guiding Principles on Business and Human Rights as 5
Human Rights-Based Approach to Development Cooperation Towards a Common Understanding Among UN Agencies 66
human rights due diligence (HRDD), corporate 57, 58; Companies and Allied Matters Act and 126–127; impact on host community 59; United Nations Guiding Principles on Business and Human Rights and 58–60
human rights impact assessment (HRIA), corporate: adoption of 73; community-based 126; due diligence and 73, 116; Environmental Impact Assessment Act and 121; human rights due diligence and 14; methodologies for 9; promise and potential of 60–61; testing projects in terms of 46

ILO Convention 169 72, 86n51
incentivising: concept of 126; socially responsible projects 48–49
India's Companies Act 2013 126, 135n147
indigenization policy: failed to utilizing private sector 31n12; of Nigeria 69; with other foreign companies 22
information, access to: Director of Mines ensuring 153; human rights-based approach to development projects 82–83; local communities and 73; in Nigeria 113–115
Ingonyama Trust 74
Institute of Directors, South Africa (IoDSA) 140
Interim Protection of Informal Land Rights Act (IPILRA) 74
International Bill of Rights 7, 17n20; of Kenya 152; of Nigeria 109
International Centre for Settlement of Investment Disputes (ICSID) 141
International Finance Corporation Performance Standards on Environmental and Social Sustainability, revised 163
ISO 26000 Social Responsibility Standard 163

Jesner v Arab Bank 17, 92, 103n15
Jindal Africa (Pty) Ltd 74
Johannesburg High Court 24
Johannesburg Stock Exchange (JSE): Listing Rules 48; trade on 141
Joint Venture Agreement 22
Jonah Gbemre (for himself and as representing Iwherekan Community in Delta State, Nigeria) v. Shell Petroleum Development Company, NNPC & Attorney General of the Federation 58, 80, 133n68
judicial and non-judicial process: access to remedies, elements of 94–101; administration of justice, effective 94–95; appropriate forums, access to 96–101; corporate liability, standard legal framework for 95–96; effective mechanism 91–94; guarantee effectiveness of 91–92; legitimacy and question of access 90–91; National Human Rights Institutions in 91
justice, administration of 93–95

Kadie Kalma & Ors v African Minerals Ltd & Ors 100, 104n67
Kenneth Gona Karisa v. Top Steel Kenya Limited 156, 160n65
Kenya: business and human rights challenges in 154–156; Companies

Act in 152–153; Constitution of 25, 151–152; environmental rehabilitation and restoration plan 154; Lake Turkana Wind Power Project 24–26; Mining Act in 153–154; National Action Plan on business and human rights 156–157; Petroleum Act in 153; policy and legal framework in 151–158; violation of African Charter 76
Kenyan Forestry Service (KFS) 76
Kepha Omondi Onjuro & Others v. Attorney General & 5 Others Nairobi 158n19
Khulumani v. Barclay National Bank Ltd 32n36
Kimberley Process Certification Scheme 8
King Code on Corporate Governance 52n35
King Report on Corporate Governance 140
Kiobel v Royal Dutch Petroleum Co. 13–14, 19n50, 32n37, 32n30, 92–93, 95, 102–103n13,n14
KM & 9 others v Attorney General & 7 others 155, 160n62
Kwale Oil-Gas Processing Plant (OGPP) 74

labour: concessions to 21; fairness concerns 151; rights 157, 162n76; Social and Labour Plan 142–143; standards, failure to adhere to 23; standards in supply chains 37
Labour Relations Act 148n23
Lagos Plan of Action 27, 34n65
Lake Turkana Wind Power Project (LTWP) 24–26, 92, 155
land, access to: area of law pertaining to 123; cultural and historical barriers to 160n74; women and 167
Land Use Act (LUA) (1978) 123–124
Larry Bowoto et al. v. Chevron Texaco Corp. et al 19n52
legitimacy and question of access 90–91
licensee/lessee, responsibility of 112
local communities 168; access to information 82–83; capacity to structure 11; corporate trust 119; corporations and 45–47; environmental democratisation in 168; Free, Prior, Informed Consent and 155; Global Memorandum of Understanding and 164–165; granting of oil licence, participation in 116–117; incentivizing socially responsible projects in 48; mines and 143; as moral agents 44; multinational companies and 14, 30, 81; non-discrimination and fairness 83–84; potential developmental projects, aware of 121; right of participation in decision making 68–77; as single dominant stakeholder 43; stakeholder approach to 42
locus standi, rules of 93, 95
Lonmin Company 23–24

Mackey, John 41
Malabo Protocol 129
Mambo and 2 Others v Limuru Country Club and ors 151, 158n11
Marikana (2012 – South Africa) disaster 11, 50n6; emergence of participatory mechanisms and 85n32; human rights standards in corporate practices and 23–24; social licence to operate, lack of 46
Milieudefensie v Royal Dutch Shell plc (1) and Shell Petroleum Development Company of Nigeria Ltd (E) 89n109
Mineral and Petroleum Resources Development Act 28 of 2002 (MPRDA) 141–142; closure and abandonment 143; equity in mining, promoting 141; for extractive industry 141; mineral rights ownership, promoting 143–144; National Environmental Management Act 144; Social and Labour Plan 142–143
Mineral Rights Board 153–154
mineral rights ownership 143–144
Mining Act (2016) 153–154, 159n29
Mitubel Welfare Society v Kenya Airports Authority & 2 others 158n19
Modern Slavery Act (2015) 163
Mohamud Iltarakwa Kochale & others v. Lake Turkana Wind Power Ltd & others 25, 33n50
moral agents 47
Movement for the Survival of the Ogoni People (MOSOP) 22, 31n13
multinational companies (MNCs): activities of 6, 16n6; challenges on profit maximisation 36; corporate culture 38, 51n21; corporate Human Rights Due Diligence 57–60; corporate Human Rights Impact Assessment 60–61; culture of information dissemination, developing 83; designing of 36; difficulties in integrating business and human rights 12; disasters of 11; duty

to respect human rights 38; ethical statements of 11, 19n54; general duty of care, violation of 80; globalization and 163; host communities and 30; human rights and 7–8; legal, political, and institutional role of 21; and local communities 45–47; local communities and 14, 30, 81; in Nigeria 45, 53n53; presumption of 11; regulation of activities of 7–8; resource governance and 7; rise in wealth 7; social license validating responsibility and power of firms 46; stakeholders, relationships with 45; violence against 44

National Action Plan on Business and Human Rights: adoption of 167; development of 15; In Kenya 151, 156–157, 160n71; Nigerian National Human Rights Commission and 129
National Environmental Management Act (NEMA) (No 107 of 1998); Proposed Regulation Pertaining to Financial Provisioning . . . (17 May 2019) 144, 149n53; regulating environmental governance architecture 144, 148n23; Regulations Pertaining to the Financial Provision for Prospecting, Exploration, Mining or Production Operations (2015) 144, 149n52; relief in respect of breach of environmental rights 95, 103n33
National Environmental Standards and Regulations Enforcement Agency Act (NESREA Act) 2007 128–129, 136nn171–173
National Human Rights Institutions (NHRIs) 61, 91
National Oil Spill Contingency Plan (NOSCP) 127
National Oil Spill Detection and Response Agency (NOSDRA) 127–128, 136nn161–163
natural resource: for economic growth and development 64–65; extraction, human rights violations in 7, 17n22; land and 157, 160n74; management, initiatives for 8–9; rights and business 157, 160n74; wealth 12
Natural Resource Governance Institute 30n1,4
nemo judex in causa sua, natural justice 94
Nestle Inc v. John Doe 41, 103n40
Ngugi v Nairobi Hospital and 2 ors 151, 158n10
Niger-Delta *see* Ogoni community
Niger-Delta Development Commission (NDDC) 128
Nigeria: Allied Matters Act in 124–127; business and human rights challenges in 22–23; Companies Act in 101, 124–127; Constitution of 59, 107–110; corporate criminal jurisdiction 129–130; Environmental Impact Assessment Act in 120–123; gas flaring in 74; Human Rights Commission in 91; indigenization policy of 69; initiatives for extractive resource management in 8; Land Use Act in 123–124; multinational companies in 45, 53n53; National Environmental Standards and Regulations Enforcement Agency Act 128–129; National Oil Spill Detection and Response Agency 127–128; Niger-Delta Development Commission 128; Nigerian National Human Rights Commission Act in 129; Petroleum Industry Act in 61, 110–116; policy and legal framework of 107–131; rule of law, control of corruption, and political stability 20; stakeholder theory in 42; transitional provisions in 116–120
Nigerian Contract Monitoring Coalition v Power Holding Company of Nigeria (PHCN) 82–83
Nigerian Enterprises Promotion Decree 31n11
Nigerian Investment Promotion Commission Act (No 16 of 1995) 142
Nigerian Midstream and Downstream Petroleum Regulatory Authority 111
Nigerian Minerals and Mining Act (NMMA) 102n4, 115
Nigerian National Human Rights Commission Act (1995) 129
Nigerian National Petroleum Corporation (NNPC) 111
Nigerian Upstream Petroleum Regulatory Commission 111
Nike 59, 85n32
Nkala & others v. Harmony Gold Mining Company Ltd & Others 24, 32n38
non-discrimination and fairness 83–84
non-governmental organizations, role of 37
non-judicial grievance mechanism: barriers of access to 73; designing and measuring 91; effectiveness of 91; *see also* judicial and non-judicial process

non-justiciability, of Nigerian Constitution 108–109
Ntsebeza v. Ford Motor Co. 32n37, 103n23

Occupational Health and Safety Act 148n23
Ogaile v Shell 80
Ogiek Community of Mau Forest 76–77
Ogoni community: Bill of Rights 22; business and human rights challenges on 22–23; environmental degradation in 6–7; oil contamination, impact of 31n20
Oguru & ors v. SPDC 88n96
Oil Pipelines Act (OPA) (1956) 89n118, 110, 118–120
oil spillage: avoidance and control of 128; cases with similar facts of 88n96; destroying farmlands 88n96; extractive companies accountable for 100; failed to prevent 97; liable for damages due to 79–80; National Oil Spill Detection and Response Agency 127–128; in Ogoni community 22; remediating 46, 47; sabotage as cause of 78, 80–81, 118; from Shell Petroleum Development Company 23, 78–79
Okogie and Others v The Attorney-General of Lagos State 109, 131n20, 131n15
Okoi v. Inah 136n153
Okpabi and others v. Royal Dutch Shell Plc and others 50n14
Okpabi v Royal Dutch Shell Plc 23, 32n28, 97–98, 100, 103n50
Olafisoye v Federal Republic of Nigeria 109, 131n19
Onwo v. Oko 136n153
Open Government Partnership (OGP) 18n35
Organization for Economic Cooperation and Development (OECD) 87n61; corporate actors, guidelines for 8, 17n27; Due Diligence Guidelines for Responsible Supply Chains of Minerals from Conflict-Affected and High-Risk Areas (2011) 18n35; Guidelines, revised 163
Organization of the Petroleum Exporting Countries (OPEC) 30n2
Oronto Douglas v Shell Petroleum Development Company 53n58

participation 68–70; in decision-making 68–70; failure of 71; mechanisms, emergence of 68; nature of 70; occurrence of 72–77; scope of 70–72; theoretical basis for 68
Pere Ajunwa (on behalf of Ijaw Aborigines) v Shell Nigeria 89n112
Peterside v IMB 125, 136n152
Petroleum Act 110; in Kenya 153; in Nigeria 110, 116–118
Petroleum Industry Act (PIA) (2021) 102n5, 110–111; abandonment, decommissioning, and disposal 115–116; access to information 113–115; environment management plan 112; gas flaring 112–113; host community development trust, establishment of 111–112; regulatory and institutional reforms 111; transparency and accountability 115
Petroleum Profits Tax Act (1959) 110, 111
Petroleum (Drilling and Production) Regulations 119
policy and legal framework: in Kenya 151–158; in Nigeria 107–131; in South Africa 138–147
Policy Framework 33n55; elements of 26–27, 33n59; objectives of 26; sections of 26; summary of 27, 33n60
political will 30; as challenge to business and human rights principles 168; to enforce laws 12; to remedy lack of 168
Port Elizabeth Municipality v Various Occupiers 140, 147n14
"presumption against extraterritoriality" rule 92–93
Production Sharing Contract (PSC) 111, 155
profit maximisation: benefits/impact of 47; essence of 40; ethical considerations above 40; focusing on 36; positive impact on immediate community 42; and societal expectations of being socially responsible 37
Profit Sharing and Risk Service Contracts 111
Promotion of Administrative Justice Act 3 of 2000 (PAJA) 94–95
Protection of Investment Act, No. 22 (2015) 148n33
public interest justification 76
public-interest litigation 94, 102
Public Protector 102n7
Publish What You Pay (PWYP) coalition 18n35

question of access: creation of 97; legitimacy and 90–91

Rana Plaza (2013 – Bangladesh) disaster 11, 34n84, 50n6; complexity in resolving problems 37; emergence of participatory mechanisms and 85n32
reconnaissance license 154, 159n40
regulatory and institutional reforms 111
remedies, access to 91, 157, 162n78; administration of justice, effective 94–95; appropriate forums, access to 96–101; corporate liability, standard legal framework for 95–96; elements of 94–101
Republic of Ecuador v. Chevron Corp. 102n11
resource governance: as challenging task 7; extractive, human rights protection with 9; implementation of business and human rights principles 5; initiatives for 8–9; irresponsible, reducing 8; unexpected resource, development of 22; *see also* natural resource
restoration plan, environmental rehabilitation and 154
retention licence 154, 159n46
revenue transparency 157, 162n77
Revlon, Inc. v. MacAndrews & Forbes Holdings, Inc. 53n62
rights-based approach *see* human rights-based approach (HRBA)
Royal Bafokeng community and Anglo-American Platinum case 143–144
Royal Bafokeng Development Trust 144
Ruggie, John G. 9, 57, 62n3
Russia, fall and influence on eastern European countries 68
Rylands v. Fletcher 78–79

Sarbanes Oxley Act 53n65
Saro-Wiwa, Ken 22–23
Satrose Ayuma & 11 Others v. The Registered Trustees of the Kenya Railways Staff Retirement Pension Scheme & 2 Others Nairobi 158n19
Save Lamu & 5 others v National Environmental Management Authority (NEMA) & another 155, 160n58
SERAC & Anor v Nigeria 96–97, 103n45
SERAC v Nigeria 135n138
Sexual Offences Act (2006) 157
"Shadow" National Baseline Assessment of Current Implementation of Business and Human Rights Frameworks 146, 150n76
shareholder value principle (SVP) 39–42; agency theory and 41; capitalism, dictates of 40; modernity and advances, evolution of 41; productivity and 42
Sharpeville Massacre 24
Shell Petroleum Company of Nigeria Ltd v Akpan 89n109
Shell Petroleum Development Company: activities of 23; emergence of participatory mechanisms and 85n32; environmental degradation and 6–7; Shell (1997 – Nigeria) disaster 11, 50n6; social licence to operate, lack of 46; stakeholder value approach and 45
Shell Petroleum Development Company of Nigeria Limited v Tiebo & Ors. 80
Shell v Isaiah 80
Sherman, J.F. 57, 62n3
Silvermine Valley Coalition v Sybrand Van Der Spuy Boerderye and Others 145, 150n68
Simplified Trade Regime (STR) 26
"smart mix" approach: creating 6; in Nigeria 107; voluntary and regulatory measures, combination of 16–17n10
Social and Economic Rights Action Centre (SERAC) v Nigeria 108, 131n9
Social and Labour Plan (SLP) 142–143
social change theory 38–39
social licence to operate (SLO) 11; granting 37; lack of 46; responsibility and power of firms, validating 46; transparency and accountability as sine-qua-non for 46
social service responsibility 47
South Africa: Broad-Based Economic Empowerment Act in 69; closure and abandonment 143; Companies Act in 140–141; Constitution of 138–140; environmental impact assessment in 145; initiatives for extractive resource management in 8; Marikana incident in 23–24; Mineral and Petroleum Resources Development Act in 141–144; mineral rights ownership of 143–144; National Environmental Management Act in 144; policy and legal framework in 138–147; rule of law, control of corruption, and political stability 20; Social and Labour Plan in 142–143; South African Human Rights Commission (SAHRC) 91, 102n7–8, 145–146

South African Apartheid Litigation, In Re 24, 32n36, 93, 103n22
South African Human Rights Commission Act (2013) 102n7,8
SPDC v Ijaw Aborigines of Bayelsa State 79
Special Representative on Business and Human Rights (SRSG): duty of 9; Guiding Principles, producing 9, 18n39; on human rights and transnational corporations 18n39
stakeholder: affected 43, 70, 119; theory 42–44; value approach 44–45
Standard Gauge Railway contract (SGR) 154–155
subsidiary corporate personality principle 41
Swedish government, human rights-based approach and 66
system of corporate transformation 38–39

tax revenue 161n77
Tel-Oren v Libyan Arab Republic 89n115
third world approach to business and human rights 20–22
tort of negligence 79–80
trade agreements *see* African Continental Free Trade Area Agreement (AfCFTA)
trade regime and human rights implications: economic integration and trade agreements 28–29; Heads of African Regional Economic Communities 28; trade agreements, conditions for 29; trade policy, key elements for achieving 29; *see also* African Continental Free Trade Area Agreement (AfCFTA)
transitional provisions 116–120; Oil Pipelines Act 118–120; Petroleum Act 116–118
transnational corporations (TNCs) 16n6
transparency and accountability: human rights-based approach to development projects 77–81; in Nigeria 115; sine-qua-non for social licence to operate 46
Trust Land Act 25

United Nations: Code of Conduct on Transnational Corporations 8, 17n25, 18n37; Commission on Transnational Corporations 12–13; Declaration on the Right to Development 86n38, 87n64; Environment Programme (UNEP) 6, 17n12, 22, 31n17; Global Compact 163; Human Rights Council 5, 16n1, 19n46
United Nations Guiding Principles on Business and Human Rights (UNGPs) 5; argument for implementation of 36; challenges of human rights standards 57; corporate Human Rights Due Diligence and 58–60; corporate-related human rights abuses, preventing and addressing 100; duty to take measures 90; Free, Prior and Informed Consent and 74; implementation of 162; influences of 37; integrating human rights 66–67; participation in decision-making 70–71; pillars of 5; principles in area of access to justice 95; release of 1; social change model and 38; stakeholder theory and 43; states and companies, responsibilities of 36, 44; transparency and accountability 46; weaknesses inherent in normative instruments 164
United States: Anti-Terrorism Act 92; Energy Information Administration (EIA) 30n3
Universal Declaration of Human Rights (UDHR) 17n20, 89n121
University of Stellenbosch Legal Aid Clinic and others v Minister of Justice and Correctional Services and others 138, 147n1,4,9
Uzoukwu v Ezeonu II 125, 136n150

Vedanta Resources PLC & another v Lungowe and others (Respondents) 99, 100, 104n59
violations of human rights: access to remedies 94–101; adverse, mitigating and reducing 10, 42; avoiding culpability for 41; by businesses 7, 9; Companies and Allied Matters Act and 124; concerns in project development 164; corrupt practices and 11; cost-benefit analysis for 47; duty to protect against 5; effective judicial and non-judicial mechanism 90–94; endemic 163; environmental Impact Assessment Act and 47, 121; in extractive resource industry 102; gas flaring as 113; Guiding Principles for 9–10; human rights agency, creation and 165; Human Rights Commission addressing 102n7; human rights due diligence and 126; in Kenya 151; mitigating and reducing 10; in Nigeria 108, 129; non-state actors

and 8, 125; oil companies and 92, 97; remedies to victims of 9; responsibility of Board and 45; rights-based approach for 64–84; rules and safeguards for 77; in South Africa 138, 140; standard for MNCs liability for 9; United Nations Environment Programme Report and 6–7; unmitigated, preventing 47; victims, inherent problems of 12; *see also* business and human rights (BHRs)

Voluntary Principles for Security and Human Rights (2000) 18n35

Wettstein, Florian 35–36, 50n3
Wiwa et al v. Royal Dutch Petroleum Company and Shell Transport and Trading Company PLC 19n52, 23, 31n24
World Trade Organization (WTO) 27

Zambia 99